A Cry From The Street

–JOHN A. GREEN –

FASTPRINT PUBLISHING
PETERBOROUGH, ENGLAND

FastPrint

www.fast-print.net/store.php

A Cry from the Street

All characters are fictional. Any similarity to any action person is purely coincidental

ISBN 978-184426-861-0

First published 2010 by
FASTPRINT PUBLISHING
Peterborough, England.

An environmentally friendly book printed and bound in England by
www.printondemand-worldwide.com

Thanks to Becky White for proofreading
and editing the book

First Edition published 1997, ISBN 0 9534593 0 6, printed
by Redwood Books, published by Aenon Trust.

Contents

Dedication

THIS SIMPLE NARRATIVE is written as a memorial, first and foremost, to the proven Existence and Faithfulness of GOD, the Father of our LORD Jesus Christ, without Whose Grace and Mercy I would have been destroyed long ago.

Secondly, I write to all those children and young people who may for various reasons feel alone and adrift in this life, that through the events and experiences here re-told some, at least, might discover the Fatherhood of God and the security of His Love for themselves.

And lastly I write for Steven, Michael, Elizabeth, James, Edward, Daryl, and Helen, that they too might better understand the Great Love of God that brought us all together.

John A. Green
Testimony House
P.O. Box 2134
Eldoret, Kenya.
25th November 1997

Foreword

Walking with my 11-year-old daughter, Elizabeth, to collect the letters from the Post Office box, I felt amusement and laughter rising within me. I felt so light-hearted at that moment, and without a care. It was about 7p.m. and already dark. The year was 1989.

The bank had rung my office at 3p.m. to say that we were overdrawn, and requesting me to normalise matters! ME! I was totally helpless to do anything! There was no cash to hand, and no means of obtaining any quickly – or otherwise! WE WERE BROKE and yet we lived and breathed AND TRUSTED in the LORD to save us – and by the LORD I mean GOD, the Father Almighty, Maker of Heaven and Earth; revealed to us all in flesh and blood, in the Life and Person of His Son Jesus Christ, in His death and resurrection. The ONLY GOD! For thus saith the LORD, the King of Israel, and his redeemer the Lord of Hosts:

I am the First, and I am the Last;
and beside me there is no God.

IS there a God beside me?
Yea, there is NO GOD: I know not any.
Isaiah 44v6&8

Our dependence upon this FACT of His Existence, and the TRUTH of His Uniqueness, has only increased with years. And certainly since my youth I have heard of many other gods, and seen them elevated to equality with the LORD, AND seen them given more and more place and prestige. YET I KNOW ONLY ONE GOD, and beside Him there are, increasingly, NO others! Only He can SAVE us.

THIRTY-FIVE YEARS AGO, when we first opened our hearts and lives to helping homeless children here in Kenya, East Africa, it cost roughly £1.50 or Ksh. 50/= per month to feed a child. We had about 20 then, and I myself, without the support of mission or church behind me, had the promise of NOTHING AT ALL from any man. No appeals were made, no needs made known to any – EXCEPT to GOD, the Father of Jesus Christ and ALL mankind. AND as I cried to Him, secretly and alone, He answered in ways that could be seen and appreciated. And so, with David the psalmist, I can say with a full heart:

I love the LORD because He has heard my voice and my supplications.
BECAUSE he hath bent down his ear to me,
therefore I will call upon HIM as long as I live.
Psalm 116v1

None of us went without from the very first day until now. And NOW much more is needed than then – or is it? Perhaps it is not more in truth. But today (in 2004), it costs £25 or Ksh 2500/= per month to feed a child here, and of course there are many other matters to see to over and above food. Promised INCOME, after 3 decades, averages 10% of what is actually needed. The remaining 90% is not in our hands to reckon with, or to plan upon. And so we are drawn each day, again and again, to the LORD, and we say to HIM alone, "O Lord, Give us this day our daily bread!" And he does. We have always eaten. YEA we have increased.

AND SO I LAUGHED. There was nothing in the post. We remained overdrawn, helpless. And no one could know – would ever know – when the need was there, and the cupboard bare! BUT GOD SAW, and sees, and His Hand redeems us out of the hand of the enemy.

He saves us – yea, and WILL save us –
you also helping together by prayer for us,
that for the gift bestowed upon us
by the means of many persons,
thanks may be given by many on our behalf.
II Corinthians 1v10-11

And so life went on from that moment until now, as I am writing in 2004. The crisis passed by – or did it continue? Even if you knew, it would be impossible to do much about it in time to save us. But BEFORE WE CALL (before the need is even apparent to us) the ONLY GOD has answered. Praise him forever and ever. AMEN.

This is the story of how I, an unwanted, 'throw-away' baby, grew to discover the Existence and Faithfulness of God, and in the process came to help many other children in desperate circumstances, sharing with them the miracle of His Love.

JOHN A. GREEN – 2008 A.D.

Introduction

Who is John Green? Who am I, and where did I spring from? Where did any of us spring from, and what for? Is there any relative reason or purpose in our consciously being here at this time? So many questions, and in a way they seem to become more acute as one grows older.

I was born into the world 64 years ago, yet that was not the beginning of who I am. Biologists uniformly take the position that Life begins at conception, in which case John Green had existence nine months before he was physically brought out of his mother's womb into the light of day. God, in Jeremiah 1v5, tells Jeremiah:

Before I formed you in the womb, I knew you;
Before you were born I sanctified you;
And I ordained you a prophet to the nations.

And in Psalm 139 David testifies of God that:

Your eyes saw my substance, being yet unformed,
And in Your book they all were written,
The days fashioned for me,
When as yet there were none of them.

In God's eyes, it seems, we all have 'identity' from the moment we are conceived. He knows all about us at that commencement of our actual being put together in the womb. But there is even something more than this in the Bible. In Ephesians 1v4 and 2Timothy 1v9 we are assured that we were known and chosen by God 'in the beginning', and 'before the world began'. At the very least, John Green was in the Maker's mind's eye before the earth was ever created – and it is not impossible that I may even have had 'existence' spiritually before a body was prepared for me on earth. After all Christ existed in that way.

So who am I really? How old am I? How old are any of us? I wonder? In Isaiah 49v16 it is written, "See, I have inscribed you on the palms of my hands."

He did it before the world began. And the name he wrote there is not, I think, the name we know ourselves by down here! No! The name engraved on our Maker's palms is the name He knows us by; the name we shall again be known by if we make it to the New Earth. Yes we all go back a long way with God. That spiritual ego that is ME is almost ageless!

So can I really be sure of who I am? Can I really know myself? Can I really know the person I was planned to be? In 1Corinthians 13v12, Paul says, 'I shall know just as I also am known.'

But for now we all see through a glass darkly, and the understanding we have of ourselves is obscured so much by our flesh in which sin has its habitation and hold.

And it is the flesh with its passions and physical appetites that is the product of the DNA of our ancestors. By it we are handicapped and manipulated into an untrue likeness, a parody of what we ought to have been, and one day will be by God's Grace. Because of this it is very easy to have wrong appreciations of ourselves.

In my own case it has not been helped by having no information about my true parents. I know nothing whatever about them, and cannot trace in any way those traits and characteristics that may have gone into the making of the body I inhabit. Thus I am totally ignorant, in many ways, as to the effect of the accrued history of sinful appetite and experience in my ancestors' flesh. This does sound a little 'way out' as I write it, but perhaps it might be tagged to Paul in Romans 7, where Paul argues that there are two Laws at work in all of us: The Rule of Sin in the Flesh, and the Rule of Reason. I am thus affected by my flesh, oppressed by and through it, manipulated by it, imprisoned and confined in it. It is through my flesh that my ancestors affect me, that the sin of Adam is passed on to me, magnified.

To know our ancestry can assist us to understand where some of the pressures that are being brought to bear upon us, to misshape us, are in fact coming from. Not to know increases the weight we carry. It increases the 'handicap', the 'weight' of the cross.

Sixty-four years have now gone by since my birth. Have I changed? Am I better or worse than when I came forth into the light of the sun?

Perhaps I have changed, but in truth I feel the same under the layers of the years laid down upon my flesh. The same, yet not the same. Still looking through glass darkly, reaching out for the day when I shall at last know myself as I am known. I will have a NEW name then. It won't be Grant or Richards or Green – perhaps it won't even be John either. But it WILL be truly MINE, and will describe exactly who I will be.

THE FIRST TWENTY EIGHT YEARS

1940 – 1968

Chapter One

REJECTED

On Saturday 11th May, 1940, a sudden flurry of activity erupted within number 30 Alleyn Park, Dulwich, in the sometime Metropolitan Borough of Camberwell, South London, England. Soon afterwards, a healthy boy was delivered of his Mother, Joyce Laura Grant, and was thereafter duly registered as John Alexander Grant on 11th June, 1940.

England was at war with Germany. On May 10th Hitler's armoured columns broke in upon Holland and Belgium. By September German war-planes were bombarding London, and the south of England. I was born into human conflict, arriving in the midst of a World War. In fact England had declared herself to be at war with Germany on the 3rd September, 1939, just about the time of my probable conception!

My Mother, whose maiden name was Dobbin, was married, and I was named after her husband. More about my true family I do not know – perhaps will never know. Within a few weeks of my birth my Mother put me up for adoption. Why she did so I do not know, but my adoptive Mother once told me that Joyce Grant had been involved in an illicit 'affair', and that when her husband realised that I was not his own offspring, he issued his wife with an ultimatum – either get rid of me, or say goodbye to him AND their six children! She supposedly chose to lose me, and if the facts of the case are true, then I will not blame her. Whatever the real truth of the matter, the fact was that I became a rejected child; rejected by my natural Father, my Mother, and her husband!

Far away in the north-east of England, another couple, Bill and Edie Green were desperate for a child. Edie had suffered six miscarriages, the last just about the time of my birth. They had not shared this latest sorrow with their parents, but Bill had suggested adoption as a way out. Thus it was that somehow they came across me, and within three months of my birth in London, I was being fostered by the Greens in a small village called Starbeck, not far from Harrogate in Yorkshire. They must have been fairly certain that the application for my adoption would go through since they told their parents that a fine son was born to them on the 14th August, 1940. It was their wedding anniversary, and was to be my birthday for the next 18 years! It also became my wedding day 31 years later! The adoption order was finally granted on the 3rd April 1941, and the following year, on the 24th May 1942, I was christened in Knaresborough Parish Church, and given the name William John Green. There were to be no more pregnancies for Edie Green, and I was fated to be the only child in an otherwise childless marriage. Their parents were never told of the adoption, nor any of their family or friends. It was a very well-kept secret, and remained so for the next 18 years.

When I was three years old I remember being parked in the hallway of a dingy house, which was my home. I was presumably put there to sleep. We were still living in Starbeck, not far from Harrogate. I was not asleep but just lying quietly in the big pram, and I can remember the stale, enclosed mustiness of that brown and cream painted hallway. Stairs went up from it to the floor above where the bedrooms were, and pale sunlight trickled meanly through the landing window and down the stairs. A fly buzzed intermittently. Voices, distant and muffled, rose and fell sombrely in the background.

Suddenly the kitchen door into the hallway burst desperately open. I screamed clambering up into a sitting position in the pram, terrified by the unnerving shouts and sobs of pain and anguish thrusting themselves upon my anxious ears. Quick steps upon the linoleum. "Mummy!" Yes it was my Mother, fleeing from some terror yet unseen. She reached the stairs and without a glance in my direction, quickly with awful panting gasps of breath raced upwards.

"MUMMY!" I remember how my little body felt encased in steel; I was paralysed with fear and horror. I sat on, wide-eyed as tears welled up and overflowed down my cheeks, little hands gripping the sides of the pram. Still she did not turn or pause in her headlong flight. She staggered, tripped, cried out, rallied, and dragged herself upward, her whole body trembling, her hair streaming in a frenzy of disarray all about her.

"EDIE!" I turned again toward the gaping door behind me. That was my Father's voice. Yes there he was. He stood swaying awkwardly in the doorway, his face red and puffy with anger. He stumbled forward, steadying himself upon the pram. "EDIE!" I stared at him as at a nightmare. His face seemed twisted – I can see it now – twisted out of shape with hate. But it was the top of his head that presented the strangest, and to me most frightening sight. It was crowned with a great crumbling mound of mashed potatoes. Creamy blobs of it were sticking to his ears, and falling sluggishly from the strands of his mousy hair. The whole scene was so unreal, but one thing impressed itself upon me: my Mother was terrified of my Father; he meant to harm her.

Now he was climbing the stairs himself, gripping the banister rails with both hands and hauling himself up a step at a time, breathing heavily. I could smell his breath; it quite overpowered the stale atmosphere of the hallway. Later I would know it for what it was – the smell of beer.

I began to bawl loudly, but at the same time I was released from whatever force had held me fast in the pram. I began to climb out of it, using the big wheels as steps and, continuing to cry loudly, commenced to crawl up that mountain of stairs. Somehow I reached the top, and looking through the banister rails of the landing, was just in time to see my Mother collapse by the side of her bed, my Father standing over her kicking, hitting, hurting her. I think that was when I began to learn about hate. I began to hate him.

My Father, William Charles (Bill) Green, was a civil servant, and my Mother, Edith Doris (Edie) Green, was a private dressmaker, working her fingers literally to the bone to support herself and me. Her husband drank most of his salary away each day of his life at that time. I grew up to know and love my Mother best. My Father was often away on government business, and even when at home was out most evenings with his drinking partners. By contrast, my Mother was always at home and we did everything together. When I was born she must have been about 35 years, still young and vigorous, full of imagination and creativity; a woman who could make happiness and laughter out of nothing at all – and most of the time there was nothing at all. She made all things come alive with simple magic and adventure. I have much to thank her for. She taught me how to pray. She was also the disciplinarian of the family. I well remember one occasion when I was naughty and had exasperated her. She got a chair and, standing upon it, took down a thick bamboo curtain rod, and taking the curtain from it, she beat me with it hard. I could not believe her later when she said that it hurt her more than it hurt me! But I do now; I know exactly what she meant!

When not visiting the provinces my Father would return late each evening from the pub to inevitably beat up my Mother, sometimes throwing the beer bottles he had brought home at her as well. He seldom spoke to me, and I cannot ever remember him playing with me, or cracking a joke. Consequently he never had my confidence and I never came to even nearly understand him until it was too late. A sparsely built, narrow man, with puffy hands, face and nose pocked, and blotchy, mousy hair, always plastered down thinly with water. A man full of curses and beery melancholy who predictably hated Jews and 'niggers'.

What other memories are there of those early years? The kitchen in that first recollected home will always be remembered. The floor was of bare flagstone, and light was let in by a big sash-corded window with cracked glass, that looked out upon a small dismal yard, with a toilet near the back wall. A rough wooden table and four chairs were the only real furnishings apart from the fireplace, with its big side ovens where most of the cooking was done. The walls and ceiling were blackened with damp, and if you came in suddenly at night with a lamp, the walls would crawl solidly with great brown cockroaches. I cannot say we ever got rid of them. It was a rather poor and dilapidated house, neglected by the owner who was only interested in the rent. It was run down, but home for all that, and it could be quite a cosy place to be. No TV of course in those days; only the radio to amuse us, and to expand our horizon beyond the small world of our existence. I suppose I was not truly aware of the very real poverty of our situation then. I remember the sitting room coal fire, and Mum's home-baked bread!

We were still in that house in 1945. I well remember the day my Mother's brother – he was then Lt. Commander in the Royal Navy Reserve, and just home from the war – came to visit us. I had a tricycle by then. Somehow my Mother had managed to save enough from her sewing to buy me one. It had pneumatic tires, I recall, and I can see myself now, proudly pedalling up and down the street with my uncle's navy cap on my head, and one hand waving a paper Union Jack. Perhaps it was D-DAY. I was very proud of that bike; there is even a photograph of me posing, seated upon it, beautifully fitted out in the clothes made by my Mother. Quite a 'little darling' was I in those days, and with a shock of black curly hair. The curls vanished the year after for some unknown reason, and I never got them back – perhaps never to be a 'darling' again either.

There are other photos too, and strangely, as I look at my own two sons and a daughter as they have grown up, I can see myself all over again such a likeness there is between us. I suppose every parent has this experience, but I count it a very great wonder. I am a most proud and thankful Father! The greatest wonder, however, is to look at a photo of me taken with my Mother, Edie Green, when I was about a year and six months old, and to see the likeness there is between us. A great surprise when you realise that she was not my real Mother at all. But then I loved her very much, and they do say that you look like those you love very much.

In 1945 we had moved to another house. It snowed that year; how it snowed! My Father had to climb out of the bedroom window and dig himself down to the front door, and then clear a path to the gate. I loved the snow. I loved the way it clothed everything with sparkle, covering every dark and ugly thing up and transforming them into light and beauty. I loved the way it felt underfoot, crisp and chill, yet delicate as lace. I loved to see the fields and trees so clad against the leaden skies. I loved the winters of my childhood; those long walks in frosty, crunchy weather; the wrapped up warmth of heavy coat, woolly scarf and mittens; snowballs, snowmen, icicles. I loved the warm fireside, and thick, hot buttered toast, toasted with a long fork against the embers in the grate. Even now I am much the same at heart, sitting here on the Equator far from those early scenes and impressions.

I was also brought up to believe in fairies, and Father Christmas! In these later years I have heard many voice the opinion that not only are such fantasies absurd, but also spiritually damaging. Children, they say, should be told the truth, and the truth is that there are no such things as fairies, and no such person as Father Christmas. Personally I see no evil in such innocent beliefs. I am more disturbed by the current children's programs – especially cartoons – that present truly fiendish imagery and violence to a child's impressionable mind. Looking at all the world imagines and invents for our entertainment and 'pleasure' it seems a world far worse than that of Noah's day, of which it is written "...the wickedness of man was great in the earth, and every imagination and intention of all human thinking was only evil continually" (Genesis 6v5).

One Christmas Eve – I think I must have been about six years old then – I was snug in bed, a rather bulky, grey-eyed teddy bear with me, both of us keeping one eye open. Slowly, the bedroom door began to open. My one eye peeped cautiously, breathlessly, from under the blankets. I saw a large wellington-booted foot secretly step over the threshold, and, glancing a little higher, caught sight of the corner of a heavy red coat. I ducked out of sight. Father Christmas had come! A sound of parcels falling; a thump, a bump against the bed; a hasty, retreating footfall; a quiet closing of the bedroom door. Then I was up, and the light was on, and there at the foot of the bed, my pillow case, bulging and overflowing with 'things'. My long winter socks, hung out for good measure, also filled with sweets and fruit and other goodies. To me, Father Christmas had come. I never considered for a moment that it was not him. Of course, I know now that it was only my Mother, in my Father's gum boots and her own winter coat, but it doesn't matter, and it has not altered the magic of that night, or of those days, and so I still 'believe' in childish things with the children. It has not robbed Christmas of its true holiness and deep meaning to me as a Christian.

That first Christmas was a 'family occasion'. It was a Holy Night, a momentous night, and I believe for Mary and Joseph it remained a night of blessing. The world has commercialised it, glamorised it, and for the most part forgotten the central point of it all.

My Mother never let a Christmas pass without putting up paper chains and other decorations. She would tell me about the Baby Jesus; this was to be His birthday. We would rejoice and be glad; we would love each other. After I would be in bed on Christmas Eve, she would turn the house into a festival with tree and holly, red with berries, and mistletoe. Christmas cards hung up everywhere. The morning would dawn with wonderful smells from her stove. Mince pies baking, chicken roasting, plum pudding heating! There would be nuts to crack, and fruit to eat. This was Christmas. Where she found money enough to buy all I cannot tell, for we were poor in those far off days, but we always had a marvellous Christmas. I always am so thankful for them, and the memory of them. Presents lovingly and secretly wrapped up as tender expressions of love and care, and unwrapped excitedly, expectantly, by finger fumbled hands! There was Love in those childhood Christmases, and a sense of warmth. A deep affinity with sky and field, with bird and beast, tree and root; an affinity which seemed to make all things and all creatures one with me, and part of me, with all the past since God in the beginning made all things.

For me, as a small child, everything around was full of mystery and magic. I have never forgotten the long walks through meadows lush with buttercup and clover, and woodlands full of filtered fairy light, carpeted with moss and fern. Sometimes we would stroll through fields of bluebells, each bell a fairy hat of radiant blue; sometimes stumbling upon strange circles of dark green, often studded with many coloured toadstools, a 'fairy ring'. Even the very birds and animals seemed to communicate, and to share deep secrets. Thinking of all this again, the magic fairy world that has woven itself so deep into my life, I feel and know that it has all helped to lead me close to the Door of the Kingdom of Heaven, the Kingdom of God and Christ – that hidden, yet very real world where all is possible, and where love and beauty dwell together. A place where lion lays down with lamb and trees clap their hands for joy.

My Father's Mother stayed with us in those infant days of mine. I mainly remember her for her false teeth, which she continually explored with her tongue, producing everlasting clickings and sucks of air. Sometimes she actually removed them, and left them clenched within a glass, pickled in Chenopod water, whilst she herself made tea upon the hearth in a big enamel teapot. All the while she would be mumbling to herself as she sat there by the grate; an old crone of bone, and stretched out flesh, every inch shrouded in black silk, her dark and greying locks falling forward over a sharp and pointed nose. Toothless she dipped her buttered toast into her milked weak tea, drooling and dripping with delight. Later she would wash it down further with a second cup of tea, this time poured into a saucer to cool it, and then slurped and sloshed greedily down between loose and blue veined lips. I often watched her thus, fascinated as by a snake. She never spoke to me, and I never did enjoy her company.

One evening when I was six, we two – young and ancient (she was 80) – were alone together in the house. Mum was out at the cinema, and Dad was, as usual, up at the pub on the corner. Granma was supposed to be 'baby sitting'. A log fell from the fire, making flames leap up the chimney and throwing frightening shadows all around the unlit room. I felt unaccountably afraid. Granma moaned in her sleep, and her head lolled onto her chest, her mouth gaping in a toothless snore. I raced scarified, up and out of the house with only my pyjamas on. I came to the pub on the corner and pushed open the swing door, and there was Dad by the bar, red and sweating, a pint of beer in his hand.

He saw me instantly and, laughing loudly, came and picked me up, setting me upon the bar counter, whilst all around him laughed and guffawed in merriment. I hated the bar, and I hated the smell of the place. I hated the curling blue smoke and the leering, bloated faces. I only wanted my Daddy; I wanted him to take me home, and to be my Daddy just for once. But he was not ready to come home, and by the time he was I must have fallen asleep, for I awoke in bed at home the next morning.

MY FIRST PRIMARY SCHOOL was in Starbeck. I was just four years old when I began to attend it and I never did enjoy going there. It was a big, grey, stone building. I hated the solidness of that building; hated its tarmac playground, and that fat hairy bully called 'Spider' Webb, who made life for all the small kids a misery. I hated the big, dark-eyed woman who was my teacher too. She loved to make fun of me because of my slowness, for I was slow. She daily found some reason to pinch me or slap me with her ruler. I am sure she hated me, too, and I am sure she did not have a reason. Years later, in London, I met her again, and I could swear that if she had been able she would have beaten me again with joy. It was my first taste of school and school teaching, and it helped to fix in me a dislike for school for most of my learning years. I certainly had to attend enough primary schools – more than five before graduating to secondary education. I remained with a learning problem all the way through the ensuing years as well, and was quite unable to read even the simplest English Reader until I attained the fifth grade at the ripe old age of nine.

In 1947 my Father was transferred to London and so we had to move. The only real thing I recall of that move was catching Sandy, our cat, and sewing him inside a cushion cover, thereafter nursing it – and him – on my lap all the long train journey to the south. It was 'Goodbye' to Yorkshire, and I never managed to return there, except for a month spent in Rotherham many years later in 1968. I have regretted our leaving there many times. For all the family trouble, they were happy years. I liked the people and the countryside in which I first felt and knew something greater than myself. But the 'mashed potatoes' were often to repeat themselves where we were going, and the family trouble was to get worse instead of better.

FULHAM, A SUBURB OF LONDON, in 1947, was to my child's eyes a very drab and miserable place indeed, with its bomb damage and grey-black buildings and littered streets. There is nothing much that I recall about it, except that it seemed to fit in with the whole impression of my Father. Pubs and my Father were synonymous; they went hand in hand. And it seemed that these particular pubs, with their green and brown walls and painted windows, and the stale smell of beer and tobacco horribly mixed with spit and phlegm always leaking out upon the pavement, were indeed one with him. He belonged more to them than to us!

From Fulham we quickly moved to Raynes Park, near Wimbledon, which was slightly, but only slightly better than Fulham to my mind. Still, it was lighter and brighter, and somehow my Father had secured a mortgage on a semi-detached house in quite a pleasant road. It was whilst being there that I got to know my Mother's Father – my 'Granddad'. I only have two real remembrances of him, though the love I had for him was enormous – my favourite person, and even now I can think of him with great affection. His son, my Mother's brother, was to become just as special as the years passed by. Yet, strangely, none of these people were truly mine and, perhaps, only my Mother strove to cover this up. To her I was her very own son. Many years later, my wife and I felt led to also adopt three boys, and as they grew and became one with our own three children, we also realised how much we also loved them – as our very own! Later we also adopted a baby girl, Helen.

I remember a day in the summer of 1947. My Mother and I took a Green-Line bus to a small place called Cheam, near Sutton in Surrey. This was where my grandfather stayed, with his daughter Winnie and her husband. He was not at home when we arrived, and my aunt said that he was in the park. This was Cheam Park, and had once been a great estate, with a grand house, but now in 1947 the house had long been but an empty shell, and the vast acres of parkland, gardens, and woodlands made into a public place of recreation and relaxation. As Mum and I made our way over the grass, I spied a great oak tree, old and spreading. Under it was an equally ancient bench on which sat, alone and leaning a little forward on a stout walking stick, an old and portly gentleman in gold rimmed pince-nez spectacles. I guessed this to be my grandfather, and slipping my Mother's hand, I ran to greet him, crying out in delight. He saw me and taking his great curly pipe from his mouth, he slowly rose, tears starting to his eyes. He seemed to come from quite a different world to mine; a world of courtesy and gentleness. History seemed to walk with him, and as we three rambled quietly in meadow and woodland, the whole park seemed to be his. He seemed much acquainted with each and every tree we passed, and even the birds and squirrels seemed to know him. Later that year, in August, he came to visit us, bringing with him a huge bag full of 'conkers' – chestnuts as they are more correctly called. He must have stooped painfully to make the effort to pick each one up, just for my delight. A few months later, joking with his doctor on a friendly visit to the Surgery, he had a heart attack and died. I was heart-broken.

In 1948 my Father's Mother also died. They had her laid out under a sheet on the big bed in her bedroom, blinds drawn tightly down, and a horrible feeling of death all around us. That was the first time for me to 'smell' death. She never changed her manner till she died, and I never got to know her or like her. Lots of my Father's family that I had never seen before came to the funeral, most of them thin, cold, and rather mean looking people. They went boldly up the stairs to look at the body, and followed it in black cars on its way, in the coffin, to the cemetery. I thought it all very dull, and VERY strange when they all came back to the house after the burial to talk and laugh and eat and drink. The husband of one angular relation, who was oppositely fat and jolly-looking, flung himself into an armchair with an "Oh my Gawd ... what a funeral! Give us some sherry, Bill!" I wondered then about my Granma. No one had visited her for as long as I could remember, and now they were all too late! Perhaps the sherry made it worthwhile to them. I never saw any of them again! As I hid under the blankets of my warm bed that night, I could almost hear her false teeth clicking.

My Mother decided that she wanted to put me in a private day school. This was to be my fourth primary school. I was nine years old, and had grown up to be very fat. I was fairly obedient, but undoubtedly selfish and inward looking, for I had very few friends of my own age, and no one to share anything with. I excelled those days in artwork, and very little else. I could not read or write. I felt academically inferior and stupid, afraid of fellow students in case they should laugh at me. For this reason school was a nightmare to me. My new class master, a thin, severe, unsmiling man, seemed to delight in asking me to stand and read, even though he knew well enough that I had a real problem. Daily I would be standing by my desk, book in hand, choking with misery and shame, whilst every head in the class would be turned in my direction in delightful anticipation of my failure, and the outcome!

"Well, Green! Come on, begin," commanded the master. Tears welled into my eyes and rolled silently down my cheeks. My tongue seemed to grow fat and fill my mouth. Looking now at the class, the master continued, "Well, boys, it seems Green still cannot read to us." Laughter now, all round the class. "How old are you, Green?"

I opened my mouth and began to stutter, "N-, n-, ni-, ni-..."

"Speak boy! Speak!"

"N-, ni-, ni-, nine, Sir." I managed at last to answer him.

"Nine, and he still can't read! Come here boy." I would go, then, slowly up the aisle to his big desk at the front of the class. "Hold out your hand. Stand still." And taking his springy cane he would cut my palm until it was red and swollen. Yet that was nothing compared to the spiteful pleasure my classmates had in me because of it.

I hated school, and hated my slowness, hated not having a Father who would come and stand by me. There were so many things I hated in my life at that time. Then unpredictably, one evening at home, I began to read fluently! I can remember the book; a small and simple reader entitled 'A Dog Called Spot'. That night when I was nine years old I read it all the way through without a single word being a stumbling block to me. It was like a door being unlocked, and a blindness lifted. From that day I read avidly anything that came to hand, quickly grasping the usefulness of a dictionary. It was a turning point in many ways, and although I was to remain behind, and never really enjoyed school life, a new world was opened up to me, and I took full advantage of it. Books became my escape from the world around me.

In that same year something seemed to go wrong for my parents and we had to leave the house in Raynes Park and move into a smaller flat not far away. We even had to sell our furniture. Once there, things went from bad to worse, and every day brought forth stormy scenes and major fights between my parents. During this time when it was my bed-time, my Mother would always come in to say 'Good night' and to remind me to 'say my prayers'. I had never heard her say any, but I believed that whatever she asked me seriously to do must have a good reason, and so I trusted that if she wanted me to pray to God, then God must be there to hear me! Even though she did not know God as a reality for herself, this woman made me 'aware' of Him, and helped me to accept that He was actually THERE! But, when she had gone, I would jump out of bed and put my ear to the key-hole to listen for my Father to come in, and make sure if he was drunk or not. I was always afraid for the safety of my Mother.

One night I was, as usual, engaged in this enterprise, when the sound of my Father's key turning the lock of the front door, was soon followed by the sound of him shouting abuse at my Mother at the top of his voice. A bottle broke somewhere, and my Mother screamed. I could not bear it. I flung open my bedroom door, and ran desperately in my nightclothes to the sitting room at the end of the passage, from where the noise was coming. Hurling my nine years at the door, I burst into the room as my Father began attacking my Mother with his bare hands. His back was to me, and I tore across the room and began pounding him on his back shouting, crying and screaming as I did so, "Daddy, don't! Daddy, don't! Don't, don't, don't!"

He turned then in a blind drunken rage, and seeing me, picked up a heavy carved walking stick and raised it to hit me. I turned and ducked behind the sitting room door, and the door saved me, as with a great tearing crash my Father brought that stick down with all his force upon the panelling of the door, smashing right through it. If he had hit me I would not have lived, and I knew it. When he was drunk he was able to kill. The night closed in around me.

The next day was to be special, both for me and for my Mother. During the morning, my Father having gone to his office, my Mother was quietly reading through the daily newspaper. I was not at school so it must have been a Saturday morning. Suddenly she gave a little gasp, putting her hand to her mouth. Her eyes were wide open. She had seen a name that she knew from out of her past. She searched for pen and paper and hurriedly began to write a letter.

After our evening meal I sat outside the back door of our ground floor flat and looked up into the gathering darkness of the evening sky. It was a cloudless night, and moonless. One by one the stars began to appear, like lights being switched on. There were multitudes, some flickering, some steadily shining, hanging there. I was mesmerised, as if I had never ever seen them before. I recalled the line of an old nursery rhyme: 'Twinkle, twinkle, little star, how I wonder what you are.'

I suddenly began to wonder what held them up, so high in the sky. It certainly was not string! Anyway, what could they be hung up to? Oh, but of course! God was holding them up. It was such a definite realisation that came upon me then, as if a voice had actually told me. Of course! He was above the stars, greater and more powerful and stronger than they were. He was stronger than I was, and stronger than the misery of my home. He would not let me down; He would hold me safely, just like he held the stars. Suddenly there was security. I got up slowly, still looking upward. Then I turned and went back into the flat. I felt I could face anything now. Yes, I could talk to the One who held up the stars. He would be my Father now.

LONDON IN 1949. It was a sunny spring morning, about a week after my 'star gazing' revelation. Dad had gone off to work, and Mum suddenly began to pack a wicker shopping basket with meat pie, boiled eggs, fresh baked bread, fruit and cake. It seemed we were having a day trip to London. It happened during the Easter Holidays. I loved going to the City of London. There was so much to see. Trafalgar Square and the pigeons; I loved the pigeons! They were so friendly, and they would come and sit on your shoulder, and even eat out of your hand.

And there amongst them soaring high above, was Nelson's fluted Column; four great stone lions keeping guard at its base, whilst Lord Nelson stood victorious and splendid at its summit. Admiral Nelson whose brave seamanship and strategy had won the day at Trafalgar, on the 21st October, 1805, in a great sea battle against Napoleon's navy. Proud and erect he stands, victor, hero, saviour of the nation. Of Lady Hamilton there is no sign, for perhaps it would not be right to remember this great man's weakness, and infidelity to his wife, and unfaithfulness to his friend, Lady Hamilton's husband! As a small boy, though, hearing of his greatness and bravery for the first time, and straining with upward gaze to catch a distant glimpse of this lord of men, Nelson was an awe-inspiring figure, and still is even today in spite perhaps of having lost a little of his 'glory' to a woman. At least I cannot judge him now, for we are all weak and frail creatures at the best, yet I wish he had not fallen into adultery. In these lawless times of the end of the age, the majority of mankind would no doubt applaud this man and woman for their love life. He was in love and she was in love; what more is necessary? One hears the same arguments for sex before marriage. I think it shows a devalued and ill informed appreciation of what love truly is. For me, Nelson and Emma Hamilton lost their 'glory' as surely as Adam and Eve lost theirs, but then we have each one lost it in some way or another. We might despair of such a state in one another, but there is little right of criticism.

It was spring. The sun shone, and the sky overhead seemed washed an even brighter, cleaner, shade of blue by the fresh showers of early morning rain. We were walking down the right-hand side of the Mall, towards Buckingham Palace. A troop of horse guards passed by, harnesses jingling, their spotless uniform of flashing red, white and stunning black, all dazzle to my child's excited eyes. Oh, what a royal sight their gleaming helmets and brass and silver accoutrements made, and what a fine, proud, heart-stirring clatter, as they jogged sternly upon their horses towards the Palace of King George the sixth. There were not many people about as yet, but plenty of birds hopping about everywhere on the pavements and amongst the branches newly sprouting with young leaves. Little brown, sharp-eyed, dusty sparrows; common, cheeky starlings, eye a-cock, professional scavengers, clothed in glossy sheens of black, brown and mauve, loud-mouthed. A hum of city business was constantly in the background as we walked, and somewhere, a ceremonial cannon was fired.

Everything – sky, birds, green grass and budding trees, buildings old and grand – all was new and fresh; full of gorgeous smells and feelings that all but overwhelmed my childish and imaginative heart. My Mother tugged me along.

"John dear, you mustn't tell Daddy where we have been." A cloud suddenly dulled the brilliance of the day. "We shall be meeting someone soon now, and I want you to be polite to him. You will be, won't you?" She looked at me worriedly, squeezing my hand a little as if to encourage a right attitude in my puzzled little mind. "He's your Uncle Dick. I know you will like him." I felt an awful feeling of insecurity assail me then. It was the first time I had ever heard my Mother suggest that I should lie or deceive anyone, and it was the first time I had ever heard of my 'Uncle Dick'.

"Look! Look, there he is now!"

We had been approaching the Duke of Wellington Steps, a huge stone stairway leading up and away out of the Mall, through huge blocks of stately government office buildings. Just come down these steps and briskly coming our way, was a plain looking man of about 45, dressed in a grey suit. He looked almost bald. He waved his furled umbrella at us. Uncle Dick? I felt more suspicion than surprise at this sudden entry into my world. The cloud had passed on, but it still seemed that the day had lost its original excitement for me. My Mother's face was shining; her eyes wet with sudden joyful tears.

"Dick, Dick! Oh, it's been so long! You haven't changed a bit! This is John." He hardly looked at me, and then I knew that the rest of the day would be lived by them alone. I was on my own. But then in many ways I had always been alone, and perhaps always would be. Mum was excited, flustered even. I had never seen her like that before. I felt vaguely alarmed.

We did not stay long that first day. We picnicked out of the wicker basket together on a bench in some vast park by the side of a placid lake. I spent a lot of the time feeding the ducks whilst Mum and Dick talked. Dad was never told of any part of that day.

Uncle Dick turned out to be an old friend of Mum's before she was married. He was also married by this time, with one daughter of about 18. We began to see rather a lot of him, but he was never very free with me. 1949 was drawing to a close. My Mother took on a new lease of life, and seemed to rise up above the drabness and brutality of her home. Later, in early 1950, she shared with me her plan to run away and start a new life with Dick. My Father was to be told that Mum and I were going to visit my Uncle Frank and his family. They were living then in Bath in Somerset. In actual truth we would instead catch a bus to Kingston on Thames where we would meet with 'Uncle' Dick. He was apparently leaving his own wife and daughter as well. I had tremendously mixed feelings about all of this.

The day came, and with one small suitcase between us, Mum and I caught the Green-Line bus to Kingston on Thames. Dick was waiting for us at the bus station, and we then got on another bus and travelled down to Chichester, and finally to a caravan on the shore at Bosham, a little place on the south coast where hundreds of years earlier King Canute is reputed to have been encouraged to send the tide back. We never returned to Raynes Park again. A week later we turned up at my Uncle Frank's and stayed with him and his family for almost a year. How my Father took it all I shall never know, and at that period of my life I didn't care much.

Soon after arriving at Bosham I was advised by my Mother that we would ever more stay with 'Uncle' Dick, and that it might be easier if I started calling him 'Daddy'. I was quick to realise the wisdom of this, but not too keen on the general idea. He was still very much of a stranger to me, after all, and I could see that his main feelings were for my Mother and I was an encumbrance!

(I guess it is going to be good for the psychologist/psychiatrist to have me share so many of my childhood feelings and thoughts. I wonder what the final opinion will be!)

The whole situation was quite immoral of course. Neither of them was able to obtain a divorce in those days, and had to live together in what was commonly referred to as 'sin', in those days. To cover this they had to 'pretend' that they were married, and to do this my Mother decided we should adopt Dick's family name of Richards. By fiat, as it were, we all became Richards instead of Green. A new beginning indeed.

This was my first introduction into the world of split marriages and adultery. I had always taken it for granted that families stayed together come what may. I had an almost intuitive feeling of the 'rightness' of permanent relationships regarding 'family', and I was not thoroughly happy with this new arrangement which immediately caused us all to live a life of deceit and shame. Shame was still a 'known' word in 1950! But I loved my Mother, and had long feared for her life, and longed for her happiness. She was obviously happy with Dick, and Dick was obviously in love with her, and treated her with sincere affection and gentleness. I was thankful for that. My Father was not that hard to leave behind, after all. At least the drunkenness was behind us. Indeed I feared my Father, and my greatest fear was that I should grow up to be at all like him. Thus I communed with myself, as I adjusted to the new turn of events in my life.

Nevertheless, I suppose I always resented Dick in a way. You see, the fact of my Mother's unhappy marriage had meant that we two had drawn closer than might normally have been the case. She had given me all the time and affection that otherwise would have been shared out with her husband. I had for years been taking this for granted. Now suddenly there was Dick. We were now both to be competitors for my Mother's attention. I was never to be close to Dick for this reason. In fact we both suspected each other I think, never trusting that the other could really love the other. The fault was mainly mine. I was too attached to my Mother. In fact, were it not for Dick I would never have obtained my independence of her. He pushed me into some semblance of manhood, and at the same time introduced me to the wider world of art, music, literature and a sense of history. Unlike Bill Green, Dick was an educated man of a more refined background. I have much to thank him for! I do thank God for each one of them now, including Bill Green.

From this time on, history, especially that of England, began to come alive for me, and to catch my whole attention. For the next eight years of my life we were to roam the English counties of Somerset, and Wiltshire. Dick was a very capable musician and leant towards the classics. He woke up my ear to sounds I had never dreamed of, but for which I discovered an immediate acceptance and delight. So also in the field of art itself, and many hours have I spent in art galleries as a result of Dick's encouragement. My previous life had only known the more bawdy jokes of radio comics, pop music of the day, and the Daily Mirror which was the only paper Bill would have in the house.

This 'new' Father of mine certainly set me free to be myself, and to explore a great deal more of life than I would normally have thought of. For this I also thank him.

He cared for my Mother and me for the eight years that were to elapse until his death in 1958; loving her and bearing me! During all that time we lived under his name. All my consequent secondary education was entered into in that name; all my academic qualifications were to be taken in that name. Strange to say John Green never went to secondary school, or passed an examination. It was a period of my life that was lived by someone else. Indeed I was not able to re-assume the name of John Green again until 1960.

Out of the city and into the country. A whole new experience was suddenly mine. I regained my love for the fields and hedgerows, and a love for the sea as well. We lived in medieval cottages, country houses, and caravans parked in country farms. The English countryside lay all around us, soaked in the past, and the peace of summers full of sun-drenched harvest fields with horse-drawn wagons piled high with corn cut by hand and tossed in with pitch fork. There were countless happy days spent in fields and woodlands, afternoons at church fetes, and country cricket matches on unspoiled village greens. Shall I ever forget the sleepy clapping and the drowsy click of bat on ball at those matches? Then there were hours spent at the scout hut, the camps, the countless chance meetings like that of the ancient survivor of the Charge of the Light Brigade who we met in the high street of Waterlooville in Hampshire one day. I was about 11 then. These were also days when I would go on long solitary rambles, and where God again began to enter my life and thought.

When I was about 11 and a half, and we had been living with Dick about a year, my Mother made a rather ill-timed and rather unnecessary attempt to reconcile me to the loss of my Father. Meeting me from school one day she began chatting about many matters on the way home. Out of the blue, after a short pause she said, "You mustn't worry dear, you know, about your Father. You see Bill wasn't your real Father." I was not actually very surprised for I had never found any likeness between us, and was glad in my heart that he wasn't my Father, as I had never wanted to be at all like him. However, the statement had another side to it by that time, and I immediately shot back a question to my Mother.

"So you are not my real Mummy either then?" It was not meant to be a question in fact, but a statement that now needed confirmation. It made no difference at all to the love I bore her; I had known no other Mother after all, and I was content with the love she had always given to me. However, this question was definitely not expected by my Mother. She looked quite upset and almost angrily replied, "Of course I'm your real Mother. But Bill was just not your Father."

We walked on in silence. I felt sick and giddy. Only that week there had been a very unpleasant scene at school where a whole group of boys had encircled a new boy, jeering and calling him 'illegitimate'. I, ignorant as I was, did not know what it meant and had asked another boy, older than I, who was also standing by watching.

"It means you ain't legitimate," he said scornfully back. "You ain't lawful because you weren't born when your parents were married proper." It was obviously a very great 'shame' to be illegitimate. It had made a tremendous impression on me, and now here I was! I must be illegitimate too! And now where did I really belong anyway? How many more fathers could a boy have? I felt that I could no longer count on the faithfulness of my Mother. I began to ransack old family photo albums that my Mother had brought with us, hoping to find one of a man I might resemble. Many times I asked my Mother to just explain who my Father really was, but she always changed the subject with the question left unanswered. I felt dirty. But at the same time I had a strange conviction that she had lied when she had affirmed that she was my real Mother. I felt cheated, and became lonely in my soul. I felt like a stateless person, a refugee without a true home or family. I was nearly 12.

Even in all the turmoil of those years, often full of personal heartaches, the three of us did attain times of great happiness together; times when we forgot the lie, and the poverty of our lives. Poverty followed us everywhere, and we moved often. Dick could not get a job, and Mum's ability to earn from her sewing was not very substantial. Debts would be piled up with shopkeepers, and I well remember being sent into shops to get groceries with a cheque; a cheque I knew would bounce. Often we obtained goods this way, under false pretences. Often we were knocked up by the Police wanting to serve us with a Summons. Then we would quickly pack up our things in the middle of the night, and move on to somewhere new. It seemed that the price of what I had first thought was my Mother's right to happiness sank us all lower and lower into shame. I managed to change secondary schools about four times in four years; one of those years being out of school altogether due to the fact that I had no clothes to wear! My

Mother often asked if I thought she had done right to leave her husband, and if it had hurt me a lot.

She was always worried about it in her heart. Then I would say to her that everything was alright, and that God wanted her to be happy anyway. Anyway? No not any way, not by any means. But I had still to learn that. Certainly God wants us all to be happy, but there is no happiness apart from Him, no happiness outside His Law of Love. And my Mother was not happy in her heart either, and never would be.

Chapter Two

LIGHT DAWNS

Really the Light had begun to dawn for me that evening when I was nine, and discovered the One who holds up the stars. I did not forget Him. He was always there in my awareness, but although I had accepted His existence, our relationship was very much one-way. I could and did communicate to Him, but there was no tangible response. I did not get to know Him from His side. He got to know a whole lot from me, and in a truly amazing sense, He filled the place of a real Father all of my developing years. I confided in Him, moaned and groaned to Him, rehearsed my joys to Him, and took him, with me wherever I went. I did not feel any holier though. I honoured and feared Him, recognised Him in all the beauty and grandeur of the world around me, and was often encouraged and comforted by the knowledge that He was there for me. Yet, for all that, I did not have any understanding of Salvation or the part that Jesus Christ should have in my life. I was still seeing through a glass darkly.

In 1955 I found myself amongst many who were to be confirmed in the Christian Faith by the then Suffragan Bishop of Sherbourne, whose name I have forgotten. It was to take place in Melksham Parish Church in the County of Wiltshire. I was in my last year of secondary school, and not doing very well. I want to record it here because it was a kind of spiritual landmark, and even today I often look back to it as such. Our family had been nominally Anglican. We had never been church-goers, however. I was 15, and my Mother decided that this was the appropriate thing to do; the traditional thing to do. I am sure she had no real idea of the meaning behind it, and certainly I did not. Nevertheless, I was sent for classes to the local Vicarage. The Vicar was an elderly bachelor called the Rev. Mr. Littlewood. He lived in a huge Victorian vicarage with enough room to take a family of at least 15. Short and a little stooped in stature, he had a round face, pink and kind, very fresh and smooth, his only hair being sown in a holy silvery ring about the bald dome of his clever head. He lived alone, looked after by a man and wife, who acted as butler and housekeeper respectively. He was inclined to be High Church and a little given to incense and the tinkling of bells, yet in every way a 'holy' man, and one whom I greatly liked from the moment we met. I made numerous visits to his sitting room in the vicarage, where he would talk of butterflies and flowers, thick black smoke curling upwards from his curly cherry bowl pipe. Invariably there would be a cosy fire in the grate, since it was late into the year, and hot buttered scones would be sitting on a silver tray with cups and saucers at the ready. They were good times for me, and I found it no trouble at all to attend the Catechism Classes because of my liking for the Vicar. There were ten of us altogether in those classes, and looking back I am sure Mr. Littlewood faithfully taught us all we needed to know. But it all passed me by; not a word of it touched my heart, or stirred my soul!

The big day arrived, and I travelled to Melksham Church. There were so many young people there; all the girls in white party dresses, and the boys, like me, in suits. The Vicar of Melksham at that time was the Rev. Cyril Witcombe. The church was packed; filled with sunlight and flowers.

The Bishop was impressive in his historic regalia. A short man, plump, with a face like a cherub's glowing with goodness and love, it seemed to me that I had to look at him! As the time came for the message, I was all attention. He mounted the ancient pulpit and began. Every word of his stirring address winged its swift way to my heart. I could feel prickles all over me. I wanted to run clear out of the church. What was I doing there? I did not know this God, this Almighty God. What had I to do with Him? How had I ever dared to think of Him as my Father?

He had finished speaking now and was seated at the front steps leading up to the altar. Already we were being shepherded towards him, and it seemed no time at all before I found myself kneeling in front of him, his hands upon my head.

"In the Name of the Father, and of the Son, and of the Holy Ghost..." Tears stung my eyes. My whole body seemed to tremble with some sudden ague, and a great terror choked me. I stumbled up, and ran out, out, out of the church. No one came after me. I began to run, anywhere as long as it was away from that man, and whatever it was he had in his hands. I have often wondered what the Bishop felt that day. Officially I was confirmed, but I knew differently. I only knew I was not good enough for God, and I had no idea how I ever could be.

The next day was Sunday, and I was to attend my First Communion in Rev. Littlewood's church. This also was traditional procedure. An elderly lady was our neighbour, and she was a very devout churchgoer, though well into her seventies and almost blind and deaf. It was arranged that she would call for me! Decrepit she may have been, but at 6 a.m. that next morning she called for me and escorted me to church. It was a bright, crisp December morning, quiet and still, yet already I could feel beads of sweat starting upon my brow. I was still very disturbed.

The church was two-thirds full, cold and grey. We took our places in the pew, and prayerfully waited. Prayerfully! Well I could not pray, I could but wait, and copy the antics of the ancient who was my companion. The service was read as usual, following the Prayer Book. It is beautiful and meaningful if you are sincerely entering into it, though I also have come to prefer the spontaneous worship of what many non-conformists refer to as 'Breaking of Bread'. On this particular morning of the 6th December, 1955, it was all new to me, and every word seemed to be taking me nearer and nearer to that very Holiness which the day before I had fled from. Suddenly I was aware of the opening words of the Lord's Prayer. "Our

Father which art in Heaven, Hallowed be Thy Name...." It was so loud, so loud in my ears. It seemed as if the voice speaking were as the bass note of some cavernous thunder. "Hallowed Be Thy Name... Hallowed, Hallowed Be Thy Name..." Over and over again! The words rolled around my head like the reverberation of some great bell.

I opened my eyes. Anxious faces looked down upon me! I felt fresh air blowing on my face. I looked hastily around me, and found I was lying now upon the seat in the church porch! I had fainted they said, and so they carried me out to the fresh air. I had not managed to take the Bread and Wine. I was still not in communion with Christ. I still did not know HIM who had died for me. Do you hear all you Christian workers, Pastors, church-goers? I could then have been called a Christian, a church-goer. I was Baptised, Catechised, Confirmed, but I had never understood about God's Lamb of Sacrifice given for me personally to cleanse me from my sin. Standing then in the midst of the people of God I was as lost as before! Truly though, Light having dawned within my heart, it never ceased to grow brighter. Now I could at least see that I was separated from God, and none of this illumination had been brought to me by man, but borne in upon me by the Spirit.

In 1955 I also finished my secondary education. I had not done well, and there was not a lot open for me to do. Eventually I found work with a wholesale grocery firm, sweeping floors, humping boxes and generally learning the business from the warehouse floor! I was not happy with the work and not happy with myself either. Weighing some 11-and-a-half stones, and standing 5 feet 11 inches, I was a rather ungainly 16 year old, peering short-sightedly through ugly steel-rimmed glasses supplied by the Ministry of Health. Friends did not come easily to me, as I continued to be shy and introspective, unsure of myself in so many ways, and ashamed of my family background. Home was such a shabby pretence, so full of hidden immorality; even my name was a sham. At 17 I began to drink and to smoke heavily in an effort to gain some kind of strength! Yes, I who was afraid of following my 'drunken Father' was now descending fast to a similar state! What about God? What about the One Who Held the Stars Up? Oh He was still there, but not close. How could such a One be close to me? Indeed I had felt rejected by Him since that morning in the church, two full years before. Yes, that was it, I was a reject; a reject with no future, and no purpose in life. I had come from nowhere and I had nowhere to go. And so, standing on the corner of the street in the town where I worked one sunny lunchtime, I was ready to put an end to the misery once and for all. I can still remember the date. It was the 24th of June, 1957. The sky overhead was blue, the sunshine brilliant. Lunchtime shoppers crowded the streets, and lunchtime traffic was plentiful and reckless. One step off the pavement into that whirling madness on the roadway, and everything would end. It would be an accident. I stood stock still, people jostling me as they passed by, laughing, talking, and living their lives quite oblivious of my own despair.

I seemed to be shut out from their world. I felt clammy and cold. I turned then towards the road, and walked into the raging torrent of traffic...

"God so loved the world that He gave His only begotten Son, that whosoever believeth in Him should not perish but have everlasting life."

The words roared into my head like an express train, pulling me up in my madness and folly. The words were not new of course. I had heard them in church a few times, and in Bible classes at school. Then they had meant nothing. Now, suddenly, they meant everything. I thought my mind would explode with the knowledge of God's love for me. I stood there and cried out to the sky above, to God:

"God, if Jesus is your Son, and if he died for me, I need Him now, to save me from myself, and from my life." I actually spoke the words out loud, though I guess few heard what I said. Vehicles were hooting their horns angrily at me as they swept round and about me, and some passers-by were staring at me as if I truly was out of my mind.

I heard no voice, and saw no vision, and trembled not at all, YET it seemed to me that at that moment when I cried out to God sunshine broke through my dark pit of despair, and flooded my life with warmth. I felt alone no more. I knew that someone had come to stand by my side, and I knew that 'Someone' had to be God's Son, Jesus Christ, who at his Father's bidding had come to rescue and save me from destruction. This I was sure of. There was much I still had to learn. The whole world had changed. I was not a church-goer, had no Christian friends, had attended eight different schools up and down the country, and met countless human beings, yet only now did I know the truth. No one had shown me this; no one had tried to counsel me in the way of salvation. God Himself, in His own time and place had done it. It was a miracle.

I found myself at the far side of the road I had thought would be my death. Facing me was the door of the Vicarage: Cyril Witcombe's door. Well, he ought to know what had just happened to me. I walked up the path and knocked at the door. Sudden doubt assailed me. What would I say to him? He would laugh at me! The door opened, and there he stood in cassock and collar, a look of some surprise upon his face, and a bowl of soup held in one hand.

"Er...yes? Can I help you?" He smiled as he said it. I had evidently disturbed him at his lunch.

"Well, I…er…hr'm…" It was ridiculous! It just couldn't possibly be said; but it had to be said now. "I…er…I've just met Jesus in the High Street! He saved me!" It rushed out quickly into the space between us. His eyes opened wider in a great joy and reaching out to me with his free hand he pulled me into the house.

"Praise God for that," he said. "Let us thank Him together." He knew! He understood! He also had found that Jesus Christ was alive and relevant. What a fellowship we had together then. I was welcomed 'home' at last. I have always thanked God for that man being there in the right place at the right time.

Two weeks later, Dick Richards died, and my Mother and I moved east to Cambridge. I never heard of Cyril Witcombe again. I had met with Jesus, and knew Him as a Saviour, but I was still very ignorant, still lacking in fellowship, and in the Word of God. There were too many pitfalls, and many wrong turnings, but in all of them

God held me up. He has continued to do so, though I have been a slow learner even in spiritual matters, and had to contend still with a feeling of inferiority which held me back again and again when I should have been going forward.

Well, I did not change a lot outwardly. I was still drinking and smoking; no doubt that will make some feel that I did not actually get saved that day in Melksham! There was change even so! From that moment I KNEW I was not alone, and I knew that God was willing to own me as His child. That meant a great deal to me then, since I felt in many deep ways a complete non-entity. I had already had three different names, and I was in danger of losing my identity. I also knew that Jesus had cleansed me from all my errors, mistakes and faults, past present and future. I only needed to stick to Him, and He would see me through. At that point I began to find confidence – not in myself, but IN HIM, who has from that time been my Strengthener. I was able to lift up my head without being ashamed for the first time in my life. I was accepted in the Beloved. I was still ignorant of what altogether pleased HIM but His Grace was enough; His Mercy was new every morning. He would take me step by step, regarding my frailties, changing me day by day.

Dick Richards, my 'Uncle' Dick, died of cancer of the lung, and I am unlikely to forget the circumstances of his death. They were to weigh heavily upon me for many a long year. In thinking of it again, something else came to mind which may have a bearing upon it all. It happened earlier in that same year. A small bird had been badly mauled by a cat, and I had rescued it. It was a pitiable sight as it lay trembling in my hands, and the warmth and soft frailty of its little body filled me with a very great sorrow, so that I closed my eyes and spoke to God in Heaven.

"Father, take this small creature to where you are, and put it out of the reach of pain." I opened my eyes, and it had ceased to move, and already I could feel a coldness creeping over its body. Life had gone from it. I was sure God had heard my request. I buried the bird feeling very small indeed, and strangely afraid of this God who was so very far away, and yet so very NEAR!

If this tale suggests that I was a very affectionate and kindly young man, then I must set the record immediately straight. I had become even more self-centred, and self-pitying. I resented the discipline of a man not my Father, and was at the time resenting my Mother for always taking his side against my own interests. This in part resulted in the state of mind recorded earlier. A late teenage, and growing independence, had produced a lot of bitterness prior to the day of my conversion. It had all come to a head one day in March, and I had raged out of the house, banging the door behind me. "I wish he was dead, dead! DEAD!" I had screamed it at the empty sky, and to the mocking crows in the ploughed fields, as I flung off down the road, alone and lonely, hurt and comfortless.

He and Mum had gone off on a holiday, leaving me behind. I was busy with evening classes by this time as well, trying to make up for lost time academically. I was partially successful, passing my O-Levels and some A's too, plus a number of other accountancy examinations. Of course it was all done in the name of Richards and not Green. Finally, I was never able to use those qualifications.

John Green has remained unqualified in everything except the word of God!

Halfway through the following week Mum and Dick arrived suddenly and unexpectedly back. Dick seemed to have aged ten years, and was grey with the pallor of death! He had collapsed at a hotel, and cancer had been diagnosed within hours. He was dead within four months!

For the last six weeks of his life he was home from hospital, and as Mum by this time had a job in a dress shop, I had to remain home and nurse him: it was at best a terrible experience. He was not supposed to know what he had, and so we all played a game of pretended optimism, when all the time I was sure he himself knew quite well what was wrong with him. He wasted away until he was just brittle, sickly, yellow parchment, stretched over bones of matchstick thickness. He was like a living corpse already, racked every minute by a cavernous, devouring, cough. Yet he never once complained or said a word; just looked at me with great coal-black eyes that seemed twice the size they used to be – beautiful eyes, liquid, sad and deep as pools. I am sure that he knew as well that I had wished him dead. I tried to talk to him then, tried to tell him of Jesus, but my tongue was too slow. At last, one night, he died. I had gone up to my bedroom to sleep a little, leaving my Mother to watch. She, poor soul, was in an agony of grief for she loved him so. Suddenly I shot up in my bed, my eyes wide open, wide awake!

"John! John! JOHN!" It was Dick's voice, loud and strong. I jumped out of bed, racing for the door. Wrenching it open I flew down the stairs. That cry had been so desperate. I flung open the sitting room door.

"Ssh! You'll wake him; and he has been so peaceful," admonished my Mother. I gasped in disbelief. Dick was in his chair as usual, for he could not lie down. His head dropped upon his breast. I thought I saw those coal-black eyes flicker. I went to him. He was dead! A chill crept over me. I felt sure I had caused his death, and that Satan had taken advantage of my bitterness, and that he was laughing now. My Mother was inconsolable. We buried him in the local church yard, without a stone, and with no one to tend the grave as we said goodbye to Wiltshire and the West of England and headed for Cambridge.

Once in Cambridge I joined a Methodist Church, and began for the first time to enjoy Christian fellowship, and the Word of God. As weeks turned into months, I was gradually given more responsibility within the church, and became first a Sunday school teacher, and later went on Note, as a Lay Preacher. Work-wise, I became assistant to the bursar of Magdalene College. It was during this period that I discovered that I was adopted! Sybil Chivers was her name, a tall, thin spinster, in her fifties, warm and lively in personality. She was the Superintendent of the Sunday school. I was 18 years old by this time.

"John! I'm so glad you could come for a moment." She was standing with her back to the tall dusty windows of one of the many 'rooms' of the rambling Methodist Church to which we both belonged. A great sombre table of some dark wood stood between us, and the diffused rays of the sun gleamed through the silver wisps of her abundant hair, framing her kind and anxious face in golden light.

"I have a little girl that I want to put in your class. She is adopted, and isn't very settled in her home, and so knowing that you are also adopted, I thought you might be able to help her. I do hope you don't mind."

A thrill of shock swept through me, but I managed to remain outwardly calm as I replied, "Yes, of course, I'll be happy to do whatever I can. But how did you know that I was adopted, Miss Chivers?"

"Oh, your Mother was just sharing with me a while ago when we were talking together. I do hope I haven't intruded?"

Adopted! So she wasn't my real Mother; I had suspected it all those years ago, but why hadn't she told me, and been honest about it instead of degrading herself. Then I rang up my uncle, my Mother's brother, my 'hero', and asked him to confirm it. He seemed cold on the telephone, and said that it was true, but that even he had known nothing about it until a year ago.

That night I faced my Mother up with the matter, and amidst many tears she confessed that it was true. She had not even confided in her own Mother and Father, and my uncle was the first to know of this deceit, in 1957.

The laws of adoption prevalent in the '50s made it difficult to find out much, but in fact my adoptive Mother was able to supply me with quite a lot of information – my original birth certificate, for example. That let me discover my real Mother's name, but sadly did nothing to reveal what I really wanted to know – who my real Father was. All my life I had needed a Father. I could not relate to my adoptive Father, and resented the next man in my Mother's life, and even at 18 was denied knowledge of the one who was my true parent. At that time the matter became even more important to me, and remained a trial for many years. I must confess I was not so concerned to find out about my real Mother. I suppose my adoptive Mother was such a very good Mother to me that it was almost impossible to miss one. I did not miss a Mother in fact. Indeed, in all the life we lived and went through together, and with all the defects and weaknesses I may have seen in her, I can only be thankful to God for this woman that He chose to bring me up and to care for me. If she made any real mistake it was only to love me too much. But I did miss a Father!

Writing now, some 50 years further on, it does not matter quite so much, yet it still claims my thoughts at times. Humanly I would like to be able to know from whence I have come, if only for the sake of my own children. Then there are times when I am assailed by a great loneliness, as a man without a state or an origin, whose name even, means nothing since it is not really his. I must suppose this to be a normal reaction, yet for me I think it would be unbearable were it not for Christ and His Word. In many ways I can see that all this has made me value home and family far more than I might otherwise have done. Originally my own early home-life used to make me vow that I would never suffer poverty, but would instead climb to the top of some professional ladder, and with the security of a good income I would keep a good home, and make security and happiness for my wife and kids. Strangely I was to put myself right out of the possibility of ever being able to do such a thing for myself.

But God has done it for me in any case. I live in a fine house with a fine car, and have had a very happy life with a wonderful wife and seven lovely children, four of whom we adopted. I have enjoyed it all without any earthly security, or ability of myself to keep any of it. God has given all this into my hands, and He keeps it going. I revel in being a Father to my children, and I revel in happiness with my wife, and the 'family' that my children can identify with, and not them only but the many other children that in these years have come to make their home with us. Another thought has been of utmost blessing to me, and that is the Fatherhood of God Himself, and the fact that ultimately I have come from Him, and that I am going back to Him. The idea of a real home and a real family that is really mine in every way, and that I am not separated from it forever, nor unable to come into a certain knowledge of it, and all that it means in the future.

My own 'orphanage' and loss of home and parents has only served to highlight the Truth which the Bible unfolds to everyone: that we have all become 'lost' and gone astray from our Heavenly Father and our Heavenly Home; that no one on earth is actually 'at home' or with their true 'family' just as long as they are not pleasing to, and living for God, Who is their true Father and Mother.

Because of 'sin' we are all separated from our spiritual and true 'home' and parents. Yet our Father, loving us, has sent His Son Jesus down to rescue us from the situation we are in, and to restore us to our Father's House, and to reconcile us into our true family circle.

Later this was made even more relevant to me by reading John 8v23:

Let not your heart be troubled;
ye believe in God, believe also in me.
In my Father's house are many mansions...

Jesus was, in fact, stating that His own home was not on this planet, but above and beyond it. He was only passing through; a 'pilgrim' anxiously looking forward to returning from whence He had come – forward to His Father's House.

So, when I read in John 14v1, "I will come again, and receive you unto myself; that where I am, there ye may be also," then I was filled with joy to know that His home is my home also, and yours also if you can accept it.

How happy I have been to be able to point my own children to their true family and their true home. We can all sing triumphantly together, "This world is not my home. I'm just a-passing through." For as Paul the Apostle says in Hebrews 14v14, "Here we have no continuing city, but seek one to come." And Peter, remonstrating in 1Peter 2v11: "Beloved, I beg you as sojourners and pilgrims, abstain from fleshly lusts which war against the soul."

Peter knows it is possible not to get to this Heavenly Home. It is possible not to be reconciled and restored to our Heavenly Father. He knew that if we do not watch our life, making it obedient to God, we shall be eternally separated from that which is our rightful home and family; eternally lost, eternally stateless, rootless, unwanted, and adrift.

Towards the end of 1958, life looked very settled. I was slowly establishing my position in the Methodist Church, and going on well with my job at Magdalene College. Then something happened that changed everything for me. It was to alter my whole course of direction for the next six years!

In my own sight, at that time, I was very righteous. In truth, however, what now took place shows me up as being full of vanity and conceit, the very elements of loathsome self-righteousness.

One day a young girl called upon the Manse of the Methodist Pastor in the area, who was well-known and respected by me. She went to him for help, for comfort, and for succour. She had once been a regular member of that particular Church, but had for some time ceased to attend. She was pregnant now, and the man was a playboy, and had run off and left her as soon as he found out her condition. Her parents had rejected her as soon as they became aware of the situation. She was alone, deserted, an outcast. She turned again to God.

"Please! Please let me come back to church, Pastor! Let me come back into fellowship. Let me break bread at the Lord's Table!"

The Pastor was hesitant. "First let me see my deacons," he said. "Call again two nights from now, and I will give you an answer then." He had prayed with her, and returned into the Manse.

Two nights later she was back. He had seen his deacons, and they had been shocked by his request. "What! Not that woman, Pastor! She is known to all of us; she is a woman of the street. People will say that we sit to eat and drink with prostitutes!"

She had seemed weaker than before. He did not ask her in, but told her on the step that he was unable to do what she asked. He was sorry, but there was nothing that he could do. She had pleaded with him, but to no avail, and at last she turned back into the gloom of that foggy, unfriendly night.

The next day they dragged her out of the River Cam. She was quite dead, she and the unborn child within her.

It sickened me. If this was the Love of God that they all spouted about from the pulpit, then I would not join with them in such a deceit. This was hypocrisy. No, I would never preach again! "Do you hear God? I will never preach again! Never again, unless you send a man to me who has never known it was ever in my heart to do so, and make him ask me to preach a gospel sermon in his church!" The Challenge was given. I packed my belongings, and I left Cambridge forever, and headed towards London.

Is somcone asking if I really was a Christian at that time; if I really did know Christ as my Saviour? Yes, I can honestly say that I believe I did know Jesus as my Saviour, but also I must say that I had still not grown a great deal. I was still very blind to what was in my nature, and I was to remain just as blind for a while longer. How wilful and stubborn we humans are. How truly Gracious and Merciful God is. I withdrew into the world for a season. I still drank occasionally and I still smoked. Are you convinced now that I was unregenerate? I will forgive you!

In the middle of 1959 my adoptive Mother decided to return to her lawful husband! He was still alive, though he had been through a physical hell, having had T.B. of the spine, and made to undergo major surgery to remove the diseased section of his back-bone, having it replaced with a four-inch bar, and a steel brace. When he had come out of the hospital he was homeless. He was jobless, and continuing to drink and smoke heavily. Once more he became ill, and this time he was taken in by the Salvation Army who ran a hospice for down and outs. He came out from there a new man, and the smoking and the drinking were gone! That was when my Mother finally looked him up again, and he, poor man, was overjoyed and accepted her back in happiness. And I got my name back! I was William John GREEN once more! I also took the opportunity to add 'Alexander' as a third Christian name; I suppose I had a desire to be what my Mother had originally called me as far as possible. I dropped the use of 'William' from then on.

The joy was short-lived, the happiness only fleeting. Bill Green died in 1961. He died in a London hospital many miles away from the new home he had so hopefully set up with his wife. He died of cancer of the stomach caused directly by his lifelong consumption of alcohol. I was not living near them when he was taken ill, and neither were they any more together as man and wife; for she had become friendly with a local petrol pump attendant, and Bill, finding out, had gone back to drink! At last she bundled him, with a suitcase of clothes into a car and left him in a neighbouring town. It was to be the final separation as husband and wife.

She visited him in hospital, and once I also went with her. It was the last time either of us saw him alive. Strange to say it was then I discovered that his Father had been a Methodist Lay Preacher! He, himself, had known the Bible, and perhaps even the way of Salvation. He was always faithful to my 'Mother', his wife, but perhaps not so faithful to himself. As I learned more of my Mother's weaknesses, I learned also to see the other side of this pathetic man, who had loved, and not been loved, turning for his consolation to alcohol.

Mum was expensively dressed on that last hospital visit, in a heavy fur coat. Left outside at the curb was a new Hillman car, bought by her latest 'friend'. Bill's eyes lit up as we came into the ward. He stretched out a hand to her. "My dearest..." His breathing wasn't good, and the smell was awful. "Please, please forgive me. Just tell me that we can come back together when I am well. I love you." Tears were in his eyes. I felt quite stifled. My own eyes were full of tears, and I found a very full forgiveness for this man that I had hated, and even wondered if I would be forgiven for it, unreasoned and ignorant as it had been. He had never been physically strong. I had known him for 21 years, and now it was the end. There he lay in front of me, his stomach full of tubes, his body emaciated. It was all the fruit of unfaithfulness. As we made ourselves ready to leave I found myself seeing as it were for the first time the great unfaithfulness of my Mother. I still loved her; I could even find it possible to understand and forgive her. But she had lied when she kissed him and assured him of a home when he was well. She had lied as she stepped back into the Hillman, and she was to go on lying for many years, until stripped of her husband, her lovers, and her home, she was confronted with God.

"All right, Bill. Now don't worry. Everything will be alright, you'll see." She waved goodbye. She knew he would die of course. How blind I had been. Why had I never realised where she was on all those empty nights when I was a baby, and she was supposed to be out at the cinema? And that was why he had drunk so much. Of course he should not have done so, but there had been a reason. My Mother I also pitied, for it seemed obvious that the love she had from her husband was not enough, and she needed more; had to have more. Perhaps he was cold and she was passionate, over emotional, ever unsatisfied. These days that is grounds for a divorce in our law courts, though not in God's eyes. Then for the first time I began to look at marriage, and I saw that it had to be a partnership, and that both partners were equally responsible to see that the marriage was a success; each one sharing in the making or the breaking.

Half an hour after we left the hospital, Bill Green was dead. Twelve years earlier I had happily endorsed my Mother's adultery, thinking she deserved a break and some happiness with a man that loved her. She may possibly have needed both, yet now as we drove along the rain-washed streets of London, I knew that she should never have given in to that need. It had brought shame, heartbreak, and death; and still her life was not ended, and her needs not satisfied.

By this time I was seeing many things in life as if for the first time, re-evaluating old standards and opinions. I was still doing much that was purely self-righteous. I assumed that because Christ had died for me, all my views, feelings and opinions, had to be right. I was not learning very well, or very fast.

Chapter Three

DRIFTING VAINLY

In 1961 I left the job I had found for myself in Local Government and became an assistant Supervisor in a Juvenile Remand Home.

In my heart I still believed and had faith in Christ, but I was quite cut off from all Christian fellowship, keeping away still from church groups. The new life that had fleetingly opened up for me that afternoon in 1957 was now in cold storage, and I had effectively quenched the Holy Spirit by giving in to criticism. Working as an accounts clerk, and studying Constitutional Law in my spare time, I had not been satisfied. I felt my life to be somehow very irrelevant; just a very minor sprocket on a very tiny cog in a vast and complex machine. Everything I did was automatically predictable, and seemingly futile.

Towards the end of the year I began to look for work in other fields, and was intrigued by an advertisement appealing for applicants for the post of an assistant supervisor in a juvenile remand home in Kent. Remand homes, in England are 'homes' for adults and for juveniles who, having been arrested and brought before a magistrate, have not been finally sentenced owing to a lack of evidence and background information both socially and medically. Thus they are remanded, put on one side for a time, to allow observations and investigations to be carried out.

The remand home in which I eventually found myself was for boys between the ages of 8 and 17 years old. My job was to constantly watch, and keep under surveillance these boys, and at the same time try to make helpful relationships with them which would assist in assessing their mental and social behaviour. It was interesting work, but frustrating too. It was a total change for me, and brought me into contact with elements of society, and personal problems quite beyond my experience. I was totally unprepared for the harsh discipline, and at times brutal treatment given out to the inmates by members of staff. I believed in discipline, and still do, but I am not the kind of person to delight in the use of violence as an answer to each and every misdemeanour.

Once I was forced to watch a boy caned in that remand home. He was caned by the Superintendent himself, a young man in his thirties and an ex-borstal P.T. instructor. He was in excellent physical condition. The boy he was to cane was just ten years old, and his crime was that he had refused to give information against a suspected thief in the home. He was placed bending over a chair at one end of the room, and held firmly in that position by another staff member. I was to be present as an 'official witness' as the law demanded. I was to protest at what happened, but no one seriously listened to me.

The boy's pants were pulled down to expose bony buttocks. The Superintendent then appeared in a spotless white singlet and P.E. shorts, white socks and tennis shoes; it was as if he had dressed especially for the occasion. It was night-time. Striding to the opposite end of the room to the boy, smiling grimly, and flexing a very springy cane, he measured the distance, perhaps some 30 feet, with his eye. With a sudden shout he sprang forward cane uplifted, and charged towards the trembling child, by this time also screaming in terror. The cane came down, curling itself around the waist of the boy, choking his scream into a strangulated gurgle of pain. The Superintendent walked slowly back, and turning again, repeated the performance, for such I am sure it was. He did this not once or twice or six times, but until the child slipped unconscious from the grip of the grinning individual who so cruelly held him there. The boy was bloody. No doctor was to see him.

On another occasion a boy ran away from the home. A 15-year-old bundle of nerves, with a mop of untidy, carroty hair, his body a constant fidget of bony self-consciousness. He was a Catholic, and had been taught many things by the Priest that made him fear death utterly. His Mother had died earlier in his life, and he had loved her dearly. She had left her body for scientific research, and there had been no proper funeral. The boy would often wake at night screaming, and crying out to know where they had put his Mother. One day a letter had come for him to say that his Father was ill and near to die with cancer, could he not get leave to return home. He was distracted and begged for permission to be taken home to see his Father. Such permission was refused. He ran, predictably, away. It was obvious that he would. Some on the staff were even glad that he had done so, not because they sympathised with his problem, but because they looked forward to getting him back for further correction! I must admit that at the time I had privately wondered if perhaps he had not been 'allowed' to escape on purpose, just for 'sport'. It may sound horrific, but I can assure you it WAS horrific. I had considered making an official report, but other members of staff assured me that if there was any kind of trouble they would also be in danger of losing their jobs, and that they would therefore not affirm anything I might say. They caught the boy, of course. They knew he would try to return to his Father's house, and sure enough he arrived, and was just climbing in through a window when they grabbed him. He never got inside, and was not allowed to see his Father; in fact he never saw his Father again! I was on duty the night they dumped him back in the remand home. The Superintendent was also on duty, plus his deputy who was an older man with a very kind heart, but who by this time was rendered often useless by excessive drinking. I was also drinking a lot just then. I had started in an effort to blot out some of the horror from my mind. We were all, together with the cook, another drunkard, in the kitchen having a cup of cocoa when the police arrived. They literally dragged the boy into the kitchen, where we were. Poor Carroty-Head; he just stood there after the police had left, head down, a picture of dejection and dishevelled apprehension. He was then subjected to more questioning, although we already knew the whole story by then. But it seemed the Superintendent believed that there was more to find out. The boy was punched, kicked and hit all around the kitchen until he just dropped on the floor. Then the Superintendent continued to kick the boy until the rest of us tried to stop him. It took all three of us, for he was a very strong man indeed. We were rewarded with curses and murderous threats. But at least we stopped him, and the boy was moved out to his dormitory. The three of us then went out to get drunk.

The next morning I was asked to move to another institution a hundred miles away. The deputy was dismissed for drunkenness, which was a fair reason if not the right one, and the cook took ill and died!

But by the time that next morning had come something had happened to me. I had woken up in the early hours with my head splitting, and my stomach heaving. I vomited all over the bed, and lay cold and empty, staring out at the stars through the bedroom window. My mind cleared, and I began to realise the folly of it all! The real problem, the real enemy was not the Superintendent, not violence itself, but Evil. I sat up in my bed now, alert. I was wide awake. I saw that drinking had been and was no answer for me or for any one; no answer for my firm friend the deputy. No answer for the cook. We had all been using drink as a prop for our own weakness and shortcoming, as a drug to shut out the truth. Drinking could not help the situation in the home. Nothing could change this horror, only Jesus Christ could do it. It was just as if the Lord Himself was putting His thoughts into my head in the frosty stillness of the night. From that time I have never touched alcohol again, seeing it as a trap, and a temptation to run away from realities in the world around us and in ourselves.

I began to read again the New Testament, and began to talk to the boys about Christ during the few weeks remaining to me at the home. Many were converted in tears before I finally left.

I was transferred to an ordinary Council children's home. The night I arrived there, there was a riot going on, and the police were trying to quieten things down! The houseparents in charge were church-going Baptists, and were certainly not violent. On the other hand they were not very close to the children either, and were more concerned for their own small family, living most of the time apart in their own private flat attached to the home. One night I arrived late after a day's holiday. Walking in through the front door, it was 10 p.m., I was conscious of the quietness in the house, though I could see the kitchen light on through the dining room hatch. I stopped to listen, and a piercing scream rent the air. It was the housemother's voice from the kitchen. I ran through the dining room doorway and looked through the hatch.

The matron, a tall, slightly-built woman in her late forties, was standing rigid with fear in front of the fridge. Facing her was one of the teenage boys from the home. In his hand, and pointed towards her, was a long carving knife; his face screwed up with hatred and anger. I said nothing, but raced round to the kitchen door and quickly stepped between the boy and the Matron. I knew the boy, and I felt confident that there was no real violence in him, but I also knew that there was often acid in the mouth of the Matron, and I guessed that somehow she had overstepped the mark of common sense when speaking on some point or other with the lad. He must have been on washing-up duty when she found him there.

"Get out of here!" he snarled at me.

"Give me the knife, David," I said, holding out my hand towards him.

"I warn yer! I'll stick yer as well, if need be! I'm gonna get this old bitch!"

"The knife isn't long enough to travel through the both of us. If you stick me it won't reach her – and anyway you don't really want to hurt anyone at all. Do give me the knife David." I made a step towards him. "Give it to me now!"

He dropped it into my hand, and turning towards the sink behind him, he burst into tears. The Matron rushed out calling for her husband. I hustled the boy off to his bed, put the lights out, and also went to bed, wondering a great deal. The next day I was called early to the office.

"Mr. Green, we feel, my wife and I, that you are not the right person for here, and we think it might be wise if you were to resign!" A parcel lay on the desk in front of the houseparent. In it were some two dozen New Testaments; ones that I had given out over the months to one and another of the children. "Also I believe you have been giving out these Testaments? We feel the children are too young to get to grips with too much religion. Please do take them with you when you go. Thank you."

We talked some more, but the result was the same. Yes, they were Christians, but they did not want God 'rammed' down the children's throats. Neither did they want any 'heroes' in the home trying to make a name for themselves with the children. I left.

Weeks went by. I remained unemployed. My thoughts constantly turned to the Lord, and I began to think of working somehow just for Him. But how, and where? I still had no strong church connection.

On Christmas Eve, I was passing through Penge, in South London, and hearing a Carol Service was in progress at the Parish Church, I went in. A man was already in the pulpit as I found a seat, and as I sat down he began to speak, ever so briefly on Love. Somehow it touched everything that I had felt, experienced and gone through up to that very moment. After the service I managed to fix an appointment to see the speaker. He turned out to be the Vicar of Penge, The Rev. John Collinson. A few days after Christmas I found myself in his house, and he listened to all I had to say very quietly and carefully, until I had finished. Then he suggested we should pray together. We spent quite some time in prayer, and afterwards he looked at me and smiled, and said, "Now isn't the time to go, John. Wait a little. You need three things. First you need more Christian fellowship; you haven't had much so far. Second you need a knowledge of God's Word; so far you don't know enough. Third you need tools to work with; spiritual tools that so far you do not have."

I felt discouraged, and left him down at heart. But of course he was absolutely right in every point. Every word he had said was true. He could certainly have been exercising the Gift of Knowledge that night. I shall ever be glad of his wise counsel. I was still out of work, and with little real idea of what I should be doing. I did not want to return to office work and columns of figures, and at the same time I did not want to go back into the child welfare scene and find myself in a spiritual straight jacket. But I reckoned without God, who was still busy arranging my steps in front of me! Within a few days a friend of mine suggested that I went to visit the offices of a certain Christian Society having a number of small homes for children. My friend thought I would find it interesting to talk to the Executive Officer, a certain Captain Martin. I was not very keen on the idea. Anyway I went, and was immediately captured. I had never heard of George Muller, and so when I was told how this particular Society ran its affairs I had no previous information to compare it with; I sat in the London Office for a good three hours listening to accounts of His Provision, and of the work of Saving Grace amongst the children. I was thrilled, and intrigued. Before the afternoon was over I had accepted an invitation to visit one of the homes situated in West Sussex – Fegan House, Buxted. All through that interview in Captain Martin's office I had been belching out clouds of blue smoke from a curly pipe, which formed part of my smoking habit. Captain Martin never referred to it at all; a very kind and gracious man, with a really exuberant and enthusiastic personality. The Grace of God is greater far than ours! Many dear people of God would probably have written me off there and then; surely he can't be saved, smoking like that!

I travelled down to Sussex and spent a delightful weekend with Gill and Alastair Davidson and their 'family' of 17 boys. It was a house full of love; it was a true family.

As they waved me off back to London the following Monday morning I knew that it was God's Plan for me to work with them there. As the train gathered speed I opened my Bible and found myself reading Romans 12v1: "Present your bodies a living sacrifice, holy, acceptable unto God..." I choked on my smoking pipe, and began to cough; my eyes were watering. I opened the window of the carriage where I sat alone, and let in some fresh air. I sat down again, startled. I glanced out across the passing countryside and saw factory chimneys pouring out thick black smoke, tainting the atmosphere for miles around. Immediately I saw a connection with myself. How could I keep on filling my body with such grime? How could I expect God to dwell in such filth? Did I want others to follow my example and spoil themselves also? I felt shocked. I quickly knocked the fire out of my pipe and put it away. Later, back at home in my lodgings, I burnt it, plus a number of others that I had, my supply of tobacco, and three packets of cigarettes. Quite a bonfire! The appetite for smoking departed; I have never ever again felt the need to smoke. One more prop had been removed, as I began to learn to lean more and more on God.

A week later I returned to Sussex as assistant to Gill and Alastair Davidson. From here on my growth in Christ and the Christian Life began to put on speed.

Chapter Four

RESTORATION

Behold I set before you this day
a blessing and a curse;
a blessing if ye obey the commandment of the Lord
your God, which I command you this day;
and a curse if ye will not obey...
Deuteronomy 11v26.

The couple I was now to find myself working with were very different to any other people I had ever known up to that time. Gill and Alastair Davidson had been missionaries in India many years previously, and both of them, though temperamentally diverse, were very committed Christians.

Just a few days after my arrival, Gill asked me if I had received the Holy Spirit into my life. Without much thought behind it I answered, "Yes!"

She looked at me a bit oddly then, I thought, and asked, "Can you prove it?"

I was quite floored by that one, and asked her what she had meant. She merely referred me to Mark 16, and suggested I read the whole chapter carefully, bearing in mind her question. Needless to say I did so, and at once was very disturbed, and began to seriously think over the matter very sincerely. At that time the 'family' attended a Baptist Church on Sunday mornings, and a Free Mission Hall in the evening. The home itself was strikingly different from anything that I had previously encountered. It was a real home and family in every way. We all lived together in the same house, eating and sitting together. There was little or no going on holiday apart from when we took all the children with us as well as a family, and no going on or off 'duty'.

There was a great closeness between the children and us, and for the first time I felt happy and settled; I began to put down roots, a dangerous thing to do!

Christ was loved and uplifted in this place, and I found myself going deeper into the things of God. The first and second needs outlined by John Collinson of Penge were now being provided within only a very few months.

Every morning about ten, we used to meet in the cosy kitchen of the old house – its cellars went back to about 1000 A.D. – and have a cup of coffee together, just the three of us; me and the Davidsons alone. The children would be away at local schools, and most of the housework finished; we had no domestic helpers. Gill would have the lunch on, and Alastair and I would be jobbing around the house or the garden. Sipping a big, comfortable mug of coffee, and munching a biscuit or two, we would talk over the day's activities and about the different children in our care. Then out would come a copy of *Daily Light* and Alastair or Gill would read the reading for the day, and the other would pray. After a while I was also asked to take a reading, but I was never asked to pray, and I was glad about it. Indeed I was always afraid they might ask me, since I was not used to such things, and was still very self-conscious. One day, however, I was planting cabbage plants in the garden, thinking over a problem we had with one of the 14-year-old boys in the house. He had been caught stealing, and was a consistent liar. We were all very concerned about him, but found him very hard to love. The sun warmed my back as I crouched on the newly dug, earthy soil, making holes with my trowel for the plantlings. A cool breeze blew in my face, birds hopped hopefully, and unafraid, looking for any worms I might be bringing to light.

"Why don't you pray for David?" The question popped into my thoughts. "You should pray for him in the fellowship this morning!" I felt surprised by this unsought conviction, and looked up, pausing in my work. Suddenly the hand-bell rang; Gill was calling us for coffee. I walked slowly to the kitchen, and crossing to the sink began to wash my hands. Now, how should I go about it? I felt I could not just pray without being asked. I fretted within myself.

"John!" It was Gill speaking from in front of the cooker where she was stirring a saucepan. "I feel it would be good if you led us in prayer this morning. We haven't asked you before, but somehow it would be so right today; what do you think about it?"

We had a wonderful time of prayer, and I was able to pray, and from that hour I believe David's life began to change. Yet, as the days passed and turned into weeks and months, I had still reached no clear conclusion about Gill's earlier comments about the Holy Spirit. I had read Mark 16 through a number of times, and had been forced to the conclusion that 'these signs' did not follow me! But did that really mean that I did not have the Holy Spirit? I did not believe this in my heart, and must be honest enough to say that I still do not believe it.

Eventually the Davidsons took me to a big evangelistic meeting in what was apparently called the Chinese Church in London. An evangelist was scheduled to speak on 'The Baptism of the Holy Spirit'. He was a small, quiet, lowly man in a battered black suit and a clerical collar. He was about 50 and came from the Middle East. He spoke nothing specifically about the advertised subject but narrated many experiences that he had had of God's Provision, and other answers to prayer. At the end of his message he asked those who were interested in receiving the Holy Spirit to go to the front of the church, where he would pray for them. I was quite determined not to budge from my seat, but nevertheless got to my unwilling feet and felt almost pulled along with dozens of others to the front. I trembled from head to foot when he prayed for us all, but otherwise was not greatly moved, and came away cursing myself for being an over-emotional fool!

Some weeks later we all, the whole family, went to an evening meeting in the grounds of the I.B.T.I. (The International Bible Training Institute), in Burgess Hill, Sussex, just a few miles from us. It was the first night of their Annual Camp Convention; a very Pentecostal gathering. As yet, however, I knew nothing of 'Pentecostals'; we were just attending an evangelistic meeting! Something like Keswick, Gill said it was! Well, I did not even know what Keswick was, or even where it was, so I was none the wiser. Anyway we went; we all went, children and all. Alastair, who was not altogether happy about this 'Pentecostal' doctrine, also went. He was a tall, thin Scot, upright and true in his character, sensitive and kind. He was one of the dearest and most graciously humble men I have ever met.

The meeting proved quite an experience in every way. It was held in a huge tent seating more than a thousand people, and it seemed even more were crammed into it on this particular night. A vast platform, disguised with gorgeous flowers, and seating a choir of Bible students, and numerous pastors, evangelists and missionaries, dominated one end. Music was supplied by a grand piano and a Hammond organ, both beautifully played. Choruses were being gustily sung as we all trooped up the main aisle, and just as we sat down the meeting proper began; someone being asked to lead in prayer. So we all stood up again, as all around us welled a sudden gigantic roar of chaotic and quite meaningless sound, pouring from over a thousand open mouths. I was appalled by what to me seemed a most disorderly scene, where it was impossible to hear whatever the 'brother at the front' was praying. I did not say Amen! At last with a few 'Hallelujah's and 'Glory's everything became quiet once more, except for an excited hum of expectation. We sat down again, and the meeting then continued along fairly ordinary lines, with good testimonies and singing, and then a message from a young evangelist from Northern Ireland. He spoke on the Holy Spirit's Ministry, and succeeded in making all of us hunger and thirst for more of Christ in our lives and experience. Many went forward for prayer after he finished speaking. A large open space had been left in front of the platform, and straw had been strewn upon the ground there. The choir sang, the organ played, and more and more people began making their way to the front. Alastair stood up slowly and a little diffidently made his prim way to the front. I felt a bit ashamed that he should be able to overcome all his doubts and fears, whilst I stayed where I was. So I also got up and went to the front to join the crowd there on their knees, and standing just as they were, seeking God. I found a small space where I also could kneel down. I could see no sign of Alastair. People were praying all around me; some were prostrate upon the ground. One woman was shouting and wildly kicking her legs about in a very indecorous manner! I closed my eyes to blot it all out; it was too fantastic – I did not like it at all. The noise was deafening. Surely God was not in all this! Suddenly my head was taken in a steel grip, and a man's voice began calling down the Holy Spirit upon me, whilst all the time shaking my head jerkily from side to side as if he expected it to rattle. I was deeply offended; what was he trying to do? Force the Holy Spirit into my head like jam into a jar? I was relieved when he finally disappeared, muttering incoherent incantations and followed by an equally incoherent group of Bible students who, I thought, were no doubt 'learning the trade'. I made ready then to depart from this awful place. I felt cold as ice and as far from the Presence of God as it is possible to be. I was already halfway up when a gentle hand was laid upon my shoulder. Looking up I saw a rather amused face smiling down at me.

"Are you going so soon? Did you receive the Holy Spirit already?" he asked. He looked very calm and unhurried; we could have been alone in his house far away from anyone, instead of in the midst of this whirling tumult. I looked at him.

"If there be any 'Holy Spirit' then I have not felt Him around," I replied truculently, and a little desperately. I just wanted to get away. The amused smile vanished, and the eyes looked a little troubled.

"Are you Saved?" he asked.

"Of course I'm saved. Would I be here otherwise?" I was still very shaken by the whole proceeding, and felt I was in the midst of what looked and felt like a drunken orgy!

"Well," he mildly began, "I've been watching you for some time, and I haven't seen you praying. Perhaps before you leave, you might like to thank the Lord for saving your unworthy soul." And he left me, open-mouthed, wretched and humbled. I wished the floor could have opened up. Why had I been so blind, so selfish, so altogether forgetful of God? I closed my eyes then, as I dropped back upon my knees, and began to thank my Father in Heaven for His Son, Jesus, my Saviour. I began to remember the long road I had journeyed upon, and the Wonderful Love, and Compassion with which He had sought me out through the years gone by. More and more words tumbled up and out of my heart. Why had I never thought to thank Him more, before?

Turn your eyes upon Jesus,
Look full in His Wonderful Face,
And the things of the earth will grow strangely dim
In the light of His Glory and Grace.

How true those words were. I no longer saw the people around me, or heard them. I was alone with my Lord.

Someone seemed to be singing loudly in what might have been Spanish. It seemed very close at hand. I opened my eyes, and it stopped! I found a ring of men standing around me smiling, and with lifted arms, all thanking God for 'filling me with the Holy Spirit'.

"Someone was singing in Spanish weren't they?" I asked, looking from face to face.

"That was you, young man! God has wonderfully blessed you this night!" I must have looked my disbelief. I looked around and saw the tent was empty; everyone had gone. We were the only ones present. It was 11.30 p.m.; I had been there more than an hour and a half since I first began to praise the Lord.

"You have received the Gift of Tongues, brother."

It was fantastic. Could it really be so? Was this the beginning of receiving those 'spiritual tools' Mr. Collinson had spoken of? A week later I was baptised in water by immersion. Yes, I know I had been baptised as a child, but then I knew nothing about being Born Again; knew nothing for myself of Jesus my own Lord and Saviour. At 23 years old I did know, and I wanted to publicly state my full intention of living a new life for Him, progressively till I died, or till He came to meet me on the earth. It was a tremendous blessing to me, and I can look back to these 'evidences' of God in my life constantly, and find strength and encouragement. Yet I was still but a 'child' in front of God. Indeed I was but a slow 'child', and many times I have felt as slow to learn the things of God as I was to learn to read at school. I remained in the children's home with the Davidsons, until February 1965. All the time the Lord continued to bless me in fellowship with other Christians, and I saw almost every child in that home come to Christ, and grow in his life, although it is also to be accepted that not all of them stood strongly in that life, and some slipped back for a while. It was a wonderful and special period of my life, and I put down very deep roots indeed. I could not envisage ever leaving.

In 1964 the I.B.T.I. Camp Convention came around again. It was in August. The Governing Body of the homes had heard that some of our children had spoken in 'tongues', and taking a stand on orthodoxy they informed us that we must cease to teach Pentecostal doctrines, and forbade us to take the children anywhere where they might hear of it. So this year we were prevented from taking the children to the Camp meetings. With me it was fully possible to go in my spare time, and I wanted to go very much, for I felt that once again God would speak to me there in those meetings. So on the opening evening I was there, no longer a stranger. There were still 'excesses' to put up with, but I was not looking at them. I was there to receive from Jesus. But I must admit that there is something in my human nature that is ever quick to find fault and criticise. It is a character flaw which Satan has been at pains to use as a means of putting me 'out of the spirit' at crucial times when God wants to bless. How he longs to keep us from God; how powerfully he comes to us through our flesh. The 'ministry' on this first night of meetings was to be shared by an Argentinean husband and wife. He was short and swarthy, with gold spectacles and gold teeth. He had a sleek moustache as well, and looked every inch a slick salesman. He held on to the microphone aggressively, and hurled his powerful voice mercilessly into it, and thence deafeningly via the loudspeaker speaker also into our unprotected ears. Before he preached, he and his wife 'entertained' us all with a musical item; he played a trumpet, and she an accordion, both violently out of key. The whole performance jarred, and I came away with a headache and a feeling of loss. I had felt so expectant!

"Hey! John Green! Wait!" I turned and found a tallish, balding man of about 43 trying to get to me through the milling crowd of campers. I stopped, wondering what he wanted. I knew him all right. He was the secretary of a small Gospel Mission we sometimes attended. His name was Bert Berry.

At last he caught up with me, a little breathless, but obviously very happy to have found me. He grabbed my hand.

"I've been trying to catch your eye all evening," he said. "I want you to come and preach for us one evening next month. I do hope you can make it?"

At first I did not realise what it was he was asking. I had never once preached since leaving the Methodists in Cambridge in 1958. I stared at him in blank amazement, and then from a great distance words began to come back into my mind.

"Do you hear God? I will never preach again unless you send a man to me who has never known it was in my heart to preach, and make him ask me to preach a gospel sermon in his church."

That had been six years ago, hundreds of miles distant. I struggled to pull myself together, and found myself refusing the invitation, and it was a legitimate refusal. We were all to be away in Devon with the entire family during September. It was just not possible to accept.

"Some other time, perhaps?" I finished off-handedly. He looked at me with a somewhat puzzled expression, but quickly gave his hand in farewell and departed, shaking his head. I was perspiring, and my legs felt weak under me. I sat in the bus going home, glad that I had been able to refuse. Yes, glad! I did not want to be a preacher now anyway. I was happy where I was. Anyway it was alright. God was just showing me that He didn't want it; if He had wanted me to go that way, He would have made it possible to accept! And so I comforted myself! Poor foolish, stubborn, ignorant child that I was. The following day was a Sunday. We were, as usual, to go to the Baptist Church that morning. We returned to the home about noon to hear the phone ringing. I ran to answer it.

"Hullo? Is that Mr. Green?"

"Speaking!" I replied, not recognising the voice immediately.

"Ah, good! This is Bert Berry again; you remember we met last night! Well I'm sorry to ring you up like this, but our Pastor has been taken unwell, and we have no one for the Evening Service. We wondered if you could come over and give us a Gospel Message? I know it's short notice."

Nothing can describe how I felt just then. "Well...er..." My voice trailed away; I could find no words.

"Thanks so much. See you this evening then." Click; the line went dead. I stood there, the phone still to my ear. This just could not be happening. A Gospel Message! It was the only thing left out the previous evening. There seemed to be such an insistence in this matter. Well of course! God hears all our words. But this was somehow different. I had issued a challenge. And now six years later I was being taken up on it. I felt very unsettled. The evening came, and I preached. I preached on John chapter 9; it was a very wobbly sermon. The Pastor apparently had made a rapid recovery, for just as I was about to stand up to speak he came into the hall and sat down in the congregation! He looked pale though, and rather serious. I felt even more nervous, and all the time, within me, a struggle was continuing. I was not going to be uprooted. I was not a preacher; look what a mess I was making of this sermon. Yet I could not get away from the terrible fact of the taking up of my own words. A coincidence?

I returned to the home. Gill and Alastair were full of chatter about such a surprising happening. I could say nothing at all! Morning came. It was August Bank Holiday Monday. Gill had decided to risk the disfavour of the Administration in London, and to take a group of the older, saved, boys to the afternoon Missionary Rally at the Bible College. I was to accompany them. I woke up that morning to find the sunlight streaming in through my bedroom window. I reached for my Bible and opened it to Deuteronomy chapter 11 verse 26.

Behold I set before you this day a Blessing and a Curse; a Blessing if ye obey the commandment of the Lord your God, which I command you this day; and a Curse if ye will not obey.

I put it hurriedly down. I lay there on the bed silent. I could not pray. I felt old and ill. I must have seemed a very miserable person that day, but no one mentioned it. Gill kept on looking in my direction. We went to the Rally as planned. We found the speaker was to be the Argentinean brother. I felt wretched. We sat on the chairs in the hot, grass-scented, tent. I could not sing. I felt trapped. At last he got up to speak. He spoke on 2 Kings chapter 7: "If we tarry here till morning light, some mischief will overtake us." He proceeded to give a fast and challenging message and appeal. I felt literally attacked personally, as if every word was being addressed especially to me. He even seemed to look and point at me at every challenge. I felt weaker and weaker, but still I resisted…and he finished. Silence in the great tent. The material of it flapped uneasily, and billowed out as if being filled with some enormous 'Presence'. The cords strained at the pegs; no one moved, no one spoke. I felt my thoughts racing. I looked anxiously around; someone will speak my name! I know it! God will point me out! I was mortally afraid, yet held in my seat, and strangely fascinated by the situation. Somebody began to sob on the other side of the congregation. Then, right at the back of the tent, a deep resonant voice boomed forth in a language that could have been Heavenly. It did not sound very light-hearted though. I turned to see who was speaking, and found a big man dressed in working clothes; a farmer perhaps. I did not know him. I settled restlessly and uneasily back in my seat. There was a moment's silence once more. Then the back of my chair was jerked backwards as strong hands caught hold of it. Someone was pulling themselves up to a standing position behind me. A woman's voice began to speak in English.

"Thus saith the Lord: 'This day I have set before you a Blessing and a Curse; A blessing if you will obey what you know to be my will, and a curse if you refuse.'"

That was that! I had to give in!

"Alright, Lord, I accept. If you want me to preach, if you want me to speak for you anywhere, any time, then I will."

Do you believe that God can reach you today, and communicate His Will to you? Well I do. I have no choice; it has been proved to me beyond all doubt time and time again. There in that tent, God – a very personal God – dealt with me in a very personal way. He desires to do the same with you. Are you ready to let Him do so, even if it may be far from your own thoughts and ambitions? He can make you, but He can also break you. Are you ready?

Chapter Five

TRANSITION

I resigned from the children's home, sold all my possessions – books, paintings, records, and so on – and in February 1965 was admitted into the I.B.T.I. as a Bible Student. Six months later the home closed down for ever, and the Davidsons themselves moved on to other ministries.

At last I was committed to a life for God alone. I had tried twice to bring it about on my own, and failed. Now it had been done for me. But Kenya was nowhere in my thoughts. It had never occurred to me that I would ever leave England. So far are his thoughts removed from ours!

I spent two good years at I.B.T.I., benefiting greatly from the concentrated life of prayer and study, and from the daily experience of His Provision. But at the conclusion of my course, I was still without clear direction as to the next step. What did God want next? I prayed, but He was silent. For some six months I went up to Birmingham as an assistant to the Hockley Pentecostal Church. Then the College asked me to return to help with Administration for a time. And there, towards the end of 1967 the Lord began once more to speak to me.

I had been working late in my office, and after a while, feeling restless, I went into the library and picked up a book with which to relax. It was entitled *'When God Changed a Man'* and was by a Pentecostal pioneer by the name of W.F.P. Burton. I was not acquainted with him. As I read, the hours sped by, and I found myself in the Congo following the life of an African slave trader to the foot of the Cross of Calvary. Tears began to stream down my face as I read, and my heart was moved greatly. That small and tattered book was God's 'still small voice' to my soul that night. As I completed the last page, I felt much as perhaps Jacob had felt on waking from his sleep and dreams. He said then, "Surely the Lord is in this place, and I knew it not." The supernatural reality of God so overwhelmed and surrounded me then, as the first streaks of morning light heralded the dawn, that I had no thought of sleep. I had never thought of Africa. I hated heat, and was afraid of snakes; even worms made me feel sick! But there was no doubt God had spoken to me. How could I be wholly sure though, and in any case 'where' in Africa?

"Lord," I prayed, "I am willing to go, but send me confirmation. I must know where I am to go. Send me a man, a man from Africa, an African to tell me clearly." And I slept, just as I was, in the chair.

Three days later, late in the afternoon, visitors arrived at the College, and I was the one to let them in through the front door. One was a tall, rather thin Englishman, who introduced himself as the Rev. Cuthbert Dawkins. I remembered him vaguely, having heard him speak at a long past College Convention years before. With him was an equally tall and wiry black African, with very bright and merry eyes that carefully looked me up and down. His name was Pastor Silas Owiti. They had just arrived from Kenya. Could they stay the night? Oh, yes of course they could, and my mind was racing ahead of me.

That evening was usually prayer meeting night, but the Principal, using the opportunity, turned it into a 'missionary' night, and Silas Owiti, our surprise guest from Kenya was asked to speak. He had joyously accepted, and gave us all a powerful missionary challenge. I was very much alert, and realised that it might be that this was the man I had asked God to send. He had not been expected and could not have been predicted. On the other hand there would be little opportunity or reason for us to see much of each other; both he and Rev. Dawkins were to leave the following morning.

After the service all the College staff were invited to the Dean of Studies' apartment for some coffee. We had to leave the Chapel in the main building and walk across a fairly large and very dark yard to get there. I had hung back after the others had left in order to turn out lights and lock a few doors. I was walking slowly and alone across the darkened yard, when I almost bumped into a solid mass in front of me. It was Silas Owiti! He had apparently turned back to look for me. He gave me a great bear hug, and putting his arm around me began to propel me forward once more.

"It's brother Green, isn't it? I was sent to find you! You know brother, we need young men like you in Kenya!"

I choked, stuttered, but was rendered almost speechless. He laughed then, and left me standing as he raced back to the others who by this time were almost entering the apartment. We were not to speak to each other again until I met him in Kenya.

But I did speak to Cuthbert Dawkins before he left the following morning, and the result was that I discovered that Trinity Fellowship, the work of Faith he ran in Kenya, needed someone towards the end of 1968, and yes, if I felt so led, then I could be that someone. However it was not as easy as it seemed. For one thing the Mission would expect me to look after myself financially; they would not give me any remuneration. And I would also have to pay my air fare to Kenya. All the money I had saved had gone into my Training at I.B.T.I. I was penniless. It seemed that if God really wanted me in Kenya, He would have to show me the way to get there. Humanly, there was no one to turn to for help. I had few friends apart from the Davidsons, and no strong church affiliation to appeal to for backing.

The first thing I did was to resign from the College!

Within a week a letter arrived for me from a total stranger. Her name was Mrs. Drake it appeared, and she was quite elderly. She wrote that another elderly lady friend of hers had met me once two years before as I ministered with a group of College students in a church in Southampton in southern England. This lady was blind, and could not see me, but she had been struck by the words I had brought on that occasion, and now, writing from Israel, had suggested to her friend Mrs. Drake that she invite me to their church down at Sidmouth in Devon. And so Mrs. Drake now wrote to invite me. She enclosed a postal order for 30 shillings, which amounted to the coach fare, one way, in those days. Needless to say I went. It all seemed to fit in very clearly.

On the appointed day I alighted from the coach at Sidmouth, and was immediately hailed by a warm hearted Welshman who had come to meet me in his battered Minibus. He had been a Pastor with the British Assemblies of God, but had now retired; he it was who led the small fellowship that had invited me down. He took me back to his home, where his dear wife welcomed me like a long lost son and fed me bounteously.

Later that night I was taken to the small upper room somewhere in the town, where the Meeting was to take place, and it was that I first met Mrs. Drake. She was then 86 years of age, blind, and almost stone deaf! She was not senile however and she loved the Lord with all her heart and soul. She was to remain a great friend and prayer partner until her death in 1976. I have kept all her letters to me over that period of time, each one brimming over with the inspiration of the Holy Spirit, and hearty encouragement. Each one written painstakingly via a hand held magnifying glass. Her prayers, on countless occasions, working most effectively for me, and for the work I was to do in Kenya. She was a Mother of hundreds all over the world, though childless herself, and the Lord raised her up. With her on that evening were six other elderly ladies. I opened up my heart and the Word of God to them. And they gave me 30 shillings as an offering. Back in the Pastor's house, eating cheese and pickles I wondered why I had come! Blind as a bat was I. Pastor Newton excused himself whilst we were eating, saying he had to make a phone call. Some 20 minutes later he returned to the room, his face aglow with pleasure and satisfaction. In his hand he held a piece of paper which he put into my hand.

"Eleven Meetings, young man! Eleven meetings ahead of you, and the first tomorrow night at Brixham just around the corner!" He had been busy phoning all his pastor friends, and had quietly fixed up a tour of churches for me, hoping that interested support might be aroused.

First Sister Drake and now Pastor Newton had become pillars of spiritual strength, and indeed over many years remained so. Only the Lord Himself could have endeared me to their hearts. The day following, I travelled to Brixham, and met Stan Hyde who was then pioneering the Assembly there. With this encounter, a firm and lasting platform of sustaining love and prayer was created. Stan Hyde and his wife Doreen, had never met me before, but it was like a homecoming. Brixham became my 'spiritual home'. From Devon and those initial 11 meetings, the Lord was to lead me throughout England to different churches and friends, and then across to Denmark as well, so that by October 1968 I had managed to obtain my air fare to Kenya, and the knowledge that many sincere people would pray for me. There were no promises of financial support; and there was nothing in my pocket when I got on to the plane for Kenya on the 12th December 1968. I didn't even have finance to get back to England!

THE NEXT TWENTY EIGHT YEARS

1969 – 1997

Prologue

LOOKING BACK AGAIN

'*The First Twenty-Eight Years*' was first written in 1987. It has been interesting to read through again almost 21 years later. Things left out and forgotten come to mind. And then again to read it with consideration in relation to my present state. What does it show me about ME? Is it a true reflection of John Green? Have I been honest to myself before God? What does it reveal – and what does it hide – about me?

I am almost certainly the issue of an unwanted pregnancy; the product of an unhappy marriage and one-sided parenting. I am also the result of a childhood and adolescence spent for the most part in the rural backwoods of my country.

England was my country of birth, and the sun-drenched, rain-washed summer fields of Wiltshire and

Somerset the backdrop for much of my childhood and early teenage growth. Through most of the fifties life in southern rural England was still slow, placid, and somehow still in recovery from the Second World War. I lived in small market towns like Trowbridge and Melksham. High streets a-bustle with pedestrian shoppers, minimum traffic and wonderful wafts of tantalizing smells from bakeries, tea and coffee shops, and a host of other mysterious sources. The air seemed fresher, cleaner than ever I can remember since. One could hear the quiet chatter of the people on the streets. Not the raucous, loud, and discordant voices raised in these present days, but a happy, comfortable murmur of unhurried humanity about their unhurried business. There were, as I have remembered previously, Church Fetes, Village Fairs, Country Shows, Gymkhanas, Cricket on the local Green. The days seemed longer then, but never boring. Golden Days.

At 15 I can remember still helping the harvest in a local farm – a farm that still used the horse rather than the tractor and the hands more than the machine. We worked in those summer fields, heavy with corn and oats and barley. Oh yes and even the hayfields. Following the scythe we would gather up bundles of what was to hand and tie them into bundles, leaning two or three together to stand and dry. Then days later pitching them up by hand onto the horse-drawn wagons to be taken off to stack or store. And the sun shone, and the sky of blue set the trees and the fields and the corn all a quiver in the warm air. Skylarks winging upwards, field mice running about in the stubble at our feet. Wonderful days, full of comfortable smells and feelings, that mingled with the perspiration of hard labour, and ended with a quiet evening with convivial friends. Some cider, laughter, a tale or two retold of the day gone by, and so to bed. I am glad to have been able to experience days like those. Days that were so soon to change and to be lost to England's senses. Days that up to that moment in time had not changed a great deal for hundreds of years into the past. I will never forget them, and I know that in many ways they are part of me now at 60 plus. And I am part of them. There was something about that time that found recognition in my heart and mind. We belonged together.

I was not very forthcoming as a child. I led a pretty sheltered life, doted upon by my childless foster mother, almost ignored by her husband. I was all she had that she could count on. I had most of her attention whilst I was growing up. She was a good mother materially and to some extent spiritually, but morally she was astray. I slowly came to see it and know it. I was ashamed of it. Because of it I think to some extent my natural sexual instincts and development were blighted. I liked girls, but was not looking for sexual relations with them – or with boys! I was not sexually preoccupied. I was not 'gay', but preferred boys' company. I wanted to have male friends who could like and respect me. In that I was not very successful. I was rather introspective, and dull. My hobbies were not very outgoing. I was very interested in entomology and philately, rather solitary pursuits. I enjoyed classical music, and drama. I was not sporty, not a partygoer, or a philanderer. In fact I suppose I was what was in those days referred to as square, and a little boring. At least that is what I came to believe. I did not have a very confident or endearing opinion of myself even. This had not been aided by suddenly having to come face to face with the fact that I had been adopted, and no longer had any idea of my origins. The relatives I had known all my life suddenly began to back away from me. Again that sense of rejection. This did not encourage me to adventure myself in amorous relationships with the opposite sex. When on two different occasions I did become seriously involved I was rebuffed. Then I retired into my shell, and entered my twenties a confirmed bachelor, increasingly alone. Not a good scenario. It does tend to show however that one IS the product of one's upbringing and environment even more than one's genes. For example if I were gay many would suggest I was the victim of genetic manipulation. But I can see how easy it would have been for me to BE gay purely and simply because of the environment and influences of my home and upbringing. I was close to falling into a predisposition that had been induced by circumstances rather than antecedents. Think about it! I had no masculine input into my life until I was 11, and what I then had I tended to resent. I was the sole focus of my Mother's attention and love. For the first ten years of my life I was brought up in the midst of violence and conflict in the home. I was of a solitary nature, concerned with the natural world around me, and rather too sensitive to spiritual influences – almost a recluse. There is little doubt in my own mind that I may very well have become queer in some offbeat or even perverted way. But I didn't, perhaps only because of the input of my 'Uncle Dick'.

WHY didn't it happen? God was busy arranging my steps – and I profited. I don't know why I profited. I am sure God is intervening with all of our individual lives, and I just do not know why some profit and some don't. But I did. And, whilst I cannot approve of homosexuality, I DO sympathize with the homosexual. I sympathize because I believe he is misguided, and because I believe he does not need to be, and should not deceive himself that his homosexuality is either normal or healthy for himself or for others. This ought to be pointed out compassionately, but in no respect accommodatingly. The modern world seems to feel otherwise. Truly we are a society more and more like that of Sodom and Gomorrah. We do not have to yield to this. I certainly believe anyone is able to find strength to resist the errors of their way. The strength may not be IN them, but it IS available to them, and may be BROUGHT into them.

There was a point where I seriously wondered if I might be 'gay'. But as my life went on I was to LEARN that we are all ABLE to become ANYTHING, given the opportunity or circumstance; but NONE of US NEED to be so. I escaped. Some escape from smoking, some escape from evil imaginations, some SEEM to escape from nothing either visible or tellable – but we are all slaves to something I believe, all handicapped, and weighted down by sin of one sort or another – BUT we CAN all escape, all overcome, if only we can catch sight of the WAY to do so.

My 'nature' does not seem to be much different. I mean I still find it hard to make friends. I still feel shy and lacking in self confidence, even ineffectual, at times. I have learnt to cover it well, and in doing so have perhaps made matters worse, since my 'disguise' is at times more off-putting than the real me. So have I changed? Have I really learnt anything? YES! To some extent I have learnt quite a lot. I have learnt to survive on this planet, in this body of death. I have learnt to HOPE, and to SEEK for progress. I have learnt to give to God my trust, and in doing so, have discovered His Power and Strength, not only to overcome, but to be FREED from sin. The Change in the area of my own soul is yet to come. I do not doubt that it will come. I long for it to come soon. For now I am often humanly lonely. Perhaps to some extent we all are.

The other factor in this first 28-year period of my life is the God factor. How did I get involved with God on a personal basis? How did it happen? Was it induced by my circumstances? Was I born with some kind of spiritual kink? I cannot honestly remember a time when I was not consciously willing to accept the idea of God, and that He was not far away. Some Religious people might say that this must have been an advantage. Perhaps. Sometimes I am not sure about that. Many people might say of me that I am a Man of Faith and that I am close to God. I must say there have been and still are times when I feel very unsure of myself and my position with God. Sometimes even jolted into wondering if God IS really there for me or anyone, and if He is not a myth! WOW, I would love to see a few people's expressions when they read this – IF they ever will. What kind of a Christian is this guy? I don't really know what kind I am. But I feel deep within that Jesus Christ did die on the Cross for me. I still do believe in God – but not without conflict and sometimes doubt.

Can this be? Yes I think so, but it tends to show me that I am not some 'great one'. I am one of the poor and needy ones. In fact I feel this more often NOW, than I did when I was 28! I do not feel the kind of Christian that might be held aloft in admiration or awe. I feel less than ordinary in fact. A door-keeper in the house of the Lord.

Was I born with an ear and an eye – an intuition – for God?

My adoptive Mother taught me to pray, being herself non-religious. Did her action plant the 'idea' of God in my infant mind – or did she merely wake up realization that was already there within me?

Did God speak to me as I searched the Heavens that night on the back steps of my disruptive home when I was six-years-old – or was it my own deep desperate need for comfort and security that gave me a straw to hang on to?

Karl Marx assures us that 'religion' is merely an opiate, a drug, a means of dulling the pain and anguish of life and living. Is he right? Did man invent God in truth as a necessity? A way of facing the odds and getting through the awful possibilities of conscious life? One could easily build a good case for such a psychological self-con. And indeed I have found as I have gone through life just how often one's mind (or is it the Devil?) can argue just such a case, in an effort to pull the rug from under one's mind and send the soul reeling into emptiness and meaninglessness, and DESPAIR. Horrifying moments. I have been in more than one moment like that – moments that at times have continued for weeks!!!! Can a Christian go through such times? Many will say NO. But some well known followers of the Lord HAVE gone through such times. John Newton did. George Mueller did. Samuel Cowper did, to name but a few. Satan – if you accept HE is also there – began by sowing DOUBT in Eve's mind, and stirring that doubt up till his hearer was willing to act as if God was a lie.

Satan won that day, and he has never changed his strategy I think. It was a good one; it worked; it can still work – why not have a go with me or you – or anyone? Be sure he does so.

I have my days I can assure you. But I have learnt that my MIND is somehow HELD firmly in the Saviour's Hand. It is fixed – fixed on HIM. But it may equally well be that HIS mind was fixed on ME before ever I was born. Yet I cannot be special in any sense. What He has done to, with and for me, He has done for everyone. So WHY have I come to SEE it, and others have not? I do not know. I cannot tell. I do not feel worthy of being able to see, and to experience, even in this often very imperfect way, the reality of His Being. I do begin to understand that none of life is by chance, but by His Permission; that no Joy or Sorrow is accidental, but allowed. Allowed in order that it should prod, prompt me closer to perceiving that He is there, and that He has a purpose to be worked out in and through me. That has been an awesome realization. For the first 28 years of my life I groped and grappled with life as I found it. But I had to be dug up from all that I had become acquainted with and taken to a totally alien situation in order to FIND His Will and Purpose, AND the power to attain it.

Chapter One

INTO AFRICA!

It was dark and wet, the night I flew from Gatwick. It was 10p.m., and I had left my 60-year-old Mother crying in the Airport Lounge. I was not to see her again until March 1972, and in all the years that were ahead until her death in 1988, I would only be able to spend a total of three months with her. I had no idea what a sacrifice that would be to her until much later on, when I also had become a parent. I was aware that she would miss me, of course, but I also knew she was not alone, and would be well cared for. For the rest I had to leave it to the Lord. Some of my friends felt that I was being selfish and just pleasing myself by flying off on some hair-brained stunt to Africa, and said so in no uncertain words. But there was nothing I could do but trust the Lord even in this. It was hard!

The VC10 taxied down the runway, and lifted off into the star-studded night sky. I was leaving 28 years of my life behind, but I hardly thought about it. I had never flown before, and was a little apprehensive as well as simple-minded about the whole thing. Where WAS the parachute? I had not heard a word of the cabin announcements being made as we took off.

"This is your Captain speaking. We have just attained our cruising altitude of 42,000 feet."

"Excuse me!" I hailed a passing Stewardess. "Can you tell me, please, where is the parachute stowed?"

She looked at me a little oddly, and said with a smile, "There are no parachutes on this flight, sir, but should you have any problem there is a brown paper bag in the seat pouch just in front of you." She passed quickly on, with a widening grin! I sat staring at the paper bag; it conjured up quite a picture! I turned to my Bible, and opened at Isaiah 42v5-7:

Thus saith the LORD...I the Lord
have called thee in righteousness,
and will hold thine hand, and give
thee for a covenant of the people.

A little later, as supper was being served, I reached chapter 43v21:

THIS PEOPLE I HAVE FORMED FOR MYSELF:
THEY SHALL SHEW FORTH MY PRAISE.

I felt assured, and confirmed in my faith. Surely God had called me to preach, and to be an evangelist to the people of Kenya. I would definitely GET THERE, with or without a parachute! I saw my name floating on Banners across the streets of Nairobi...wow! How vain-glorious and ignorant I was. Truly His Ways are not ours and His Thoughts far from our own. We know nothing as we ought. The night sped by, and I awoke to find we were nearing Entebbe, Uganda, where I and a few others were to get off. I had to change to a local flight to get to Kenya, my destination.

As I walked down the steps of the V.C.10 Jet that had flown me the four thousand odd miles from England, non-stop to Entebbe, Uganda, a soft warm rain was falling. Yet the rain that was filling my eyes was not from above, but from within, where a spiritual dam just seemed to burst. There, standing on the shiny runway outside the toy-like Airport building, were African people all with smiling faces, officials and air hostesses running forward with huge umbrellas. And suddenly I had 'come home'. These were my people, and it just didn't matter that they came from Uganda, and not from Kenya, my ultimate destination. Africans were my people, and standing there in that warm, friendly rain, I knew it as surely as if God Himself had said it to me out loud!

PRESIDENT MILTON OBOTE was President of Uganda at that time, and as I, and those others who were disembarking with me, walked through Immigration and the transit facilities, we all bumped into him in a very informal kind of way, and he greeted us all quite jovially!

Soon afterwards I was safely installed in the little DC4 that was to fly me to Kisumu in Kenya, just an hour away. I was accompanied by only one passenger, a pregnant Friesian cow! The Flight Attendant gave me a sweet to suck whilst we took off; the cow got a bale of hay! The aircraft kept fairly close to the ground so that I could, for the first time, see clearly the countryside below. I was a little disappointed to see the houses covered in corrugated-iron instead of grass thatch; somehow I had not expected it, and it seemed so un-African. At last the plane touched down at Kisumu Airport. The sun was shining here, and Rev. Dawkins of Trinity Fellowship was there to meet me. It was Friday, 13th December, 1968.

"ONE THING I SHOULD ADVISE YOU ABOUT, JOHN, and that is your relationships with the African."

He was sitting opposite me, wiping his mouth with a linen napkin. The meal, served upon a beautiful mahogany dining table, antique and heavy, had ended. The African servant quietly cleared the remains of the delicious fruit salad.

"You see," he put the napkin down and continued. "You see, they really do not seem to think that lying is wrong at all. You really should not trust them to mean exactly what they say, and you should take care not to let yourself get too involved; you might suffer a broken heart."

I smiled politely. Inside I felt suddenly weak. My heart grew cold, and my stomach turned slowly round, constricting as it went. The room seemed suddenly airless, suffocatingly hot.

I felt dumbfounded. This was my first night on African soil, and I was sitting in the house of the founder of the mission I had come to join. How could he be saying all of this? Only a few hours before he had met me at Kisumu Airport from the small DC4 that had ferried me into Kenya from Entebbe. Now here he was facing me across the table, elderly, fresh-faced, though a little crinkled here and there with the passing years. His eyes, blue like a Norwegian Fjord, were kindly eyes; love and humility radiated out of them. But surely he couldn't really mean that you should not give your heart to an African!

A soft breeze, warm and fragrant with scent, drifted momentarily into the room through a still open window. Coffee was now being brought in. It was dark outside now, and cicadas chirruped noisily.

"I…er…hrrh…" he cleared his throat, and smiled shyly at me. "Er, I do hope I haven't depressed you? There is so much we can do to help our African brother – but, er, well…" He stopped, looking helplessly around the room, apparently stuck for words. I continued to stir my coffee. The ticking of the sideboard clock seemed to increase a little in volume.

"He thinks a bit differently to us, you see; we mustn't expect too much from him, or judge him by British standards of behaviour."

He chattered on. Looking back now, I can be sure that his love for the Kenyan, and for the African in general, was ever deep and sincere – he was just afraid that the young man in front of him, a 28-year-old from a very different culture, was going to be disappointed that Africans were not Englishmen and women. He was right to be apprehensive, as I was to learn as years passed by, but that night laid me low with doubts and fears. I lay on the comfortable bed, sweating in the unaccustomed heat. Kisumu lies on the Equator, about three thousand feet above sea-level, and on the shores of the Kavirondo Gulf, a gateway to Lake Victoria.

How can you really love without getting 'involved'? Without trusting and believing? Even if it should mean a broken heart, surely that was why we were serving God, to love and not be loved; it sounded well enough – well enough to be ideally true. I had come to lay down my life for the African, regardless of how I might find him, or what he may be like! I was absolutely bursting apart with noble sentiments and romantics. But at 28 I still didn't know myself very well. God had still to show me a great deal about myself. Indeed, after all that has happened through the years since that first steamy and uncomfortable night in Kisumu, I feel that the whole exercise has been to get me to see myself more clearly. Certainly I believe God has led me to step along this road since the very day I was born. Rev. Dawkins was to remain a very close friend and counsellor, until his death in 1997.

Three days after my arrival in Kenya, I was driven up to Maseno, some 4,600 feet above sea level, and about 20 kilometres north of Kisumu. I was to stay in the main mission house with another young Englishman who, as it happened, I had been with at I.B.T.I. some while before. The house was in fact a very large bungalow set in a couple of acres of lawn, with a high cypress hedge all around it. Maseno was, and still is, an administrative centre, and is known largely for its Training Colleges for Government administrators, and teachers. Recently the Teachers Training College has been upgraded and expanded into a University.. There were few local shops, but it did have a post office, a police station, and law courts.

The house was spacious, sporting three bedrooms, a sitting room, office, large kitchen, dining room, and bathroom. My friend and co-worker greeted me with open arms, not only as a new arrival, but as one who he hoped would ease the financial burden. The cost of up-keeping this enormous house and its two permanent servants was considerable, and my friend had very little backing to draw on. The mission itself did not contribute to the running cost of the establishment, each missionary being entirely responsible to pray in his needed support inclusive of the cost of his housing, and in this case the actual running cost for the work itself! It was a very new concept for me to adjust to, and certainly on my initial arrival I had no idea at all how God would take care of me! I had literally promise of nothing at all, and had spent all my savings in flying out to Kenya. I had an English sixpenny piece in my pocket and that alone was my entire fortune in this world! My friend was wonderfully depressed when he discovered my unsupported and unsponsored estate. He was receiving some £25 a month from his church in Birmingham. He estimated we needed £90 a month each to pay for all the expenses. I was more than shocked by this revelation, for it seemed that even before I arrived costs were not being met, and that there were some cumulative bills! I had known I would need to trust God for my own personal needs, but I had not realised I would also need faith for the running of the entire Mission! I had arrived early on in December

1968, and that month I was to receive gifts from praying friends in England amounting to £15, a far cry from the £90 apparently needed. I felt that if the Lord was not sending in the required funds, then the cost of our way of life must be too high. Certainly it seemed almost a waste for a household of two vigorous young men to be waited on hand and foot by two servants and in so large a house. I timidly suggested that we look for a smaller house, ditch the servants, and cut costs. My friend thought this to be impossible; to him he would be failing in the Mission's eyes if he ran out on the responsibilities given to him. The days and weeks passed, and bills mounted. During this period the work of the Mission was also in abeyance since the schools and colleges in which they ministered were on Christmas Holiday. Time hung heavily upon me. I began to seriously question if I had been right to think God wanted me in Kenya.

Looking back then, as I have now in writing all this, I could not but be re-assured that Kenya was the right place for me. But there was a lingering question as to whether I was in the right place in Kenya! Initially, though, I am sure now that Trinity Fellowship was the right 'Door' to enter in by, and that the Lord had made no mistake, whatever the difficulties.

It so happened that my bedroom in that large house in Maseno, was also the office! It was a very large room, about thirty feet square; one side given up entirely to windows, with french windows leading out onto a wide veranda. There were three large desks arranged on that side of the room, near the windows, and also many filing cabinets. My bed was cosily situated in a far corner of the room, away from the 'business' area. The walls were covered with large sheets of soft boarding, on which were pinned ordinance survey maps of the various areas in which the mission operated; the boards themselves being hung on heavy copper wire from nails. I am mentioning all this because of a very strange and quite nerve shattering event which was now to take place in that room.

Every morning I was woken up before dawn by one of the African servants bringing in a cup of tea. I had asked him not to bring it on a number of occasions, but he always insisted. So one night I decided to prevent this disturbance by simply turning the key in the lock of the door; and this I did before going to sleep. It was about 10 p.m., and I was soon asleep. Suddenly, I found myself half awake, with the sure conviction that the door had opened into the room, and that someone had entered. It was still dark outside, and no light filtered in through the curtain less windows. I began to say, drowsily, that I didn't want tea.

Immediately, the entire room erupted into frightening noise and activity. Dull thumps and loud crashes resounded all around the room, and something enormous and heavy jumped onto my bed. A scream of fear and terror escaped from my mouth. Blackness, thick and impenetrable, crowded down upon me. I was going to be murdered! MURDER! Murder! Oh, God Help me! Jesus! And then I was shouting loudly in a totally incomprehensible language and tongue. Silence. A stillness so intense, so profound that I dared hardly to breathe. My heart was pounding; a cold sweat was upon my face. The light switch was on the other side of the room near the door. It was still pitch dark, a darkness that could be felt; horrible and terrible as a panther crouched and waiting to pursue!

I flung myself from the bed headlong into the engulfing nightmare, racing for the wall, and for the light switch. I found it and light came! I held my breath then, wondering what or who I should find to be with me in the room. I was leaning with my back against the still shut door. The room was empty! It was quiet as death itself, yet a sense of waiting and watchfulness pervaded everything. All my flesh crept and moved upon my bones; fear gripped me in a vice. I felt weak. Only my eyes moved. Every piece of soft board, six separately hung pieces, had fallen to the floor. One was lying upon my bed, face down. My eyes brought back the message bluntly. "You chump! There are your murderers! A few pieces of badly hung soft board!" But my eyes could not convince the rest of me, could not calm my spirit. The door was shut, and the key was still turned in the lock. I moved slowly to inspect the boards. The copper wire had just snapped with age! But no. There was no thinning of the wire where it had parted, and the two ends of each wire gleamed brightly just as if they had been cut! Each board's wire had separated in exactly the same place. No one board had touched or had been touching another, yet they had fallen together! An accident! It could be nothing more than that. An evil-looking African mask, the only thing remaining on the walls, looked down mockingly. I was still trembling! And what about my friend in the next room? Why hadn't he heard my shouts and screams for help? He had heard nothing. I returned to bed, but I left the light on.

The next morning I re-hung the map boards, and removed the mask from the wall, and out of the house. Nothing of the sort ever happened again, but I know that on that night I was very close to losing my mind. The only thing that saved me was the Name of Jesus, and the strange words drawn out of me in that unknown tongue. I remain convinced it was a serious attack of the Enemy. Many years later I was to learn from the previous tenant of that lonely bungalow that he and his wife had experienced many strange and terrifying things in that very same room. He believed it then to be seriously 'haunted'. Today it is a Night Club.

All this happened in February 1969, just three months after my arrival, and made me even more anxious to leave that house and find another. On the other hand I was beginning to get out and about, and had already fallen in love with the country and the people. Mainly my work for the Mission, was office-orientated during those early months. Debts continued to mount, and eventually, towards the end of March I began to pray for help. "Father, please help me. If this is not the house you want me to live in, please find me another one, preferably rent-free, and somewhere near to the people you have sent me to, and where they will feel free to visit."

During an afternoon walk some days later I found myself just inside the gate of the C.M.S. Mission Hospital, looking rather aimlessly at nothing in particular.

"Do you want to look inside?" The voice had a strong accent, Canadian as it turned out, and sounded slightly amused. He was tall and not a lot older that I was. It seemed he was the new doctor to the hospital, and was looking around at his new kingdom. A key was in his hand, and I realised he was talking about a small mud cottage just to my right; I had not immediately been aware of it. It had a corrugated tin roof and seemed rather deserted and neglected. The mud walls had been plastered on the outside and whitewashed some years before. It was about 20 by 40 feet in dimension, with wooden shutters serving as windows – a very common and usual African house. If it was empty it could even do for me.

"Well, do you want to look? I'm just going to do so myself." We introduced ourselves to each other then, as he unlocked the door. Roosting bats flew squeaking out as the light shone in.

We entered and opened the window shutters. The place was filthy. There were walls dividing the interior about eight-feet high. These provided two small bedrooms, a living room, scullery and bathroom. There was no ceiling, just the bare rafters and the underside of the tin roof; no doors internally from one room to the other, just openings. There was electrical wiring for lights, but none seemed to have been fitted. The kitchen was outside. The toilet consisted of a grass-roofed closet of mud and sticks enclosing a 'long drop', a 20-foot hole in the ground surmounted by a rough wooden box with a lavatory seat fixed upon it. The whole place, including the house itself, stank of rottenness and rat and bat droppings. Not very inviting; not as grand as the mission bungalow. But it was not grandeur I was looking for, and it was in the right place locationally, with people passing all the time to the market and the hospital. It could be just what I was seeking.

"How much do you think it would cost to rent this place?" I asked my doctor friend.

"What! Surely you can't want to live here? You must be joking!" He looked at me incredulously.

"Seriously! How much?" I repeated, smiling.

"Well, if you really are in need of a place, you can have it rent free as far as I'm concerned. I wouldn't feel right charging anything for it."

And so I moved in! I tried to get my colleague to agree to go with me, but he felt strongly that the responsibility for the Mission House was his. He stayed on. But I moved, and took the office with me.

The house needed a lot of cleaning, and the varied aromas of its past occupants took some weeks to fade away! But it was paradise to me. I bought rush matting from the local market to make a ceiling, and some white paint for the walls. I borrowed a bed from the hospital, and my doctor friend provided a table and some cowhide chairs.

I was home and free! I had arrived at last! Or had I?

In actual fact the Lord was not yet finished bringing me to the place where I would really understand His purpose in calling me to Kenya. Events were awaiting that would completely take me by surprise, and which would lead me into a life quite unlooked for. Soon I was to see clearly and it would be as sensational for me as for the blind man who had been blind from birth!

JUST A FEW DAYS after my arrival in Kenya in 1968, I found myself waiting on the porch of the Mission

House, Maseno, for some visitors. They had promised to pick me up around 8.30a.m.

By 10a.m., I'm still waiting and the sun is now well up. No I am not impatient. Life is just as it comes out here, and it is foolish to bring time into it.

A car swings dustily into the drive, and a wiry African in his mid-forties jumps out with a huge smile, his hands waving in joyful greeting. It was Silas Owiti, again!

"Praise the Lord! Are you ready?"

And so we begin. Out of the drive, and down the hill from Maseno, down two thousand feet into Kisumu's heat. There we picked up the wife of this human dynamo, plus a few more African brethren. We are on our way to a village meeting miles away on the plain, the other side of Kisumu. No road here, just a dusty, crater-pocked track.

"Hey, careful!"

We plunge down the bank of a stream, fortunately dried up, and shoot up the other side. The bridge has rotted away! The plain is hot. Dust swirls behind us. Passing a rural market with countless dilapidated stores selling anything from matches to Asian rugs, and besieged by a mass of villagers from all the country round about, we pass on, waving to the many people who recognise us along the way. Just a week ago, many of these people found Jesus as Saviour in a great open-air convention not far from where we are heading.

Suddenly we have arrived, over an open patch of scrub, and right into the centre of the village. Around us are the homesteads with their mud walls, and thatched roofs. Cows, dogs, cats, chickens and children are into everything. People come running to greet us, the women so clean and bright in their gaily-coloured dresses. The men can't really compete. All have been expecting our arrival, and have been constructing a 'church' of branches and rush matting. We are soon led to a special hut set aside for us to sit in, out of the sun, and where we can wait for the meeting. Only two windows, and I am made to sit next to one of them, since they are sure I must be suffering from the heat. Droves of flies descend upon us, but soon go unnoticed as more and more village people crowd into greet us, each one clasping our hands, and praying the special Blessing of God upon us as we stay in their home. About noon the meeting begins. One after another, new converts stand up to testify to God's saving Power and healing touch. No sooner one sits down than another is up. Over 70 people have come to the meeting. At 3 p.m. I am asked to preach, and I stand up to give God's word. At the conclusion many respond and come forward for prayer, some for salvation, some for healing. Here, under the rush-mat ceiling of this makeshift church, men and women reach out and touch the one who loves them, and find a Blessing. 4 p.m. and we are served with the meal prepared for us: tough beef curried with rice, and thick greasy gravy.

'Afters' is sweet tea, and fresh bread and margarine. Great is our joy together. No colour question here; no barrier of custom and tradition. Jesus has been found in the midst, and we have an instant union. We sit, we talk, eat and drink together; every one of us made in the image of God. Night falls, and the mosquitoes begin to bite. Still we linger on. The darkness is deep now, so that the stars seem white brilliants in its depth, whilst the whole atmosphere breathes with the sounds of night and mystery.

Finally we get back into the car, and turn for home. It is midnight! All this is a long way from Starbeck in Yorkshire! A long way from Fulham in 1947.

Christmas came and went, and yet another letter home was written:

MASENO, Western Kenya, January 1969.
Since coming here I have been much engaged in correspondence, and with sorting out last year's finances for this infant mission. However the Lord has been leading me outside into the land around us, and a picture is building up of the Work. The great problem is with the young people. There are not enough schools or teachers, and still education must be paid for. Many cannot afford it, so that even if they have the brains to pass the Primary School Leaving Certificate and to go on to secondary school, they may not be financially able to do so. Instead they will join the ranks of idle school-leavers who are jobless. Over 100,000 school-leavers a year are going on to Kenya's streets. It costs approximately £50 a year to keep a boy or girl at a school here, and the average monthly income of the working man is only £8. Obviously few parents can afford education for their children. Crime and manifold anti-social activities such as alcoholism are on the increase.

Recently a Kenyan friend and I finished a day's meetings in a secondary school some miles away from here. Sundays are difficult days for transport if, like us, you have none of your own. Sometimes one is lucky though, and can pick up a fast Peugeot taxi somewhere on the road. These cars are roomy, usually overfull, and very recklessly driven! They are also cheap. On this occasion we were able to wave one down after only a few minutes of standing by the roadside. It was late afternoon. The two of us got in, my friend in front next to the driver, and me almost in the boot. The road was of tar macadam, and there were quite a number of people about and a fair volume of traffic too. A few miles along we picked up a young African family of three, husband, wife, and young son. Again we set off, and gathered speed along the straight road.

Suddenly the husband of the family just arrived began to cry out, and to struggle in his seat, just behind the driver. There were ten of us in this nine-seater, plus bags and packages. It was jammed packed. The man began to hit out at those nearest to him, and then grabbed the driver by his collar, as if to choke him to death. The vehicle swerved all over the road, but the cabby still managed to hang on to the wheel, and eventually brought the car to a standstill by the kerbside. Everyone tumbled out of the car, and dragged the offender out after them. He then began to weep uncontrollably and to plead for forgiveness, but the driver was in no mood for such things, and leaving the man and his family ushered the rest of us back inside and drove off. Looking back I could see them still, the man was staggering into the road in front of the oncoming traffic, trying to wave down another taxi, his wife hysterically trying to drag him back, the child screaming with fright. Then I remembered again my own childhood, and how I too had stood by and watched a helpless Mother wrestle with a drunken husband.

Bars here are open most of the day, Sundays included, and liquor is cheap and plentiful. Drunkenness is rife everywhere, and at all social levels. With it come rape, murder, and robbery. Less than a mile from where I was living, a man was attacked and cut to bits with knives, and not much further away a girl was raped by her own school teacher.

Sin is as great here as elsewhere, and alcohol is eating into many hearts, and lives, to the injury of the nation.'

One African poet has written:

If only you knew the horror that is wine
You would curse it.
You sway, you fall on your face,
You are covered with dirt.

By July 1969 I was firmly established in my new little mud house in the Hospital compound. I wrote:
Recently a small team of us went some 90 kilometres into a very rural area. We went for two days, and we went especially to hold an evangelistic outreach amongst the people. We went with Jesus and the Bible, nothing else. No microphones, no loudspeakers, no films, nothing at all. It was a forest region. Many people are brought in to help with the conservation programme, and there are many large work camps where hundreds of men, women, and children are living without church or shepherd. We visited some of these camps and we saw well over 50 take hold of Christ in a definite way.
One woman who gave her heart to Jesus during those days also came to us with her baby. "Pray for him," she said. I told her that Jesus told us that we should allow little children to come to Him, and I asked her if she would trust me to hold her child. She quietly put him into my arms, and we gathered round to pray for him. His stomach was about two times its normal size – the Mother told us that the child had passed nothing for ten days! He was crying loudly. In Jesus' Name we prayed. We prayed in faith for that child, for his complete healing. His cries reached a violent pitch as we continued, then abruptly ceased, giving way to smiles and whimpers of joy. I gave him back to his Mother. Half an hour later she returned with him to show us that he was quite normal! Apparently he had passed an enormous quantity of worms soon after we had prayed!

Just a few days ago I was preaching the Word of God to some 1200 souls some hundred kilometres away in another part of Kenya. My message had to be translated into two tribal languages, which made preaching a bit slow and difficult. Yet even so more than a hundred came forward to receive Christ as Saviour on that day. As many more came out for prayer for many problems they had such as illness and a longing for a deeper spiritual life. We were many hours praying with and for them, some ten other African Pastors praying along with me. We specially thank God for the many works of healing that were accomplished on that occasion; one child in particular was sensationally healed from chronic convulsive fits.
Space will not permit me to tell of everything that has been happening. Surely God is moving, but we must admit that Satan is not idle at this time. One of our prominent Statesmen, Mr. Tom Mboya was shot dead on a Nairobi street the other day. Tension ran high. There were riots, smashed windows, and even fires. Additionally, many were injured and even killed by way of retaliation. There is no doubt that this was not some isolated chance murder. A wind of change is blowing. The future only God Himself can see. For myself, I remain the same, unchanged in the knowledge that this is the place and the time for me to be here. My average monthly income, still as unsure as when I first arrived, amounts to about £12 sterling. Yet God has not permitted me to suffer in any way, and I am even stronger now than before. His Grace is sufficient, and He is ever faithful.

Writing yet again, in August:

We are flying along the road towards Kisumu once more. This time we are travelling in style in the Mission's mobile film unit. This has been loaned to us by the Oral Roberts Organisation. Painted a dazzling white, with bold red lettering proclaiming that 'God is Good', it is a real attraction. With us are three African evangelists and eight nurses from the local mission hospital. We are on our way to a large open air rally beyond Kisumu.

The rains have begun now but it seems no cooler. The nurses are singing for all they are worth, and it seems as if our vehicle will lift off from the ground with the Glory of God any moment! Soon we are all singing, filled with the Joy of belonging to Jesus. Through the suffocating streets of Kisumu we go, our onward rush making the only breeze, and now out along the road towards Nairobi. People stop and turn to wave as they hear the happy song that is left behind in our wake. Speeding on, we pass a busy market with all its bustle and business. Now we turn off onto a subsidiary road, and continue into the interior of the flat country of the Plain. Not so dusty as it was in January. The Rains have produced mud. It's still very hot, but humid as well. Now we turn again onto a rough track, and bump and jolt along into the bush countryside. Flies are here, and mosquitoes. This time of year seems to be a good breeding time for them, and they come in their multitudes, big and hungry!

We have a loud hailer fixed to our roof, and as we go along we are announcing the meeting that is to take place. We are to show a film this night, and people from miles around will come to see this 'wonder'. Ooop! Even the rough track has vanished now! We go on almost blind, guided only by tree and bush! The sun is already going down behind the low hills. It is 6.30 p.m. Suddenly as always, we find ourselves right in the village we have been making for. A meeting, the afternoon one, is still in progress, and so we continue on a little into a clearing and begin to unload and get things ready for the film. Darkness falls very quickly, and it is best to get the screen up, and everything fixed before night arrives.

These mosquitoes certainly bite.

Three of us put up the metal frame of the huge screen, and carefully raise it up, securing it with guide ropes. Soon all is finished, and the projector all ready in the van. This unit is really compact. At eight o'clock we begin to show the film, perhaps to a thousand people or more who have been slowly gathering from miles around. We cannot see the edge of the crowd. The sound track is in English, so, from time to time, we have to interpret the action and the story. Hardly worth it, you may be thinking. Yet as the film ends hundreds come to Jesus in answer to a brief appeal. Many will be saved this night; many will be healed as well. By 10:30 p.m. all is ended and we are packing away the equipment. Our nurses have been singing gospel hymns over the loud speakers as we did so. We are all tired. Each of us has been busy. This is the third day of meetings here. Just as we are ready to leave, our African hosts come to insist that we stay for a feast of roast duck, with all the trimmings. It is already past midnight! And those mosquitoes! Fellowship is sweet. We arrive finally back at the mission at 2 a.m. On the way we find three secondary school boys looking for the police station. Apparently their school, unstaffed at night, was being attacked by a group of drunken men, not unlike those outside the house of Lot. Evil is ever present and the battle always raging, every hour of the day and night.

Although as the year 1969 wore on, I had these opportunities to enter into the evangelistic scene in and around Kisumu, I was actually more and more tied to the office work of Trinity Fellowship. I began to feel that I was not making any headway, and that the early vision of becoming a 'Famous Evangelist' seemed in error. My heart was often heavy with misgiving, and I must confess that I had often begun to think of England. During this period

Robert Langton and I played host to an elderly brother in the Lord from Dagenham in Essex, England. His name was Alfred Webb, and he was well-known and respected in the British Pentecostal Assemblies of God. Alfred was probably nearing 70 when we met him in Nairobi. He wanted to visit the offices of a Christian Newspaper in Nairobi, and one of our first assignments was to drive him there. The offices were on the third floor of a fairly old and musty office block in the city centre. No lifts, so we had to use the uneven stair cases. He was a little overweight, short and short-sighted.

On the way back down he slipped and slid from the top to the bottom of the second flight of stairs. We were shocked…but he bounced immediately up and continued on as if nothing had happened. In the afternoon we took him to the Nairobi Game Park; he wanted to see real lions in the wild. We were driving the mission's minibus, and we were fortunate. Almost immediately on entering the Park we came across a pride of lions feeding on a recent kill.

"Stop! STOP!" cried out our elder brother, and pressing his camera into my hand he said, "Here! Go and get me a close up!" Well, I was not too keen on even getting out of the vehicle, let alone getting a close up. The camera had no telephoto facility. However, Brother Webb was not the kind of man you could easily withstand. It was not that he was overbearing – far from it – but he was a man of faith and never looked at impossibilities. I looked nervously at my friend in the driving seat, and slowly got out of the van. I was about 20 metres from the lions. One gigantic male with two females, one on either side, grunting as they tore at the flesh of their kill. All were lying down. I put the camera to my eye and inched my way towards them. I am quite sure I was not at all supposed to do what I was doing. Suddenly I saw the great head of the male lion look up. He stared at me. I stopped. I lowered the camera. I found I was now about five metres away. I crouched down and again put the camera to my eye.

"Go nearer, brother, go NEARER!" urged my respected elder brother from the minibus. The lions resumed feeding noisily in front of me. I crawled forward. I was VERY CLOSE. I lifted the camera, and as I did so the lion lifted up his head and saw me. His wives stopped eating and also looked my way. It was now or never. I focused quickly and pressed the button. The male sat up on its haunches and growled. I backed slowly, then turned and fled to the van. I have never been so scared in my life. All three lions had got up and run after me. Now they were sniffing round the car. The photo came out well, and many years later I was to find it enlarged and framed on Pastor Webb's sitting room wall. He never said thank-you. I was just a lad to him. He had seen no danger in the adventure at all.

Towards the end of his stay I confided in him that I was feeling that I may have made a mistake in coming to Kenya. We talked for some time and right at the end after we had prayed together, he said,

"Young man the problem is that right now you are just a clerk – but you will be a Departmental Manager if you persevere. Change is just around the corner. Hang on. Kenya is the place for you."

The next day he left for other African Countries. I did not see him again for three years. This happened in the second week of August 1969.

Chapter Two

A CRY FROM THE STREET

On the 25th August 1969, I was standing outside my little house in Maseno, Kenya talking to Frank, one of the young students from Maseno Secondary School.

As we talked, someone began to cry and scream, and to make a big noise on the street nearby. Normally there was always a steady stream of passers-by, shouting and talking loudly to each other. On this occasion the cries seemed out of key with the rest of the daily hubbub – full of pain and misery. Frank and I ran the short distance to the fence to see if we could see anything. The cries were getting perceptibly louder by the moment. They were issuing from the mouth of a young boy of about twelve years who was being slowly helped along the mud road to the hospital gate by two young women.

"Oh it's just Wilson!" smiled Frank. "He's probably been at the bhang (marijuana) again!"

"Do you know him then?" I asked, curious. The boy's right big toe seemed to have been broken, hanging at an angle from the rest of the foot which was held out tortuously in front of him as he hopped heavily between the girls.

"He's an orphan," was the reply. "His parents were supposed to have been poisoned a few years back; he just seems to run around on the loose most of the time."

We watched them go by and along to the hospital gate. Twelve years old, alone in the world and a drug addict! I was startled. The hospital admitted him for the night. It seemed he had indeed broken his toe, and badly smashed up a good part of the rest of that right foot. He had been heedlessly kicking a boulder in some kind of drug-induced trance!

I decided to pay him a visit later that evening, and Frank agreed to come with me as interpreter, which was just as well since I spoke no Swahili, and the boy spoke no English! We found him awake and drug free, looking a bit wan and miserable. We sat on his bed and began to chat with him about his life. We talked of Jesus, and the Love of God. He wept a good deal, and finally asked Jesus into his heart. We prayed with him, and left him. Frank went back to his boarding school to get ready for the first day of term, and I returned to my now empty house to sleep. But first I knelt down to pray a little; it was about 9 p.m.

"You could have that boy to stay with you, couldn't you?" The question pushed itself to the front of my mind. "You could send him to school; give him a chance in life."

"Me, Lord? Me take that boy into my house? I hardly have enough to even keep myself."

"You have enough spare room though, don't you? And now that you have brought him to Me, are you prepared to see him just stumble out of the hospital back into the dust of his old life?"

I got up then. I got dressed again, and walked back to the hospital ward. Wilson was still awake. I called to one of the nurses, and with her aid I asked Wilson if he would like to come and live in my house and go to School. His face lit up with joy

"Can my little brother come too?" he asked, eagerly!

A brother! He had not mentioned having a brother before. Now what was I letting myself in for? One boy was one thing, but two!

"Lord, I didn't know there would be two!"

Yet on that fateful evening in 1969 the Lord put them both upon my heart – just them. I had no idea that there might be others; no idea of starting a home for children.

It did not dawn on my consciousness that this was but a 'Beginning'. I had finally returned to my house that night wondering how on earth I could support two growing boys. The next day I made extensive enquiries and discovered that Wilson had an aged grandmother living not far away. I discovered my way to her tiny mud and wattle hut, and found her living in abject poverty with eight small children, one of whom was Zacaria, Wilson's ten year old brother. He was crippled, and apart from a ragged vest was also naked and dirty. He had lovely eyes! The toes of both feet, and one heel, were in an advanced state of decay owing to long neglected 'jiggers' – minute parasites that attack the extremities, laying their eggs in the flesh. The other children, some of them two or three years old, were children begotten by wayward daughters living away from home! She would have had me take all of them away if I had been able! But I only took Zacaria; I had to carry him all the long way back to the hospital, and my house. Wilson arrived the next day!

Two days later, on the 29th August, a letter arrived from a lady in Derbyshire.

Dear brother Green, you visited our little church in 1967, and your name suddenly occurred to me again this week in our Prayer Meeting. I asked Pastor if he knew where you were, and today he advised me you are in Kenya. I feel the Lord would have me send a small gift to you, with His Love.

A cheque for £15 was enclosed. I had never received money so late in a month before, since I had arrived in Kenya, and I had already received as much as I usually could have hoped for. Suddenly the Lord had doubled my income! Two halves made a whole or one adult! Good book-keeping, Lord! It was a very pointed provision for the children I had just taken into my care. There was also a parcel in that post. It came from Manchester. Inside were three pairs of khaki shorts, and four shirts. Each of my two 'sons' found themselves instantly kitted out in new clothes for daily use. That first night they had started out sharing a pair of my pyjamas! Thus a 'Testimony' was raised up to the Lord: a Testimony of Provision and Loving Care. From then on I began to call my little mud house 'Testimony House.'

By December, six more children had found a home with us. We had become a family of nine. Just before Christmas I was to write to friends:

Already I have eight boys in my care; all of them with stories like Wilson's and Zacaria's, orphans and throw-aways! My little house is filled with noise and activity.

Who were these eight boys? What were their backgrounds? Well I have already told of Wilson, and his brother Zacaria. Then came Daniel, a shy and introspective 14 year old. His Father had been a witch-doctor of some renown, but had apparently died from a curse put upon him by a colleague! Don't laugh will you, for curses are very real to those who believe in them, and very effective. When Daniel came to stay with us he was quite alone, and suffering from a lame leg. He said that he had a splinter of bamboo in it, but there was no swelling, no wound, and no sore to be seen. He could not put the foot on the ground and hopped along with the aid of a large pole; because of this he obtained the nick-name of 'Hopo'! He was quite sure that another witch-doctor, the one who had cursed his Father to death, had 'magicked' his foot! A year after coming to us he was still hopping along, and eventually I persuaded a rather sceptical doctor to examine this troublesome foot. He was sure the whole thing was purely psychological. However, eventually he did an exploratory investigation under local anaesthetic, and lo and behold, lodged inside amongst some of the dorsal bones was a quarter-inch piece of bamboo! There was absolutely no indication of how it had got there. The doctor wonderingly removed it, and in no time Daniel was running around normally. He continues to run today, even long distance! He is saved and loves the Lord Jesus.

After Daniel came, David and his elder brother Johanna arrived. David was about eight, and Johanna ten. They ate out of dustbins to survive, their Mother having run away from home with their younger sister and brother. Their Father was mentally deranged from smoking marijuana, and drinking raw local spirits. David had arrived first, being deposited naked upon my doorstep, where I found him curled up and asleep very early one morning. It was mid-October, and cold. A day later he led me to his brother!

THEN came Luke aged 14, and also Jacob, 10, and his elder brother Moses aged 14. Luke was also an orphan, and had smoked marijuana for years. He was very slow mentally, and had been badly abused by his Father till he had died. He was now just a wanderer. He completed his secondary education with us, and then went to polytechnic where he qualified as a Painter and Decorator. He now works for us as an Assistant in our Maintenance Department. He is married and has one son. He did not yield his life to Jesus until he was 40! Jacob gave his life to Jesus early on, and his brother followed him. Today, having been to college and trained in Bible School, he is back-slidden. His brother, now married and with a large family of sons and daughters, is pastoring a church, and running a children's home in Nairobi. Both these boys never knew their Father. Their Mother was a prostitute. Out of those first eight boys only four can be said to be pursuing their Salvation today. But we believe they will ALL come to know the Lord one day.

That night, in 1969, when I prayed by my bedside, I understood so little about what my involvement with Wilson would mean. As far as I was concerned, I was just helping one homeless kid! After all I was otherwise quite busy caring for a mission office, plus a fair amount of teaching and preaching.

Since moving into my small mud house, I had taken on the Chaplaincy of Siriba College, a large teacher-training establishment, and also that of the C.M.S. Mission Hospital where I stayed. Maseno was then, and to a large degree still is, an administrative and educational centre, set in a very rural area some 4,500ft above sea level. To the south-west is Kisumu and Lake Victoria, and to the north-west is Uganda. When I first arrived there it was still very much like an enclave of the old colonial days. The National School was run like an English public school. The Headmaster, himself an Englishman, was Mr. Bowers, and he and all his staff would be out watching cricket on the school ground every Sunday afternoon. Boys all in uniform, complete with blazers and straw-boaters! Maseno was also the seat of the Anglican Bishop of the area, and the Archdeacon, The Venerable Kenneth Stovold, and his wife became my close friends. Ken would often stroll around in gaiters and clerical apron, as if he had just stepped from a novel by Trollop. He was every inch a Churchman and Bishop-maker! In fact he had a great deal to do in preparing the then Bishop of Maseno, The Most Rev. Festo Habbakuk Olang to become the first African Archbishop of Kenya. But Maseno was in transition, and the colonial atmosphere and most of the 'left-over' colonial personnel had all gone in a few years. Things were changing. It was August 1969.

It was too late to get the children fixed up in schools that year, and with the fees so high out here, I was not sorry, as it would have been a great amount of money to find, and already my tight budget had been made to expand past breaking point. Hallelujah! Our God is the same every day, for even though my monthly expenditure had more than doubled, He met it! Some days, however, it was not so easy to trust! For example, some weeks earlier, I only had 10/- cash in hand, and nothing whatever in the bank. Our daily expenditure was 10/-! We held our breadth! The next day we still had 4/- in hand; nothing came in the post, or to the door. On the third day 1/- remained, when suddenly 50/- was put right into my hand – one week's housekeeping! Oh, how we praised the Lord! One week later, when we were in the same position, a letter came with a further cheque for £6! That's how it is most of the time; the words of George Muller could have a direct application. I quote from his diary:

"The Trial still continues, it is now more and more trying, even to faith, as each day passes. Truly, the Lord has wise purpose in allowing us to call so long upon Him for help. But I am sure God will send help, if we can but wait."

Well, there is little else possible, at such times; except to wait!

My vision was to see a Christian orphanage begun, preferably in the form of cottage homes. Together with the homes, I wanted also to see a school! School fees were, and still are, too costly to think of sending all the boys likely to be cared for to a state school. We needed a free school! At first it might only cater for primary level, but if the Lord tarried I wanted to see it go on and include secondary. In addition to, and in support of all this, I wanted to have an active Evangelistic Centre, eventually able to train and encourage young men and women to communicate the Gospel!

At the beginning of August I had been frustrated, confused, and unsure of what God wanted with me. By December I had a definite Vision before my eyes, and was already started along a road previously unimagined in my wildest dreams. And what of Trinity Fellowship? Where were they to fit into this?

By the middle of September 1969 I had realised that the Lord wanted me to go on sheltering children. I then wrote to the Committee of Trinity Fellowship suggesting that they permit me to commence an Orphan Home under their auspices. They replied that they did not feel the Lord had given such a Vision to them as a Mission, and that their mandate was purely and simply to evangelise. I then tendered my resignation, and this was accepted. Initially they felt I was very much misled in this action, but I am glad to say that over the years we have maintained close ties.

Still, I had put myself in a difficult position. In September I had already five children in my care. Having resigned I was without an official backer in Kenya, and according to the laws of immigration in force in Kenya one cannot remain longer than a month in the country after having resigned from whatever employment one was engaged in initially, as an expatriate. This includes missionaries and voluntary workers who all must have some kind of immigration permit giving right of residence in the country.

Of course I got busy writing letters all over Kenya to various Missions and Christian organisations asking for assistance in obtaining cover so that I could continue on, in faith that God would provide for the children's work that had started. All that wrote back replied negatively, each insisting that they were concerned only in preaching the gospel and not in social welfare. Had I realised it, I believe that if I had written to the Government of Kenya instead, I would have received almost instantaneous assistance. I did not realise it.

At the eleventh hour, just a few days before I became an 'illegal alien' I received a visit from an Anglican Priest. He was an African brother, and arrived pushing a bicycle on a very hot and dusty afternoon. He brought a letter from his Bishop requesting me to visit his office some three miles away. I did not know him, and in fact did not even know at that time that there was any Bishop living anywhere in the area. I went. It was a weary walk in the heat of the afternoon, but we, the priest and I, had happy conversation as we walked together.

We eventually reached a small red brick building which was the Diocesan Office.

I was shown directly into the Bishop's presence. He was the Bishop of the Diocese of Maseno North as it was then called and his name was Festo Olang. A year later he was to be appointed the first African Archbishop of the Church of the Province of Kenya. He put me immediately at ease, with his grace and charm. He had heard of me, and of the children, and that I had left Trinity Fellowship. He wanted to know what my plans were. He hoped I would stay in Kenya. He said that he had prayed for eight years for the Lord to burden someone to help the destitute in the locality. He wondered if, maybe, I was the answer to that prayer. We talked together freely and at length, and finally he offered to apply for a permit for me from Immigration under the Church of Kenya. I would be responsible for carrying on the children's work already started, and for finding the finance for it.

In December the Mission Hospital on whose compound I then lived, offered me a larger house, rent free, and in February, they offered an even larger one on a temporary basis! By July 1970 I had some 27 boys between the age of 8 and 15 years staying with me. A few extracts from my diary for that period might be of interest at this point.

1970

January 3rd

We received our first Luo boy to-day, aged about 10. He is called Christopher. He does not look too well. We now have nine boys. Wilson's behaviour has really improved. I do pray it might continue, and that the Work of Grace in his heart will grow rapidly.

January 5th
M's parcel arrived at the Post Office in Kisumu today. Had to travel in by bus to fetch it. Once home again, we unpacked it, and found it to be full of very good and usable clothing; every article has already been distributed! We still need shorts!
A cheque from Brixham Assembly of God in Devon, England, also arrived in the post. It is so encouraging the way these dear folks have taken me and the children upon their hearts! Thank you Jesus!
January 22nd
We had only 20/- left in cash. Nothing in the Bank, but I felt quite light-hearted and happy. An old gardener from Siriba College had just come to ask me to help him pay his son's school fees. I explained that my situation was such that I could not help him. He persisted in his asking none the less, and said that even 20 shillings would be a help at the least! I told him that it was impossible; that I could do nothing for him. He left at last, bent with worry. As I sat in my chair, one of the boys came and sat on the arm.
"Dad," he said, (they all call me dad now!) "doesn't the Bible say that you should give to the one that asks?"
"Why, yes, indeed it does," I replied, quite blind to the direction the words were leading me.
"Then why didn't you give that man the 20/- that is there in your shirt pocket?"
Why? Because I feared! Surely God's Word is sharper than any two-edged sword, and this child had turned it on me. I was run through!
I gave the bank note to the boy, and he ran off after the man with it. An hour later the hospital messenger ran up to the house with a letter that had just arrived. It was from a sister living in Denmark, and contained a cheque for $40. The most remarkable thing about it was the fact that it had been posted sea mail on 26th November

1969! Truly before we ask, He answers! Both comforting and challenging.

January 27th
Three parcels of clothing arrived. Two from Denmark and one from England. The greater part of the contents were at once useful and even I have been well provided for! We do give thanks to Him who moved hearts to help in this way. Amen.

February 10th
After supper we had prayers as usual. John and Luke had had a difference, and were ready to fight. Luke is always too complacent to see himself in the least bit wrong, and John has so little self control that I fear for his sanity at times!
I spoke on David and Goliath, using Okila Olindi the young man that helps me, as the interpreter. It was received very well by all, and after a short prayer all except Luke and John made a public decision to ask Jesus into their heart.
We admitted another boy into the family.

February 11th
Prayed alone for some time.
Our situation has never been so bad. We have received only 85/- since the month began. There is nothing at all in the bank, or in hand! Humanly, there is little or no hope that we can escape catastrophe!

February 12th
Received 85/- through the post from Plymouth, England. Praise the Lord!

February 16th
Two parcels arrived. One from Denmark again, and one from a West Indian sister in England. There was a Christmas cake inside!!

March 8th
On returning from shopping to-day, I carefully looked into the daily diet and food arrangements. I found that our daily expenditure had risen to 30/- per day! Afterwards shut myself away to prepare the message for this evening. Finally led to Proverbs 4v20:

"Keep thy heart with all diligence,
for out of it are the issues of life."

Was interrupted by a boy from the secondary school. He was a Christian, and had fallen into sin at school. He was very upset and tearful, and wanting counsel and prayer. We prayed together for some time and He seemed much encouraged and assured. After he left a number of my boys came to ask who he was, and if he was having an evil spirit!

March 28th
Moved into a larger house. We presently have twelve children, and now have room for many more!

And so life went on, and the family continued to grow. With that growth responsibilities increased, and being still young in this business of trusting God, I was not always free of worry and at times even doubt about how we would all survive.

But not everyone was happy about a non-Anglican being given Church property to start an orphanage. There were many malcontents, and at times the atmosphere within the Hospital compound where we all stayed was not too friendly. Once again the Bishop asked me to his office, and I went with some foreboding, wondering if perhaps he was regretting extending his aid to me. Once there he sat me down and explained that his wife had been warned of the problems building up against us.

It seemed that a friend of hers who lived near to us had come to her and said,

"Tell your husband, the Bishop, to help John Green, for he is doing a good work amongst us, but some want him put out of the Hospital, and even out of Maseno because of it."

He and his wife had then discussed the matter carefully. They were both leaving Maseno within days and going to Nairobi, where the Bishop would take up his position as the first Anglican Archbishop of Kenya. They would live in the Archbishop's mansion. They would offer their own family home, a rambling farmhouse, to me at a nominal rent of a few shillings a month. His thought was that if he, a respected Kenyan from the locality, offered his own house to me and the children, it would silence all the opposition effectively. He did not let the thought of the wear and tear on his property stand in the way but risked it all in the Love of Jesus. We shall always be thankful to him and for his graciousness to us all.

Satan had once again been confounded. His evil designs had once more turned into Blessing against him.

The words of David to Solomon in 1.Chronicles 28v20-21 came so clearly and forcibly to mind as the day ended.

BE STRONG and of good courage, and DO IT.
Fear not, nor be discouraged, for the Lord God, even my God
Will be with you. He will not fail you, nor forsake you
Until you have finished the work. ALSO the princes of the land
And all the people will be wholly at your commandment.

At this time we were trying to teach some of the children ourselves since many were totally without education. We had a pretty mixed bag of children as well, and from many different tribal groups within Kenya. Some of these groups were not naturally friendly to each other. There were often disagreements, and even fights. On one occasion one got hold of a very nasty rock shaped like a stone age axe head, and imbedded it in the head of another of the boys. Blood was everywhere. It was dead of night, and we were far from a hospital at that time. I boiled water, and washed the wound with disinfectant; it was very deep. Then I sterilised a needle and got some thread and sewed it up. It healed perfectly! Another time, I was returning from shopping and found a 15-year-old with his left hand holding a rock, and in his right a bread knife, which he appeared to want to use on another boy trapped against a wall. I dropped all my packages and jumped between them.

"You can't do that!" I said breathlessly.

"I can and I will. He's no good I tell you. Why do you want to save him?" shouted the assailant.

"If you want to hurt him you will have to hurt me first," I replied. (It re-called that incident in another children's home that I related earlier, when I had once again jumped in between opposing forces! This time, however, I could see the matter through). The boy still stood defiantly, pointing the knife at me. I continued to talk to him.

"I want to save him because God has put a love in my heart for him, just as He did for you," I said.

Yes, there could be tense moments in those early days, as the numbers grew, and the mixture became greater. Some were still hooked up to marijuana and alcohol. Some even drank petrol. Some were still stealing. It was a rather 'hairy' situation as God slowly worked out some 'order' from the 'darkness' of their lives.

Just before moving from the hospital compound where everything had begun, I collapsed. I had been sewing chair covers on a hand sewing machine. It was about 4 p.m. Some of the boys who were present in the room with me say that I suddenly stood up and began to order everyone out of the house, actually chasing them out. They all thought I had gone suddenly mad, and ran hastily out. I shut the doors and windows upon them. I went to the bathroom and began to comb my hair. By this time they had got a medical officer from the hospital to come. He forced his way through a fan light window and opened the back door and let the others back in. I fought them like a wild animal apparently, though I have never been able to remember any part of the episode, until they overpowered me and stuck a syringe in me. I then collapsed in a heap. When I awoke I was fine. Cerebral malaria they said. Shortly afterwards we left the hospital compound forever and moved into the Bishop's family home. It was July

1970. Writing to friends, I had mentioned that our new 'home' was three miles off the main tarmac road, down a very rough mud track. "Please pray for a car, as transport especially during the rains is going to be a problem."

In November I suffered a further attack!

I was standing cooking in the kitchen one lunchtime, and just dropped like a stone onto the ground. The boys carried me to my bed and then one of them ran the three miles to the Church House and told the wife of the Archdeacon there that I had died!

She, poor lady, was distraught, and got into her VW Beetle and chugged down the mud track to find out herself. She was a little into her fifties then, plump and over anxious by nature. By the time she arrived an hour or more had gone by and I was just coming to. I felt as if I had been drugged! She insisted on taking me back to the hospital. It had begun to rain, and the already muddy road became a quagmire. She got stuck in a rut half way back, and since we had taken no one with us, she asked if I would mind getting out to give her a push! I did so, and we managed to get free and go on. A mile further on she suffered a flat tyre; and she had a bad heart; she was sorry to have to ask me, but would I mind assisting her to change the wheel? I did so, and at last we reached the hospital, much wetter and muddier than I bargained for. The young African doctor looked me over and asked how old I was.

"I was thirty in May," I told him.

"Ah, yes," he replied, wrinkling his brow professionally. "It's pretty certain you are commencing epilepsy; it often begins about your age." He gave me a packet of Phenobarbital tablets and told me to let him know if I had any more attacks. It was still raining.

"I do hope you don't mind," said the Archdeacon's wife, "but since I should be alone on the return journey, I think I won't risk taking you back. I'm sure you'll be alright, won't you?" She peered a little anxiously, or was it fearfully, at me through her spectacles.

I hurried home. On the way I considered the situation. If I did have epilepsy then I was not a fit person to look after all these boys. If I did not have it, then I did not need the tablets. I took the packet out of my pocket and looked at it as I walked along. I emptied the tablets into my hand, and threw them into the next puddle. Whether I had epilepsy or not the Lord only knew, and only He could sort it out. I never did have another such attack. Neither from that day did I ever have malaria. Praise the Lord indeed!!

During October, I had written a circular letter to friends. I had started it off with a few lines of a poem by Lenri Peters of Gambia:

'What does it cost, to be loved and left alone?'
I was sitting with Okila Olindi in the Hospital Land Rover. The morning was hot, and we were parked in a back street of Kisumu where many stores and emporiums are situated. Across the street I caught sight of a boy of about ten going into an open-fronted drapery store. He was in rags; dirty, and gave one the slight impression of a down and out animal more than a human being. His stomach was terribly distended, and he seemed to stagger often as he lurched along. As he entered the shop he began to ask for money, holding out his hands in the usual way beggars seem to have. The storekeeper cuffed him soundly and he fell back into the littered street. No one noticed

him, fallen amongst the rubbish. He got up, and came uncertainly towards us. We tried to speak with him, but his language was not one that either of us could understand. He went on sadly from us, lost, unwanted, and uncared about; one of so many.

Then a few days later I was travelling back to Maseno from Kisumu by bus. Hot, overcrowded, and slow, we churned our way up the tarmac road. Suddenly some passengers began to point ahead, and there in front was a man walking; he was quite naked. People seemed shocked. The bus passed, heads screwed around on long necks to see better. Then we also had stopped.

It was a Police Traffic Check Point. As the passengers turned their attention to the Police, into the bus swung the same naked man. He could not have been much more than 20 years old.

"Ladies and Gentlemen, this is a bad world."

A policeman yanked him back, and out of the bus. He turned and ran like a mad thing down the road away from us, as if he would attack a herd of cows a mile away. He had spoken perfect English. The people were quiet, too shocked to speak. The Police laughed. But no one seemed to care very much.

What does it cost to be loved – and left alone?

What does it cost to be concerned, yet not to be involved?

The answer is very short.

It costs nothing; nothing at all.

That love is worthless.

And all the time since then, I have been more than ever haunted by the thought that there is no one to care. No one to care.

Yet there is God! Yes. God cares.

It is just over a year now that the first two boys came to my little house in Maseno Hospital. The one only twelve years old, yet tainted with women and strong drink, a taker of drugs, almost an old man already. And the other, his young brother, crippled through

neglect, and well taught in the art of a lie. What kind of miracle was it that God put in their way? Not the kind commonly heard about from evangelistic platforms. Some look down their noses, and label it social welfare work; not really the same as preaching the gospel.
Is God's care so little thought of? In the lives of these first two boys, lost and alone, Christ came and worked a miracle. Oh yes, there was deliverance, and there was healing for crippled Zacaria who walks and runs to-day, but that is not the miracle that I am thinking of right now. The miracle to me has been the sunshine that has replaced the cloud and storm that was upon their faces, raging out of their eyes. Yes, God cares. He cares as He looks down from Heaven, but who will let Him care through them on earth? Christ was One that let God care through his life. Christ! God's Love shone through His life and everything that He said and thought.
Recently a Pentecostal Preacher over here from the States said these words:
"It's no use preaching only!
It's no use praying only!
We've got to do something with it!
And it's the doing that will cost, not the other two."
And so we have increased the number of boys over the last two months, and we now have thirty-five. Certainly it has meant that our financial needs each month have nearly doubled, and this has caused some heart-searching moments. But how is it possible to turn boys away, often naked, and always in some awful need, when there is space to house them? Jesus would not have let material considerations hinder Him. I don't feel we should either. He hasn't let us go hungry, and every day our daily needs are met, although there are pressing needs often!

Yes they were often very pressing.

One morning we awoke to a total lack of any money anywhere. There was only maize flour in the store cupboard that day. Our African cook poked his head early round my bedroom door.

"What will be lunch today?" he asked.

"Just cook the maize flour; there is nothing else, and no money to buy more yet!" I answered him.

He looked a bit doubtful. We had never just eaten Ugali (a kind of stiff pudding made from boiling up the maize flour with water). He hesitated, then, withdrawing his head, closed the door behind him.

Later, about 11 in the morning, one of the boys ran in with a letter, just one letter, from the post office. It was from England, and had been written by Pastor Stan Hyde of the Brixham Pentecostal Assemblies of God. It had been posted some seven days before.

He wrote that all the brethren in his church at Brixham had been much in prayer for us, and had been impressed as they had prayed with a verse in Psalm 50: "He owns the cattle on a thousand hills." As they had continued on in prayer, this verse had continued to make itself noticed, until they had all felt that we must need meat! "So, Brother John, WATCH OUT FOR MEAT! MEAT IS ON THE WAY," he ended, using capital letters by way of emphasis!

Well, I thought, and where will I look out for meat! Will it just fly in through the open window! Please note my frail humanity! At that moment in time, with the letter still in my hand, there was a knock at the back door. On opening it, I found an African servant with a fat goat trailing behind him at the end of a rope.

"Are you John Green?" he asked.

"Yes," I replied, looking cautiously, even covetously, at the goat!

"Well, the Archdeacon has sent this goat to you," he said, handing me the end of the rope. It seemed that on the previous Sunday, just when the folk in Devon were praying for us, this goat had been given to the Archdeacon of the Anglican Church. He himself did not like goat meat, so instead of slaughtering it, he had turned it loose into his garden where it promptly began to devour everything in sight, including his wife's rose trees. When this good lady discovered the damage she was filled with horror, and told her husband to get rid of the goat promptly! He then instructed his gardener to bring the goat down to us. Just as I was being exhorted to "Watch out for MEAT", the meat was in fact walking down the road towards us. We ate it for two days!

And so we lived. And so God took care of us. He was our only security.

Chapter Three

MARRIAGE

During the month of August 1969 I was a Bible teacher at a Christian Youth Camp. Some of the campers came from quite far, mainly secondary school boys and girls. During the early part of 1970 I received a letter from a Christian Union in a boys' secondary school in Machakos, some 40 kilometres south of Nairobi, almost 400 kilometres distance from Maseno, where I was living. Some of their members had attended the '69 Camp, and had been pestering the Union to invite me down to the school for some special meetings. So now they were finally writing to ask me to accept an invitation for a Weekend Challenge at their school during the month of June 1970. It was a long way to travel. But the cost of transport was enclosed in the letter! It had been sent by the C.U. sponsor, a European teacher at the school. And so I went. I left my boys in the capable hands of Okila Olindi and taking two fast taxis travelled the distance in some four hours for a staggering cost of 30/-!!

I arrived on the Friday evening, and had a meeting that night, and again on Saturday, a big afternoon rally at the neighbouring girls' high school, with further meetings through Sunday. It was very taxing, but very enjoyable as well, and it opened my eyes to the fact that there was a great deal of error and confusion abroad spiritually. Many came to me privately, between meetings, saying that they felt very mixed up spiritually, and that they were in danger of falling away from the faith. It seemed that many different evangelists visited the schools, each with his own brand of doctrine. One in particular had been a regular visitor to the schools. He claimed to have the Gift of Prophecy, and began telling the young Christians what they should or should not do in their daily lives, as direct guidance from the Lord. Many of these directions could find no scriptural foundation or confirmation. The brother claimed to actually hear the Voice of the Lord, audibly, and said that if others did not do so it merely showed spiritual immaturity. The schools in Kenya are very open to Christianity, and all are welcome in His Name to preach, sometimes without a great deal of discernment. I realised as never before how much I needed to pray that I might always rightly divide the Word of Truth, and be kept from error.

On the Sunday evening my hosts had decided to invite a couple of African young lady teachers to have supper with us, and to spend the evening. They taught at the girls' school. Only one was to arrive. The afternoon rally had been over for about an hour, and I had just returned to my host's house on the compound of the boys' secondary school. I was relaxing in an arm-chair, sun streaming in through an open window. The Bible was open upon my knees and my eyes were closed as I quietly enjoyed the almost unknown luxury of peacefulness.

She entered the room silently, and stood framed in the doorway looking a little uncertain. I had opened my eyes to just find her there, as if by magic! I was a little startled to see her! She was dressed in blue, I remember.

We looked straight at one another, black and white, African and European, woman and man. She could just as well have been Eve, so unannounced and sudden was her arrival before me, and so surprisingly riveting of my attention. My heart must have missed a beat or two!

"She will be your wife!" The words rang out within me.

"Nonsense," was my mute rejoinder. "She's black! And I'm white! Such a thing just isn't on!"

She was walking towards me now, across the room.

"You must be John Green; I'm Esther Iguru," she said, sitting down in another chair close by me. I felt quite undone and a bit harassed! Where was my host? He and his wife came in just then.

"Oh so you've met! Good, we'll have an early meal and then we can fellowship the whole evening together. Sorry Josephine couldn't come," he rattled on, and the hours sped by. We talked of the Lord, about the children left behind in Maseno, about the Schools. At 11 p.m. Esther stood up to go.

"She will be your wife, you know." That inner voice again.

"It's no good, Lord! I am not pursuing the matter. And if she is to be my wife, she is the one who will have to start things off, not me."

She was saying goodbye now; handshakes all round, and she was gone.

The following morning, squeezed into my taxi, I could only think of her. As we moved slowly through the town towards Nairobi, I looked for her face amongst the crowds. This was ridiculous! We had only just met; we knew nothing about each other. I set my thoughts upon Maseno, and the children waiting for my return.

A week later a letter arrived. It was from Esther. She was herself confused by the self proclaimed 'prophet' ministering amongst the school children. Could I help her to clear up some misgivings she had. She enclosed a number of unused postage stamps! I immediately wrote back and a fairly regular and lengthy correspondence began!

It was quite platonic in substance, and very spiritual. But all the while I was clearly aware that once again my words had been taken literally!

Early in September I felt unable to leave the matter in doubt any longer. I sat down one afternoon and wrote, "Dear Esther, what would you say if I asked you to marry me? Yours sincerely, John." I posted it early the next morning. However, immediately it had gone I suddenly felt how totally unprepared she would be for such a letter and how she might even take me for an insincere kind of person. I sat down and wrote seven more pages to her, explaining how I had arrived at such a proposal.

Fortunately she received both letters in the same post. She replied by telegram.

"I think we had better meet and discuss this!"

So off I went again, this time to Nairobi. We had arranged to meet in Uhuru Park, in the City and under the shadow of the huge pseudo-Norman Anglican Cathedral. Initially, though, we would rendezvous outside the New Stanley Hotel. I was terrified that I might not recognise her! But I did. We walked together to the park and sat under a thorn tree, and there we talked. Well I talked first, and tried to put all my thoughts together into some sensible and romantic declaration of love. All the time I was nervously plucking up blades of grass; I think the ground must have been quite bare by the time I had done, and Esther had said, "Yes, I will marry you!" It all seemed so right, but we still hardly knew each other. It just seemed that everything was 'arranged'. There was nothing left to do but get on with things. The next day Esther fixed for me to meet her Mother. We would meet in the Nairobi Wimpy Bar!! And so we did. My future mother-in-law spoke no English, and I did not speak anything else. So, in the midst of a busy morning in that Wimpy Bar, and quite loudly, was interpreted and broadcast for all to hear, the request of a very nervous white man for the hand in marriage of a very pretty young Kikuyu teacher. All the questions of my future relative had to be answered right there. I think I must have been far more red than white by the time the interview was over. It all caused quite a stir, and a lot of amusement! BUT that dear lady also said "Yes," and the matter was settled. I returned to Maseno on 'air'. We would be married in August the following year, 1971.

Esther Iguru continued to teach English and Home Science at the girls' high school in Machakos, 400 kilometres away. We did not meet often! Occasionally I would travel down for a weekend, usually with a few of my boys with me, and sometimes she would also drive up alone to Maseno. She owned a little V.W. Beetle in those days. We never managed to see each other entirely alone; there were always plenty of eyes looking at us. If I went down to the school, all the students would observe us closely, and of course I had my boys with me! If Esther came up to Maseno the entire family would want to be with us all the time, and even if I asked them to leave us alone they would still keep an eye on us from a distance! A novel way to carry on a courtship!

At school, Esther lived in a nice and well-appointed teacher's house. She had a well-equipped kitchen, and everything was clean and orderly. A far cry from our household! Her Mother and Father had separated quite some time before when she was still in primary school, her Father marrying again. She had worked hard at school and won a place at a university college to train as a teacher. She earned a good salary. I wondered at times how the Lord would assist her to adjust to such a very different life-style. I had not felt like asking her to give up her profession, so hardly pursued. Well, the Lord would have to work all that out. We had agreed to marry, and marry we would.

But there were problems just around the corner.

Many of the children we then had in care were real vagabonds! Orphaned and destitute they may have been, but they were also well versed in iniquity. Many people seem to have had the idea that the children we took in were all angels who had suffered shipwreck. Once safe inside the 'Home' they would be restored and shining examples of decent society. Such change was not always quickly evident. Sometimes it did not come at all. In more than one, old habits died hard, and there were outbreaks of rebellion. Our friend the Archbishop got to hear of some of the escapades of these wayward youngsters, and he took exception to it. He felt that since we were actually living in his family home he was himself in danger of getting a bad name as a harbourer of undesirable elements. He asked us to leave his house. He gave us only seven days notice to remove ourselves from his property. We had nowhere to go. It was an unexpected situation.

I walked miles that week, looking for alternative shelter for myself and the thirty-five youngsters I had become responsible for. Not until the afternoon of the sixth day did I find anything. The 'anything' was a two-roomed sports pavilion on the playing field of Maseno National School. Mr. Wiessler, the Headmaster, generously gave us free use of this building until something better was available. It was a real squeeze! We had to use the two rooms for sleeping, and the veranda for everything else. Fortunately, there was a toilet and a shower attached which we were able to use. And more fortunately it did not rain during our stay. We thus camped out from the 26th June until 10th July 1971. On the latter date we all moved once again to what we hoped might be a more permanent site. It was an anxious time of upheaval and apprehension; my wedding day was planned for the 14th of August! It almost looked as if I would be bringing my wife to live in a tent! I wondered if she had ever been a Girl Guide! Naturally I was sharing what was happening step by step, but I am sure she had no really graphic comprehension of what things were like. As we began our camp, like a tribe of refugees, we had no assurance of when we would end it! But another friend was working hard for us. He was Mr. Benjamin Ogutu, then Principal of Siriba Teachers' College. Not far from his home, some eight miles northwards, there was a deserted colonial administrative centre. It had not been used for some ten years, and many of the seven buildings were in bad repair, but they were brick-built, and iron roofed. He had been trying to get the local County Council to agree for us to use it. He succeeded, and it was offered to us, rent free. The complex stood on some three acres of land, on top of a rather exposed hill. It was known by the name of 'Ramula', the Place of Gold!

When we moved there, like a collection of tinkers and gypsies, we were met and welcomed by the local Chief of the area, and the Parish Priest! The air was fresh and invigorating, and the views magnificent, and the problems legion!

Water was three-quarters of a mile away, at the bottom of the hill. Toilets were noted to be three decayed wooden shacks tottering dangerously over long drops (holes) of some 20 feet, some distance from the house we would be living in. The houses themselves were long neglected; windowless, doorless, and ceilingless. Plaster falling from the walls, and floors cracking. Bees, bats, lizards, rats, and invisible ticks, snakes and even larger wild animals such as leopard were all long-time residents unwilling to be thrown out! It was depressing. My heart felt cast down. What was happening?

Initially the Lord seemed to have expanded and carried us on to bigger and better situations, and now, suddenly, we were like outcasts. Yet He was with us; He was providing still for our daily wants, and surely this was shelter for our heads. We moved in.

On the 20th July we had a visitor. This was Mr. S.M. Ndunda, the Assistant to the Chief Children's Officer in Kenya.

Apparently there was a new department in the Ministry of Home Affairs which had been set up to monitor what had been noted as a growing incidence of children in need within Kenya. He was delighted at finding us, and was a very great encouragement to us, and was the very first link in our relationship with Government.

Life went on. We managed to get most of the boys into local schools and a few we kept at home since they were older and had no education; these last we endeavoured to coach so that they could eventually also enter normal schools later on. In between we tried to repair what we could, which was not very much.

My house consisted of three rooms. One was a dormitory for some six children. One was my office, and a kind of common room for the family of six, and place for other workers to also meet and pray, and the third was my bedroom. This was the house to which I was to bring my unsuspecting bride. The windows were mere wooden shutters, and there were no ceilings to hide the blackened rafters and the grimy underside of the tin roof. Bats swooped around at night inside, and countless lizards and other livestock, to say nothing of rats! The rest of the children were scattered in the other houses, and I had some three adult African staff assisting as house parents. It was not the best of arrangements but it had to work out, at least for a time.

On August the 13th I travelled up to Nairobi. I was to stay with Rev. and Mrs. Edward Weaver at Thika Road Grace Baptist Church. With me were Micah Amukobole, my Best Man, and Frank Oyungu, that young man from Maseno School who had been with me when all this had first begun. Mrs. Weaver was still busy making the wedding cake that evening, and I was feeling a bit nervous.

And so the 14th dawned, bright and sunny.

They had put up a large crusade tent in the grounds of the Mission. They thought the church would be too small to meet all the expected guests. They were very right; more than 700 people turned up; Esther had endless friends and relations it seemed. I felt a bit lonely, just for a moment or two! Pastor Weaver started a regular evangelistic meeting at about 10 a.m. and preached for souls, and many did indeed respond, and then the wedding proper. Esther looked wonderful in her wedding gown; she had actually made it herself. But the veil was very thick, and for a moment I feared it was not really her beneath it, but after all was said and done, I lifted the veil to see that dear face, and we kissed. A real 'fairy-story' it seemed to me. Hundreds of smiling faces and countless hands all wanting to greet us, and to congratulate us. The sun shone down on us, and the hours passed. We were still there greeting people at 6.30 p.m., only finally managing to get away in Esther's little black beetle car about 7 p.m. Even then we gave a lift to a relative! We had a quiet and personal supper in town, and then went to a Nairobi Hotel for the night. Married at last, together at last, and no one, absolutely no one to disturb us. The next morning we were to travel back to Maseno. A teacher friend of mine, Paul Pibworth, and his wife, had offered to let us have their staff house at Maseno School for a week, whilst they themselves went on holiday. We would spend our honeymoon there. Whilst I was paying the bill at the hotel, Esther standing by my side, another guest picked up Esther's suitcase by mistake and went off with it. By the time we discovered it, the lady had gone, and we understood she would not be back for ten days! Well that was a good beginning! The most important things were Esther's Bible and her wedding dress which she was planning to wear at a special reception at Maseno that the Amukoboles had arranged for our children and local friends. It was a frustration and a disappointment, but not the end of the world.

By the end of that next week Esther had been introduced to her new home, and became an 'instant Mother' to some thirty-five children! She had managed to get a transfer from Machakos Girls School to one near at hand, and so continued to teach, leaving the home every morning in her little car, and returning in the evening, often very tired. I was not very happy about it, feeling that she could not be the Mother that was needed, and be out all day, and too tired at night to take any interest in the children.

One morning she returned home after about an hour of leaving, looking very shaken up and upset. A bus had run her wilfully off the mud road and into a ditch. It had been a terrifying experience for her, as she was quite alone.

New children were also being admitted during late August and September of that year. We took in our first girls – sisters of some of the boys that we already had with us in care. We were very short of funds, and some of our African staff became involved in immorality and theft. Even some of the older boys were stealing at this time. A lot of prayer was going up, and at the same time the local population began to resent us. First they sent a party of Elders to talk to us. They had thought we would come and build a Hospital for them, and that we would take in only children from the locality, and from their particular tribe, and from the local church denomination. When they found that we were not building, and that children were coming from all over Kenya, and from different church backgrounds, even none at all, they had become resentful. The Chief grandly exclaimed that I was 'A teapot without tea!' After that passers-by would take up rocks and throw them on the roofs of the houses at night, and in many other ways showed their annoyance at our being in their midst.

Then on the 17th October I fell ill with a kind of dysentery, and shortly afterwards Esther got it as well. We could not eat anything and became worse until, on the 27th October we were admitted into hospital. By this time I had been diagnosed as having pleurisy and pneumonia with unknown complications. Esther also with an unknown infection, but with the disclosure that she was also pregnant! Later in the hospital they discovered that we both had tick fever brought on by an infestation of invisible ticks that were all over us, and which we must have picked up from the house we lived in. We were very ill. But we recovered and later went to convalesce for a few days at friends who were then also teaching at Maseno National School, Mr. and Mrs. Brian Wilkins. It was the 3rd November, and we had been married barely three months; it had been a trying and demanding time.

As we ate supper at our friends' home in Maseno, a car drew up outside, and the brother we had left in charge of the home whilst we were in hospital ran in.

"I'm leaving!" he said. "Those boys are rioting, and one of them tried to kill me." It seemed one of them had been rude and he had taken a piece of four-by-four timber to beat the boy with, whereupon a whole group had jumped on him to stop him from doing so. He had run in fear, and on the way had notified the local Chief who had now gone up to the homes with his men to put down the 'rebellion', and to take possession of the home.

We got up immediately, heedless of the remonstrance of our hosts, and drove the eight miles back to the home. It was pitch dark when we arrived, and as we turned into the entrance we converged upon a group of men on foot, armed with sticks and clubs who were also just arriving; these were the Chief and his men. I jumped out of the car and shouted to them to go away, that we were now back, and that there was no rebellion or riot. The children ran to meet us from where they had been gathered in the shadows. We were home again. From that moment it was as if the Lord gave me and Esther extra strength, for we felt completely well and restored, and did not again succumb to any serious sickness.

A few days later all the money we had was stolen from our own house during the night. We never discovered the thief.

These were dark and desperate days, when the Lord tested us again and again as we stood alone and helpless.

One night about this time, Esther woke me up in the small hours. "What would you say," she asked, "if I decided to leave teaching? We wouldn't have my salary any more, remember."

I felt overjoyed. I had wanted her to leave teaching for a long time, and be full-time with me in the work. As to her salary; well we had never needed it before, and since it had been coming in, the donations from other sources had practically ceased! To me it was an answer to prayer. She resigned the next day.

Our first Christmas together was great. It seemed that most of the hurdles were behind us. Oh, we were still quite poor, and even the day before Christmas Eve we had nothing in hand to buy food for the holiday in front of us. But the Lord provided. On Christmas Eve our friend Micah Amukoble arrived with a goat! It was a real 'family' occasion: Mum, Dad, and a VERY large family of children. On Christmas Day we ate together outside in blazing summer sunshine under a canopy of cloudless blue. A little moment of heaven.

On January 21st 1972, the roof blew off our house!

Esther and I arrived home from Kisumu and found our compound beset by a strong tropical storm of wind and rain. As we drove in at the gate, the roof of our house lifted, and was flung across the compound to the road, narrowly missing our car as we turned in. It landed up in the field on the other side of the road. For an hour we sat and watched an avalanche of water pouring into our house, and imagined the havoc there would be inside. We felt stunned! The books, all the office records and files. The bedding; everything soaked through, and saturated with rain, and a horrible filth which washed down from the walls and rafters. It was a hard blow. We had so little money at that time, and many large bills loomed over us. Now this – the loss of even those small personal possessions that we had.

In the gathering darkness and dripping of the abating storm, we slowly moved the soggy, sodden mess that was what was left of our home into another smaller house. At midnight we laid ourselves down on the still wet bed, but not to sleep immediately, for as we lay there we suddenly felt the Spirit of Victory, and Praise around and about us, and knew that the Lord was very close. Realising this fact, we also realised that no bad thing can come from Him, Who is our Life. And so we also knew that Satan had only been permitted to do his worst by our Father in Heaven, Who knew we could not be harmed by it. He trusted us with this calamity! If God be for us, who can be against us? We praised the Lord.

We had returned to a fundamental Truth, and realised that our life and self-respect, and our possessions, were nothing compared to His Love, Grace, and Redemption.

We were then facing possible court action over one or two large debts which had been accumulating, yet that night we felt the whole problem had somehow mysteriously lifted as we lay upon our damp mattress, Praise Jesus!

The next morning we received a letter in the post. It enclosed a cheque for £350. We had never received so much money before, and this one Gift cleared all the debts!

But the local clamour against us continued and increased as the nearby Anglican Church suffered a split in its ranks. Each side wanted to claim the Children's Home as its own! I decided to go to Nairobi and discuss the situation with the Children's Department Headquarters. We just felt that we could not progress in the midst of narrow-minded tribalism and church politics. I found the officers there very understanding and sympathetic.

"Why not register the home privately?" I was asked.

"I am not a Kenya Citizen!" I replied.

"Try!" it was suggested! So I returned to Ramula and, getting my little committee together, we agreed to apply officially for Private Registration of the homes. At this point, we agreed to call the home "*Testimony Faith Homes*" (previously it had been known locally as Maseno Christian Children's Home).

Official registration under this name was granted by the Kenya Registrar of Societies on the 11th March 1972.

On this day, Testimony Faith Homes officially severed its connections with the Church of the Province of Kenya, and became for the very first time an independent entity of its own. Yet we cannot but be grateful to all those who nurtured us and sheltered us, and protected us in those early years. Through Trinity Fellowship, The Board of Maseno CPK Hospital, the Diocese of Maseno North, and Maseno South, the Most Rev. Festo H. Olang, The Ven.

Ken Stovold, Mr. Benjamin Ogutu, Mr. Olly Wiessler, and many, many others who gave support, encouragement, advice, and friendship, the Lord created Testimony Faith Homes.

It was now an established interdenominational work of faith in God for the reclamation of the lost and destitute children of Kenya. But local feeling was still strongly against us being there at Ramula.

Chapter Four

INTERLUDE

In March, 1972, Esther and I were given an unexpected opportunity to fly to England for some months. I had not been back since December,'68, and it seemed very opportune indeed, since Esther was expecting our first child, and we would be able to delight my Mother, who had been unable to attend the wedding, by letting her both meet her daughter-in-law, AND her grandchild!

A fellow student, Duncan Munn, who had been with me at I.B.T.I., had made this possible for us. He was married now, and they had a baby daughter of their own. They were feeling led to serve the Lord in Zaire, and they had offered to hold the fort for us in Kenya whilst we were away as part of their orientation. On the strength of all this I was able to write to friends in the same month:

This month, on the 10th Duncan and Christianne Munn, together with their three month old daughter, Fiona, arrived here by air to join the work. They have come out in Faith, to give themselves to these boys and girls in a very primitive situation, in order that Esther and I can be free to journey to Europe. We have long prayed that God would set us free to come and present the work personally for the first time, but only this month has the prayer been fully answered. We shall be leaving for England on the 28th of March! Please pray very much for Duncan and Christianne, that God will continue to provide and care for them as He has for us, whilst we are away.

Duncan and his wife, Christianne, had little idea of what they were walking into. They had little idea of the true situation. I am sure they thought all our children would be little angels, all saved and cleansed and filled with the Spirit of God. They were not prepared for the mixed multitude, and the enemy's war effort. They were very brave; and we were very glad to have a chance to get away!!

As we left for Nairobi, and the flight to England, we had quite a few misgivings. Our heart was a bit heavy too at having to leave behind so many we had learnt to love deeply in our spirits. We passed out of sight, down the winding mud and rock road, coming first to our nearest local 'town', Luanda. How often we had come here, sometimes even on foot, to do our weekly shopping, just five miles away from where we stayed. One hit the railway station first, with its collection of market women, and beer parlours. Then the flour mill, and so on up the hill to the Asian shops, and lastly the big sprawling Market, with its gaping trading area imprisoned with closely huddled open-fronted shops, and beer parlours. Long dead motorbuses and old cars slumped rottenly in the rutted roadsides, rust and oil settling into dust and mud. Buildings, paint-peeled and wearied by scorching sun, sledgehammer rain, and hail. Rags and bare feet. This was Luanda.

Centre of local trade and commerce for miles around, and the main market to which all came to see and sell what there was – vegetables, fruit, cattle, native medicine, soap, rope, and a thousand other items. Flies, mosquitoes, dust and noise. Rags, nakedness, sickness. So many people seemingly mad or possessed, pass by shouting, cursing, blindly capering to some unheard jig. Young children, and teenagers, struggling endlessly in the hot sun; pushing home-made wheelbarrows up the hill from the station, burdened with the merchandise of Asian traders who may give them ten cents for an hour's toil. Children already addicted to strong drink, drugs, and women. Venereal disease a fact of life before a boy is twelve years old! Many orphans; many starving. That was our local town. But Nairobi, even in those days, was no better; it had to be worse in fact!

Only a week before, Esther and I had seen three teenagers drinking methylated spirits in the main street of our capital city, each of them raving, all of them thin and gaunt, like skeletons on the run. Of course we might discover such scenes even in the west, and in the more developed countries of the world. Yet wherever one finds such corrosion of human life and existence it is a tragedy. How active Satan is; how bent on destroying mankind. But God is stronger; we had already begun to prove it in our home. We sped onwards. Soon we were in the aircraft, Kenya left behind. It was the end of a chapter.

A letter sent to friends from Duncan and Christianne Munn three months after Esther and I left for England in 1972, read as follows:

It seems such a long time since we arrived here at the village of Ramula (25 miles north of Kisumu). In fact it is only three months, but what packed and testing ones. On the compound are living 20 or more children aged from six to eighteen, all with distinct personalities, and we are still getting to know them. All are either orphans or neglected; our aim is not just to provide a 'home' for them, and to raise their material and moral standard, but to see them truly transformed by faith in Jesus Christ. With big moral problems, mainly stealing, this aim would seem well nigh impossible to achieve, but one must never underestimate God's Love for a soul, or His power to change. It is very encouraging to realise that before his conversion, George Muller was a profligate swindler of his own father, yet once saved, became founder of the famous orphanages that bear witness to his great faith in God.

Our first big test came in a combination of crises. Baby Fiona suddenly taken dangerously ill with Meningitis, a shortage of staff just as the holiday help also left, and an ultimatum from a creditor. We felt overwhelmed.

Anxiety was dispelled and prayers answered when Fiona quickly recovered, a fine young Christian joined the staff and a very large donation came just in time to pay off the creditor! How we thanked God and rejoiced!

They had a great deal more to go through, and experience, before the year ended, poor dears, but they held on, and won through. We carried on a lively correspondence with each other, their letters often frantic cries of frustration and despair, as well as shouts of Praise and Victory. Mine not always as helpful or as patient as they ought to have been, and often moved by anxiety about all of them huddled on that unfriendly hill so far away from us both.

On arrival at Gatwick Airport that March, we entered into a late winter scene of snow, ice, and cold. We were met by brethren from my old Bible School where we stayed for a few days before bussing down to Cornwall where my adoptive mother was then living. All the trees were leafless and looked charcoal black against the snowy landscape. Esther thought there had been an enveloping fire that had burned the trees; in Kenya most of the trees are evergreens and never noticeably shed their greenery! There was a lot to see and much to learn, and we were not alone! We had brought one of the boys along with us to England as well. This was Johanna, one of the first eight boys that I wrote about earlier. He was a rather surly, rebellious youngster of twelve. Esther and I had felt that it might help him if we took him with us on the trip, to try and prove to him that we really did care about him. We thought it might soften him up, and bring out a little sweetness in his life. We were 'greener' than we knew. It was not a success, and indeed he did his best through the months ahead to both embarrass us, and those we stayed with. It was distressing, it was heartbreaking, and it put quite a strain even upon our marriage! Many friends did not understand how we could have brought such an uncouth and difficult child with us. Neither did we at times. We certainly often regretted it. Johanna was, nevertheless, to remain in our home until he completed secondary school in 1980. He then left us to make his own way in life. He left in the gall of bitterness. We wept for him. In 1987 he was arrested for armed robbery, and imprisoned for ten years. We tried to contact him without any success, and then this year a letter suddenly arrived from him. We had never given up hope. He is in his forties now! He writes:

Dear Dad and Mum,

I have always known you both loved me, and that you brought me up in the knowledge of God. I would surely have died in sin, if you had not done this for me, and if it were not for you and God, and Jesus, I might have died in the prison.
Because of this, I and many others in the prisons have been Saved, and Accepted Jesus as our Personal Saviour.
I am busy now telling others how I have spent ten years in prison, and how I found Jesus there. Thank you for loving me, and for loving God. Since Jesus came into my life, even immediately as He drew me to Himself, I have been able to give up the things I used to do and be.
And YES, if it were not for HIM, I would have died in sin, in the prison, BUT He has set me free. I am out of the prison now, and I am working! I am a new person.
Your son always,
JOHANNA NANJELO.

Johanna has not been the only child we took with difficult background and damaging habits. Many have resisted, and still resist the Gospel, and the work of the Holy Spirit in their lives. Not all are saints, and not all become angels whilst they are with us! Some have told us that they feel there must be something wrong with us spiritually when they find out that we have ungodly children living in the homes. They seem to assume that the Holy Spirit, if He is with us, must automatically convert all ungodliness into holiness of life. It has not been our experience. That there are sudden and instantaneous conversions and sanctifications we do not deny, but we feel that generally spiritual growth and substantial change is often slow. Poor Duncan and Christianne had to learn this, and they certainly had many surprises!

THE RETURN TO ENGLAND. The three of us rested together at my mother's for about a month, before I began itinerating amongst friends and churches. Esther remained with my Mother until the birth of our first child in June. Steven Iguru Green was born to us in Truro Hospital, Cornwall, south-west England, on the 16th June, 1972. Later that year he was to be dedicated by our beloved brother, Stan Hyde, at Brixham in Devon. My mother travelled up for the occasion, and made a decision for Jesus during the meeting! So many joys were in store for us as we travelled round. Such a delight once more to see Sister Drake and dozens of friends whose faces we had never seen before, yet who had prayed for us, and supported the work. But one of my happiest moments was to meet Dave and Joyce Bargh in Rochdale, Lancashire. Their support and friendship had meant more than we could put into mere words, yet neither Esther nor I had really known either of them.

Way back in 1969, the Bank in Kisumu wrote to me saying that £50 had been deposited in my account by SUREHEAT. It was such an unusual announcement, and name, that it caused considerable speculation. What was Sureheat? Was it a Race-horse?!! It took quite a time for the bank to come up with the answer. When it did we discovered that Sureheat was the trade name of a central heating firm run by Dave Bargh in Rochdale, Lancashire. In 1972 we were to not only meet Dave and his family, but we actually stayed with them for almost three months! The Lord raised up such friends! Such families!

It was in fact while we were staying with Dave and Joyce that we received a letter from an Australian friend of ours then working in Kenya with his wife. He had come across a house that was for sale and which to him had seemed just the kind of place we could have used as a children's home. He wrote:

I have just been to Eldoret for the weekend and heard about the African Inland Mission selling its place, which is a good old house with five acres of land - for Kshs. 19,000/-. It could be an asset for you!

We wrote back straight away, and after a week received a letter from the owners of the property.

Dear Mr. and Mrs. Green,

First of all let me say that the property has been up for sale for three months and several people have already shown interest to buy. One person in particular has been trying to raise the money.
A valuation report was done by a local valuer, and he said Kshs. 95,000/- was the present market value.
If you are seriously interested please let know immediately and what terms financially.

A sketch map of the floor plan of the house was enclosed, and it seemed just ideal for us. That evening a sister in the Lord pressed ten new pence into our hand. It was not much, but we saw it as the 'earnest of our expectation'.

We wrote back again putting in a definite bid for the house at £4750 sterling. We had exactly £40 in hand!!

The reply returned to us swiftly enough.

Your offer of £4750 is a little too low, but we would be able to accept £5000. We might add that we have an offer for Kshs. 95,000/- to hand here now! Also the length of time to pay the total sum is a little too long. We would require 50% down with the remainder to be paid in six monthly instalments.

We confirmed the offer of £5,000, with 50 percent to be an initial down payment. It all seemed like a dream! After all we had only £40! We had never seen the property with our own eyes! We were seven thousand miles away!

In December 1972 I was to write a circular letter. We were then in Denmark, and getting ready to return to Kenya.

The last time we wrote to you it was August!
We sent you a plan of a house in Kenya, and told you of this new property that was offered to us at Eldoret, about 70 miles north-east of our present compound at Ramula. We told you how we felt about the house, and why we wanted it for God, and we told you the purchase price. What we did not say was that we had to pay the first FIFTY PERCENT of that price before the end of September. If we did not do that then we could have no hope of getting it.
Of course we did not have the money we needed, but we did write back to Kenya, and we said that we believed God wanted us to have the house and that we believed He would supply our need. Little did they know that we only had 40 pounds when we wrote, and no idea how or when the rest might come! BUT they agreed to accept our letter and miraculously we were soon able to write that the £2,500 down payment had been found, and was being transferred to Kenya. The LORD performed HIS word to us. Gifts of money came from all over England and Europe; some great – one of a thousand pounds just into my hand – and others small but just as precious and meaningful. None of the donors realised the urgency of our need at that time!

They did not know how much we especially needed, yet ONLY that amount came to hand. The Lord did not provide for the full price at that time!

On the 24th December the four of us, Esther and I, Johanna the young boy we had taken with us from Kenya, and Steven our son, now six months old, all arrived back at Nairobi Airport. It was very hot, and the sun shone gloriously!

I had planned to go direct to Ramula by taxi with all of us together, but there were no taxis, no buses, or anything available. All had been booked in advance by people leaving Nairobi for Christmas! However, on Christmas Day, I managed to find a taxi to drive me and Johanna the 250 miles for 25 shillings! Esther decided to stay in Nairobi with Steven, so that she could spend a little time with her Mother, and then join me in ELDORET the following Thursday, December 28th , provided I had managed to move by then!

Johanna and I arrived at Ramula about 8 p.m. on Christmas night. It was a complete surprise to all the children, and to Duncan, and Christianne, for we had had no means to warn them of our plans. What a welcome we received! Oh, it was good to be HOME!

Christianne Munn had her chin in plasters, as also did Wilson! Their car – Esther's in fact – had been hit by a bus not many days before and was a total wreck! Christianne had been driving. Wilson had been in the back. It was amazing they were not more seriously hurt. On the 27th I arranged for a lorry to drive me, plus seven boys and half of the furniture the 136 kilometres to Eldoret!

On the 28th, Esther and Steven arrived, and on Saturday the rest of the family arrived from Ramula. We began then to settle in. The house was beautiful to our eyes, but very bare and empty, so vast it was. The gardens full of trees and the Peace of God. It seemed a real refuge.

The following March I was to write of it in the following terms.

HERE WE ARE, in our mansion! With its colonial pillared porches, its stately trees soaring upwards, spreading peace and thanksgiving into the sapphire vault of heaven. And the spirit of the wind moving every blade of grass and single leaf to whisper, sing, and sometimes shout the Praise of Him Who makes all this to BE! Yet nothing is ours! Given into our hands, these things are daily passed on to others. The shelter of the house, the peace and joy of the garden all have been given to us, yet the greatest blessing has been in passing it on to the children that share it with us, and also to the great 'outside' that we seek to welcome in at all times of the day and night. And not only the house and grounds are passed on to others, but all our life and living. Every day the Lord fills the larder with food, and every day it goes. Nothing is put by for the day of 'want' – cannot be put away – there is only ever just enough! Have we amassed a great fortune whilst away visiting friends and churches? Have we come back to the delight of a fat, secure, bank balance, and financial security? Some might believe so! But no! All the offerings put into our hands passed on into the buying of a mansion; not for us, or for any individual. Nothing was banked; nothing laid up for a rainy day! Still each sunrise comes, as for the flower of the field, and the bird of the air, filled with expectancy, and renewed and necessary HOPE.

We named the house 'TESTIMONY HOUSE' in memory of that first small home in Maseno. It is a beautiful house, though built of sun-baked bricks of mud. The original builders had trekked up from South Africa about 1908 and began to put up the first rooms, planting ornamental trees and shrubs ready for us, 70 years later. A house with a past; a homely, family house. Comfortable, and friendly. A real GIFT. A Gift from the LORD.

The balance of the original purchase price took almost three years to come in, instead of the agreed six months, the owners graciously and patiently waiting! But it came in. We never mentioned the purchase again after the March letter to our friends in 1973. At the last we still needed £1400 to finalise. Only the LORD knew of the outstanding debt.

Finally the owners asked us to finalise within a month. We could say nothing. WE waited. Towards the end of the third week we were in prayer, when out of the blue a sister in Christ called and left an envelope for the homes. Inside was a cheque for £1000! Two days later another lady arrived, this time from Nairobi. We had never met her before. We showed her round, chatted over a cup of tea, and she left. As she was getting into her car, she put her hand into her bag and withdrew a previously labelled and sealed envelope, which she gave to me. Inside was a cheque for £300. The following day, in the post, arrived $300 from America! Another sister! This time, the wife of the brother of a friend of ours. She lived with her husband in Seattle. There she had become organist and choir director to a Presbyterian church; the cheque was her salary! And so the house was paid for, all £5,000. Its present market valuation, with all the extensions and improvements is, as at 30th December 2003, well over £300,000 – an almost unbelievable appreciation!

But before we arrived back in Kenya, and came into the possession of the Eldoret property, we had spent a month in Denmark! There are many dear praying friends in that country, and I think it is right to mention here just how it is that an Englishman should have been given so much love and Christian care by the Christians of Denmark. There is no doubt in my mind that the Lord forged this link, and fellowship.

Whilst I was being led around in 1968 prior to coming out to Kenya for the first time, I had received an invitation to go to Denmark to help with an Evangelistic Tent Crusade in a small town called Ejby, on the Island of Fyn. I had been there before in 1967 in the company of a few other students from the Bible College, and had even had meetings there during that time. Eva Vosegaard had been our Bible College Secretary, and her home being in this small island, she had been burdened to reach the people with the Word of God. Now, once again, she was inviting me to go and stay with her family and to minister once more in the tent meetings. When that letter arrived I only had enough money for the passage by sea to get there! But there was at that moment no other engagement made in England, and so I decided to go. Only one soul made a decision in that tent meeting. But Marinus Lund, who was conducting the Crusade, enthusiastically invited me to stay and visit more churches. Through his warm hearted kindness to a very raw missionary recruit I was able to travel over more than half of Denmark, meeting countless other members of the Christian family. Marinus Lund himself was a particular help and encouragement to me and I shall always remember him with thankfulness of heart. At the end of November 1968 I had received in good will offerings in Denmark, not only enough to travel back to England, but enough to fly out to Kenya. No more, and no less! And from that time the Lord used friends made during those months both in England and in Denmark to provide for all that has arisen since.

Thus, in 1972, we planned to make a return visit to Denmark. Marinus Lund was to be my interpreter, and we were to travel all over the whole Country this time. Imagine our feelings when on arrival we were given the tragic news of Marinus's death in a car accident just a few days before our arrival. It was a hard blow. But the Lord still had us to go on as planned. During that month our friendships and contacts were cemented and strengthened. We have remained astounded at the way the Christians in Denmark took us and the work of Testimony Faith Homes upon their hearts.

Before we left that December, we were asked by some of the churches in Denmark to try to contact an elderly lady missionary working in Kenya, near to a town called Eldoret – the very town we were moving to! It turned out we would be living just ten kilometres away from this old saint of God; her name was Elizabeth Boys. We came to know her very well indeed later on.

Much later still, in 1976, Eva Vosegaard came to spend some weeks with us in the homes. She was busy all the time taking notes, and on her return she published a book in Denmark entitled '*Father of the Fatherless*'. Thus our name became even more widely known in a country not my own. God works in a mysterious way His Wonders to perform. And since that book was published another has been also published there, and many articles printed in magazines about the work of the homes here in Eldoret; these the product of the fertile and creative mind of Anne Lise Madsen, who for many years with her husband was a missionary in Tanzania and Kenya. It has been our joy to have such a happy continuation of friendship and fellowship. Denmark has kept close to us, and to the work. Praise the Name of Jesus.

FROM A RENTED MUD HUT, via other rented houses in strange places, hostile environments, storms, and sickness, we had now come to an eight-bedroomed, stately house in five acres of parkland, within the boundaries of a growing municipality, with running water piped into the house, electricity, and even good medical help on the door step. Now we could believe for a more settled and harmonious existence; now we could grow, and develop. This was indeed a turning point, and a consolidation.

Yet our entire existence remained firmly grounded upon the Lord. There remained no financial or material security on which we could rely for our ongoing existence or progress. God alone would continue to hold us up.

Before giving some glimpses back into those years after our arrival in Eldoret, perhaps it would be good to reprint here a Statement and Explanation we put out about the work in 1973:

THE REASON WHY we call this society 'Testimony Faith Homes' is because we want it to be a Testimony of Faith in God! We want it to be a message of HOPE, and ACTUAL LIFE, to all those who come to know us, and who are able to SEE what GOD has done, and is NOW doing amongst us.
We want it to be a WINDOW through which people can come and look and see the LIVING GOD; that HE is there, and that HE answers prayer.
AND MORE THAN THIS, that He CARES for all those who do not care for Him, as well as for those who DO care for him. Many have come to stay with us in the Homes, and yet have NOT cared about God, and even today some may be with us who do not

KNOW God in their life, or appreciate Him at all. Yet we can truly say 'THANK YOU' to God because here we ARE, and every day food comes to us; every DAY provision of every kind comes to us, and provides for ALL our needs, whether it's clothing, or food, or school fees – whatever it may be. As we pray, so our God has Provided, in the Name of Jesus.

No, of course, money doesn't suddenly appear growing on our trees, or falling like rain from the sky, so that we just go and gather it. Food doesn't just miraculously appear on our shelves or on our plates. Our God uses PEOPLE to actually BRING our needs to us. As WE pray, God, by His Spirit, INSPIRES PEOPLE!

People anywhere and everywhere to come and bring, to come and GIVE, to come and BE His ANSWER to our prayer. So many times we had NOTHING here, and people, often complete strangers to us, have come to the door, bringing exactly our need. We THANK GOD for the people that He uses to supply our needs; channels of His Love and Blessing.

ONE MORNING, we were praying in my office. We usually gather there to pray after the children have gone to school each morning. This time we faced a rather difficult day. We had spent our last shilling the previous afternoon, and we had eaten our last food at breakfast. The children had all gone off to their various schools, and we would see them all again at lunch time. LUNCH TIME! Well where was lunch going to come from? We were sure the Lord would supply it, BUT from WHERE we still had no idea. AND SO WE BEGAN TO PRAY. We prayed for our lunch!

As we continued in prayer we heard the sound of a car driving slowly up our gravel drive. We ignored it, and we went on praying. It stopped, and after a short while we heard it drive off again. When we finally rose from our knees and went out of the office, we found piled up on our doorstep more than 40 loaves of bread, milk, sugar, jam, and even maize flour. It was our lunch! We never found out exactly WHO had brought it all, BUT it was an answered prayer! This is the way God takes care of us. It is NOT an isolated incident, but a very usual one. Only ONE PERCENT of our whole need to run the children's home is actually promised or guaranteed. For the rest we TRUST IN GOD, to 'Give us our daily bread'.

"And a man shall be as an HIDING PLACE from the wind..." Isaiah 32v2

A MAN, a hiding place, a SHELTER from the wind, the tempest, the storm of life – from the heat and oppression of life. In a sense that is EXACTLY what WE seek to be here: a shelter from the storms of life. Many of the young people that come to live with us, and who become part of the home, have come out of various storms and troubles of life. Some have lost their own home; some have lost their own parents and loved ones. It is impossible to perfectly replace somebody's home or parents, BUT we TRY!

Some have been the victim of circumstances and difficulties, perhaps because of argument between parents that has ended in separation; perhaps because of sickness in the home, that brings death or mental incapacity; perhaps because of such poverty that there is no longer the ability to support life.

Testimony Faith Homes is a place to run to: a hiding place. We do not advertise very much, and few are actually aware that we are here!

A person can hide here from the past, whether fearful or distressing. No reporters come to dig up past sorrow, pain, or shame. From here a new beginning can commence, new self-respect and self-assurance, can be built up.

JESUS CHRIST is the MAN who is a Hiding Place. GOD HIMSELF has provided and given HIM to us. ANYONE can run to Jesus and find a HIDING PLACE, a place to begin again in; a place to be built anew in. He is the SHELTER to which ANY may run and find rest from the turmoil and the battering of life; a place to gather strength in.
Christians believe that Jesus Christ now lives in them, by the power and agency of God's Holy Spirit. IF this is so, then each one that is called a 'Christian' ought ALSO to be a hiding place for any of his fellow men that might need one.

"And each one of them shall be like a hiding place from the wind, and a shelter from the storm; like streams of water in a dry place, like the shade of a great rock in a weary land (to those who run to them)."

THUS each one of us that has come to join hands in this Society, believing themselves to be a Christian, has also contracted to BE what Jesus IS: a Hiding Place! A place of refuge and of peace.

Chapter Five

GROWTH

DURING FEBRUARY 1973 many of the children who had not trusted their lives to Jesus just suddenly opened their hearts to Him. I wrote in the diary:

Many of the senior boys re-dedicated their lives, and more than six asked to be baptised. The whole spiritual atmosphere of the home changed almost overnight. Even the Headmaster of the local primary school has testified of the change in them at school.

Writing later in the same year of 1973, in the month of May:

"A certain man had a fig tree planted in his

vineyard; and he came and sought fruit thereon, and found none." Luke 13v6

This home, This Testimony Faith Home is a garden. Oh yes! And we are all gardeners here, for we have Christ within. And you also are gardeners if it be that Christ is alive in YOU. What of your Garden; what of the trees YOU tend and care for in Jesus' Name? We watch over the youngsters here just as the gardener in the parable watched over his trees. We watch with love and longing – longing for the FRUIT to appear. We watch with love and FEAR – fear that the fruit will fail to be there on time! For the Owner comes suddenly to His Own.

For three years I also came to a particular boy here in the home looking for fruit, but none seemed visible, though the tree was strong and flourishing with ordinary life. Then while we were in England last year, God came and confronted this 'Tree' and shook it, but still no fruit appeared, and the request came to 'cut it down' – to send the boy away! Then Esther and I had taken to prayer, and wrote back to Duncan Munn saying,

"Give him another chance yet – another year. We will pray, and perhaps in a year things will have changed."

But the year has now finished, and the 'Tree' still fruitless; indeed now bent and crooked, having, under promise of fruit, robbed us of £30. Loving care, prayer, and effort, all produced no fruit. Again the owner came, again shook the tree, confronting it yet again with its lack, and looking for repentance. But none came. 'Cut it down,' came the order.

We sent the boy away. A boy who would not, could not (?) come and yield that which was necessary for continued life. We have had to cut him out of the family. Even George Muller felt himself left with no other choice on occasions when the offender refused to repent.

The rotten apple had to be discarded for the sake of the rest that might be contaminated! BUT it is HARD when we seem to fail. When it appears we did not rescue the perishing! But we can of course do nothing of ourselves, and even God Himself will not FORCE His Salvation upon a soul.

Just now (May '73) we have TWENTY children in the home with us. Each one of them has come from a background of difficulty, and many from very bad lives indeed. Each one is a matter of definite prayer; each LIFE a BATTLE GROUND on which a victory is being fought and believed for. But we can only HOPE to touch those who are willing to come. Not all will be willing! Not all will be thankful for a home or even Christian Love. Writing in his book 'Born Old', Dave Wilkerson says,

"Our children were hard to work with, and they weren't likely to thank us for anything we did for them. We weren't convinced they needed our love or understanding; not after doing without them for so many years . . . just when we thought we were getting somewhere they might say, 'Thank you Buddy', and take one fast slide, BUT SOME GRAB HOLD!"

In January of 1974 we were joined in the work by a young secondary school leaver, Francis Wainaina. We had known each other in Maseno where he was at school, and then met again in Eldoret where he came to work during school holidays to help pay for his school fees. He was a very bright young man – university material. But he was also born again, and towards the end of 1973 he asked us if he could come to spend the December holiday with us. He had completed his O-Levels and so we agreed. I wrote in the diary for December 1973:

We have welcomed Francis Wainaina as our guest until March next year – though we have prayed he will become much more than a guest!

And so he did. On the 25th January he formally made the decision not to proceed with his education, but to throw in his lot with us, and work with Testimony Faith Homes. He put out a number of 'fleeces' and the Lord answered each one positively for him. He was to remain with us until August 1981. In 1975 Francis married Elaine Johnson, then teaching at Moi Girls' High School, Eldoret, and almost immediately they found themselves 'instant' parents of their own family.

Their wedding day was on 30th August 1975 at St. Matthew's Anglican Church in Eldoret, and of course we ALL attended, Elaine's parents having flown out from England for the occasion.

On the 29th October, 1975 Gideon Rotich, a local social worker employed with Eldoret Municipality called me on the phone and asked me to meet him in town; there was something he wanted to show me. Later I was to describe this encounter:

ROTICH, the social service officer, and I left the car at the roadside, and walked on up the hill. It was about 11 a.m. On either side of the road tall fields of maize rustled in the wind that swept over the steep incline we were climbing. The road had been tarmac once. Now, long neglected and broken up, it led us to the Municipal Rubbish Dump. The smell of it and the acrid blue smoke of endlessly burning rubbish blew down upon us we walked.

"Come with me," Rotich had said, when we had met earlier, "and I'll show you a sight!"
At last we reached the sloping summit, and there stretched out before us under the blue vault of a sun-drenched heaven and margined by maize plantations, was the DUMP! Acres of it. Smoking, burning, rotting! No TIP, this, but truly a DUMP. Everything was just dumped on the ground. Dumped and burned; dumped and rotting away; dumped and POUNCED upon, searched, and rummaged – for FOOD!!
There was a place like this outside Jerusalem – The Valley of Hinnom (Gehenna) they called it. HELL! Next to Jerusalem. AND THIS! The vivid sapphire and emeralds of sky and fields – then the charred, littered, defiled earth, enmisted in slowly curling smoke, huge carrion hawks circling always watchfully.
"Well, here we are!" commented my companion. "And there THEY are!"
Yes, there they WERE! People! People who lived from this rottenness!
Like wraiths they moved in and out of the haze, tattered, ragged, thin and gaunt. PEOPLE, and CHILDREN, scattered all over that putrefaction. Children jumping and scuttling in and out of the rubbish like great rodents; some naked, some in rags, hair matted, bodies caked in grime. The youngest seemed about 5, and the eldest 16. And above their age, young and ancient of days roamed rapaciously amongst a sea of urban filth.
We came upon them quietly, walking. None of them were supposed to be there, and if we had gone in the car all would have run, thinking we were the Police come to beat them and arrest them.
"Where are they all from?" I croaked, wide-eyed in horror.
"From the north, from Turkana. From the desert lands and poverty even greater than this," my friend replied. "Many of the children are

orphans who have been abandoned or stranded here by their parents. Others have family either here, living off the dump with them, or back up north, even poorer."

I looked and wondered how, after being in Eldoret so long, I had never heard of this stricken place. But now the Lord had shown me! Before that day had ended we had arranged to transfer FIVE of the children into the Homes.

A week or so later we began to rent another house! It adjoined our property, separated only by a 50-foot tarmac road. We moved in, or rather Francis and Elaine moved in, on the 15th November 1975. And with them went those first five boys from the rubbish dump. A new home was started, and we called it Jacaranda Cottage.

It had been empty some time, and we had been praying about buying it, but funds did not come in. Then someone DID buy it, and it was to them we applied for permission to rent since they themselves did not seem to want to live in it. They agreed, and at the same time we took out a six-month option to BUY. Of course we told no one. We called it 'Jacaranda' because of the many Jacaranda trees that adorn the garden; in fact the house seems to stand in a glade of them, the beautiful blue blossoms seasonably covering the ground like a carpet as they fall, full blown, from the branches.

By 1976 I was able to write to friends the following Update:

Jacaranda Cottage really does belong to us now. Much prayer round the world has gone into securing this small house for Christ.

Beginning as it did, as a shelter for the boys from the Rubbish Dump, Jesus seems to have put it upon many hearts.

In taking this house, and the 'rubbish', we took on a tremendous additional burden – more than £200 a month extra expenditure was going to be needed in order to pay for the rent, water, electricity, and food. We believed that this is what Jesus wanted us to do, so we did it! We were severely tested!

Immediately income dropped to a bare minimum. The monthly standing accounts could not be met for the month of November, and by the end of December we were feeling desperate!! Only enough came to provide for daily food. We seemed poised on the brink of certain collapse. We COULD only continue to wait upon the LORD. Suddenly about this time, a sister dropped in and left an envelope. She had no idea of our situation at that moment. Inside the envelope was a cheque for £1000 sterling. The accounts were all paid! Jacaranda Cottage was secured for months ahead – and we took some more boys from the DUMP!

By the end of March we found ourselves again in need, but AGAIN the Lord undertook for us, and friends in England, hearing of us from an old acquaintance and brother in Jesus (Leslie Pick of the International Refugee Mission) forwarded gifts amounting to yet another thousand pounds sterling! But we still had nothing in sight which would actually buy the property. As we entered the month of August we were confronted with a crisis situation. The owner of the cottage informed us that he had a buyer, with the money in his hand.

"Mr. Green, either buy now or move out in three weeks!" he said.

It was an ultimatum. We had nothing in hand, and nothing in sight. We resorted to prayer, whilst the nightmare of seeing the whole Jacaranda family camped in tents on our lawn was ever before our eye.

Then the 'Wilde Ganzen' flew.
In Holland there was a Christian radio and television programme. It went out to the nation every Sunday evening just for ten minutes, presenting challenging projects from the world mission fields. The sponsors called themselves the Wild Geese, and when they went on the air they said that the Wild Geese were flying.
One Sunday evening, unknown to us, they 'flew' for Jacaranda Cottage. They had been telephoned about the home and the dump children by a Dutch missionary friend of ours here in Eldoret. He had often visited the homes, and was especially concerned about the dump children that we had rescued from the rubbish.
We had no idea that he had phoned. Neither did we know of the programme. During the week following the programme being broadcast, the sponsors in Holland received EXACTLY the purchase price being asked for Jacaranda Cottage, PLUS a further £500 which we discovered later to be the cost of the legal charges!! God thinks (knows) about everything! And so we have paid the owner; Jacaranda Cottages is OURS – THE LORD'S!! A MIRACLE once again. The surprise, delight, excitement that was ours cannot be expressed. Our wonder to see HIM working in the hearts of people complete strangers to us, in a land untravelled in any way by us, cannot BE described. Jesus is WONDERFUL.

And on the 1st September 1976 Francis and Elaine were praising the Lord yet again, this time for the safe delivery of their baby daughter, Rosemary.

The homes were expanding, and our personal family was also growing! Esther and I welcomed our second child, Michael Waweru into the world on the 27th January 1974 and on the 13th January 1977, Elizabeth

Mugure was safely born to us. Our blessings were multiplied!!

Jacaranda Cottage was to continue on, and during 1978 we were able to extend its accommodation so that today some 38 children are able to find shelter within its walls.

Francis and Elaine remained as house-parents in Jacaranda Cottage for seven years until June, 1981, when Francis felt led to join the Anglican priesthood, and to leave for training in U.K., together with his immediate family. They were difficult to replace. Not everyone wants to live in with other people's children, and to forego personal privacy, freedom of movement, and financial gain. Two couples were to attempt it. They were Hans and Sonja Jensen from Denmark, and Bob and Joy Grahamslaw from England. Neither couple stayed very long, nor in between the Jacaranda 'family' had to be looked after by one of our 'single' members of staff, as a stand-in houseparent. It was not easy for the children either! Then, in 1986, Joshua and Miriam Mbithi offered themselves for the job of 'Mum and Dad' in Jacaranda Cottage, and there they remained for almost 19 years. It was to be quite a challenge for them, but Jacaranda had been Miriam's home many years before, so she at least knew a little bit about how it would be.

When we opened the home in 1975, Elaine asked us if we could let Miriam, who was then part of Testimony House family (she had come in 1973) go with them to start the new family. We agreed, and Miriam was to stay there until she completed her secondary education, and even on a few more years, whilst she was completing her nursing training. Miriam was about 11 years old when she first came to Testimony Faith Homes. She came from an area south of Nairobi, towards the Coast; a dry, arid region. Her Father had had been a casualty in the Kenya Army, and had been invalided out without pay. He was mentally unstable and disabled. Her Mother had died in 1972, and the elderly Grandmother, the only able relative, found it too difficult to look after Miriam and her siblings. She asked her Pastor to help look for help, and soon afterwards it was arranged for Miriam to join us. Later her young brother would come too.

After completing her Nursing Training, she joined Kijabe Hospital near Nairobi, and it was whilst working there that she met her husband-to-be, Joshua Mbithi, a young pastor. They married in August 1985. I remember the wedding day very well indeed.

She had to be married near the home of her husband-to-be; some 440 kilometres from Eldoret, on the other side of Nairobi. I felt very glad to be standing next to her, so beautiful in her wedding dress.

As the procession made its way towards the church door, I looked back over the years to 1973, when Miriam had first come to stay with Esther and me. She had been 11 years old then, shy and skinny; nothing at all to look at. Now here she was by my side, a woman entering into married life. What a change had taken place. She knew and loved Jesus! He was the one who had been working the transformation in her. She had trained as a nurse too, and had in fact only just graduated, and now she was getting married.

We had entered the church, small, built of wood and mud, with a roof of iron sheets. Slowly we went towards the front where the pastor was waiting with Joshua the bridegroom. Esther was also at the front with five of our boys that had come from the home, and who had grown up with Miriam. Slowly the bride and I walked up the aisle, the bridesmaids, my daughter Elizabeth amongst them, following. The church bulged with well-wishers, friends, and relatives of the bridegroom. Outside, the sun was shining on a dry and dusty landscape. We have got to the front now, and Joshua catches my eye for a moment, and smiles.

FLASH! Cameras begin recording the scene. The choir which had been singing all the time continued, and there was an expectant and excited hum everywhere.

"Who gives this woman to be married?"

"I do!" I replied, and handed Miriam's hand to the pastor. I was a bit croaky. It's not every day you give a daughter away! And to all intents and purposes I *was* her father at that moment, and as I looked across at Joshua I felt glad that he was to be her husband; a fine young man, already in full-time service for Jesus.

Silently I lifted my heart to the Lord. "Thank you Lord, for underwriting Miriam's life for us, and for bringing us all together in Faith on this day to witness a new Jesus-family being born. Thank you!"

FLASH! It was my camera this time, and me taking a picture of Joshua slipping the ring on Miriam's finger. Now they were one; now they were actually married, and their faces were radiant with joy. Oh Happy Day!

We had left Eldoret on the Thursday morning. I had had a heavy heart about it, for there was virtually nothing in the bank, and no cash in hand – I had to use what we had just to get us all to the wedding. I had never before left the home in such a fix. I did not want to go – would have given anything to stay. I worried all the way to Nairobi, and was miserable and irritable of spirit – a bad travelling companion, and I knew it. I - I - I - and more I! Yes, of course, I had left God right out. It would have changed nothing if I had remained at home.

Once in Nairobi I endeavoured to put my 'worries' away, but they still nagged at the back of my mind. I could get no news until Sunday evening, after we arrived in Nairobi on the way home again. Esther was the one that phoned home. Nicholas Mwangi, my deputy at that time, answered the phone.

"How's the 'old man'?" he asked, meaning me! "I bet he's just been worrying all the time about how we are! Well tell him he needn't have bothered! As you left here the Lord supplied our need almost immediately, and we received enough to provide all our need for the weekend AND for the week ahead!"

WONDERFUL. Of course it was. But it was also a rebuke to me. I should have had more faith – should have realised He had us all in the hollow of His Hand.

And so the work expanded, and grew on. And the numbers of lives leaning upon God increased, and the costs of keeping them all together also increased. Our utter dependency upon God continued.

In February 1975 the diary records:

February 3rd
No money! LORD, do a miracle for us!

Went to town. Post revealed one letter containing 1,000/- from Sister R. Later received a further letter, this time from friends in Seattle USA, enclosing $150.
Isn't God WONDERFUL to His Children!
During the afternoon the Police phoned asking us to take 2 boys (twins) whose mother had deserted them. They were just four months old, one seriously ill with what was termed 'bronchitis'. The mother has been arrested and put in prison. She is a well-known lady who is a 'roamer', a prostitute really, and a drunkard. She has a brother who has 11 children in his own family PLUS some SEVEN more belonging to his sister.
He has tried to get her to settle down, giving her land of her own, and even building her a house. All to no avail.
(Later we were to discover that one of the twins – the one with 'bronchitis' – had a congenital defect in his windpipe making it difficult for him to swallow, and also inducing the 'bronchitis'. Doctors said this had been caused by the 'drinking' habits of his mother who must have been on raw spirits most of the time.)

June 8th
Received 1,000/- from Alliance Girls High School.

June 9th
Michael, our little son, stuck a screwdriver into the electric heater whilst it was switched on – and blew it up! We thank God for saving his life!

June 12th
Bills amounting to 12,000/- outstanding today.

November 4th
Esther's watch stolen from the bathroom! Francis and Elaine's house broken into, but nothing taken.

November 15th
Francis and Elaine moved into Jacaranda Cottage with Miriam, the twins, and eight small boys from the rubbish.

November 17th
Francis unwell. Doctor diagnosed Malaria.

November 20th
Drove Francis to Kitale Hospital. He has taken a turn for the worse. Doctor here immediately diagnosed acute appendicitis.

November 21st
Had his operation and was fine. Appendix was gangrenous!

January 7th 1976
Esther and I went to Ambira more than a hundred miles west of Eldoret, and admitted a boy from there who was in need. On the way home we saw a very emaciated young boy at Luanda Market, but we were afraid to bring him home with us!

So often one can find oneself shying away from the thing that God wants. This is mainly because of human fears and failings. Such was the reason for the following article and story that I wrote back to friends during the later part of that month of January 1976:

'Which now of these three, thinkest thou, was

neighbour unto him that fell amongst thieves?'
And he said, 'He that shewed MERCY on him'. Then Jesus said unto him, 'GO, and do thou likewise.'
Luke 10v25-37

Fix your hearts and minds on this word MERCY. It is one with and the same as LOVE. And it is indispensable in the Christian life. It is this having of MERCY upon our neighbour which is the measure of our LOVE for him. Thinking of this man who fell amongst thieves, it is forced upon us that it was not his fault! It HAPPENED that he met them, and that they violently robbed him, and left him for dead. It could have happened to anyone. But most people were unsympathetic to this man's adversity, passing him by. Of course the actual situation is not limited to being robbed of money. There are many ways we can be robbed; many ways of falling amongst thieves. One could be robbed of sight, of hearing; or robbed of mental or physical health until totally crippled and helpless. How many people pass by cautiously – yes even hurriedly?!

Both the Priest and the Levite turned away – passed by! Both the spiritual and the material man passed by. WHY? Both could have been 'good' men, even 'kind' men, by most standards. Why DID they turn away? Why DID they pass by? One did at least LOOK – concern was evidenced, be it only such a little. BUT he hurried on, just as I also did, very recently!! They did not want to be INVOLVED more than necessary. The Priest may have thought the man beyond spiritual help, or that he himself was not spiritually equipped to answer the need.

The Levite may have been unwilling to take a burden which might cause him more expense than he was prepared to give; more energetic physical activity than he thought he could spare.

JESUS, in Mark 12, is seen to note how the rich give much. They could spare a lot, because being rich they still had much left to spend upon themselves. In their giving they were not denying themselves, because self was still well taken care of. BUT the WIDOW gave MORE than they did because she gave ALL, her EVERYTHING. He was her joy, and her Passion.

Her loving was an act of selfless GIVING. Jesus loves that way; GOD loves that way. He says we must also love that way. DO we? We say we love Him, but DO we show it in the way we love others, in the way we DO MERCY to them? With her two mites the widow risked her life, her family, her home, EVERYTHING.

Jesus says that when we show love and care for others we show it to Him. Think of that! What is the quality of our MERCY? Does it stop short when it begins to mean personal sacrifice, inconvenience, HURT?

THE SAMARITAN thought nothing of himself, or what others thought about him. He took up the burden caused by that chance happening, and dealt with it; going out of his own way in order to do so. The full application of this will, I hope, be plain to you as you read on. During this time many of us here were deeply moved and blessed by NOT just passing by! Even though, by stopping, we had to face our poverty of spirit, and be humbled!

How often we are cheated by our wicked heart. We can believe in our ability to go SO FAR . . . then we have to go a step further than we had planned or thought would be necessary, and we don't want to! How many times must we forgive? How many miles must we walk that are extra to what we had agreed initially? How many times must we miss the T.V. programme, interrupt our reading, or go without a meal, or miss an appointment, or even forgo that hard-earned rest? How many times must we turn aside from our own way in order to attend to someone else's problem? And if I said the answer must be AN ENDLESS NUMBER; COUNTLESS TIMES, *how willing would you find yourself? And I am asking myself again, even now, how willing will I be the* NEXT *time?!*

It was about 6 p.m. that afternoon we passed through Luanda Market. The sky was black, ominously full of storm cloud.

Already a fierce wind was blowing; dust and refuse swirling about the deserted market place. The last shoppers were going home. We were parked just opposite, getting petrol. A country bus pulled out from across the road, suddenly revealing to my gaze a small boy. He seemed about to fall. Naked except for a too small, torn and tattered shirt, he staggered a few steps and stopped. Feet splayed out, swollen knees pressed together, he seemed paper-thin. A gust of wind blew, and he staggered yet again. His right arm was bent double across his breast, clutching in the claw-like hand what seemed to be a piece of rag. In the other hand he held a piece of bread. His right eye was swollen, and closed up.

"Look at that boy!" I cried out to Esther, still sitting in the car with another of our boys, Peter, who was just 17. They looked. Petrol was given by this time, and I was paying the attendant. Out of the corner of my eye I could see the boy jerkily making his way away from us on the other side of the road. I got in the car and pulled across to intercept him. He looked at us uncertainly, even vaguely!

"Peter do get out and see what you can find out about him!" I said. Peter got out of the car and tried to talk with the boy, but it seemed he could not get any answer from him, and he turned quickly to some passing women, homeward bound from the market stalls. Then he was back at the car window, supporting the boy with one arm. He stared at us pathetically with his one eye and holding out his hand asked for food; he looked even worse close to.

"He has fits!" said Peter. "And the people around say he is well-known, and is always just around."

FITS! He has fits! Then he must be epileptic. Fits! NO, it was impossible; without fits maybe we could have taken him away to help him. BUT with fits! Why this would be too great a RISK; he might be with us, helpless, all his life! All OUR life. Think of looking after him for evermore.

"If he has fits then we can't do much for him." I said out loud. "We'll just have to leave him. A pity, but after all what else can we do?"

Peter got back into the car. We had looked, we hadn't liked what we had seen, and we drove away! We drove away into the gathering storm, into the oncoming night. A night and a storm that the boy would also meet, but where, and how? We drove away, afraid to get involved in something too big for us! In something too big for Jesus too?? We drove DOWN HILL! And the storm broke upon us, and night came.

I tell you, dear ones, I was very unsettled, but I did not turn back. We drove in silence, and in the rain, and it was like driving through the tears of this world's sorrow and despair. My own soul was distressed. Jesus would not have passed by! I had not asked HIM though! I had not wanted to get involved. I had looked at that broken down skeleton, with its history of fits, seeing its sores and wounds, and although I had been sorry, I saw only defeat there. The physical reality of that boy's situation seemed to me then more than the power of a Risen Christ.

In bed that night I tossed and turned restlessly. Esther also was disturbed, and Peter told us later that he had prayed for a long time before he could get to sleep; he just couldn't get the thought of the boy out of his head!

"I feel I must go back for that boy Ess," I said at breakfast the next morning.

"Well I think the same," she replied. "I could not sleep worrying how he managed with all the rain; I was just fearing how WE would take care of him – BUT I know Jesus can heal him."
And so I drove back the hundred kilometres to Luanda. Peter, John and Moses Otunga going with me. We arrived about 2 p.m., and after a 40-minute search found the boy in the same condition, stretched out under a lorry, moaning. The market was thick with people, all of them passing by! Some turned to look, but went on. We had done the same the day before!
No one seemed willing to say anything about him, but after a while we found someone who knew him, and she took us to the grandmother who lived a mile away. She, an ancient of many years, told us that the boy had been ill SIX years. The father and mother did not exist, the father being dead, and the mother having deserted. He was an orphan.
"What could I do for him?" she asked us. "He was always falling down and always being robbed of whatever he had. I am too old to help him."
We have brought him home.
People backed away from me when I lifted him into the car. Peter put the boy in his own room, and has become more than brother to him. He had put us all to shame with his love and compassion for this broken life.
We have PRAYED, and he is much better. He is called HOSEA, and he is about 14. He looks only 12. He rested without moving for two days, without any fit. The doctor called and said it was a case of gross neglect. The third day he had four fits. We prayed more. The next day three fits and we went on praying. The next day two fits and prayer continued. He was completely delivered in the end. Doctors in Nairobi that we took him to said that he had

cerebral damage, and would be a 'cabbage' for the rest of his natural life and recommended heavy sedation.
We ignored the opinion and the drugs. He grew up to learn Swahili and English, and to handle his own financial affairs, working a full labouring day each week of his life. Years later he was to return to his home area and build himself his own house, much to the astonishment of all those who still remembered his past. Hosea remembered it all very well, and glorified God always for the Salvation and the Healing he received from Jesus.
He taught us a great deal. He is not the only one from whom we have learnt of the Love and Mercy of God. Indeed each and every child that has ever come to be with us has had a problem; sometimes more than one! The disfigurement is not always an OUTWARD ONE; there are often INWARD ills to deal with. We have had to learn patience, and sometimes long suffering, and often seeming inability to help has left us weak and wasted in heart – yet never without HOPE.
WHY, one has just now come in to see me, as I am writing this. Last year he was in the grip of alcoholism; a thief thrice in prison. NOW he is working in a steady job. He has just come to thank us for the years gone by, the hurts suffered.
"I have joined a church now, as well," he said, his eyes shining. There were tears in mine. We have believed in, prayed for, and endured his wayward life many, many years. Thank you Lord Jesus.

In 1974 we had admitted another child who was to teach us many things over the years, even to the present, for he remains very much with us in the family. His name is Paul, and he came to us when he was only four years old. Initially we had no idea of the extent of the problem that would unfold, but by 1984, ten years further on, we did know, and I was able to write to friends all about Paul, and how he had affected us, and indeed our entire attitude once again to physically handicapped children.

LIFE – I will that no man should perish!
TO BE OR NOT TO BE? That is the question that is often asked in our world, often in the connection of whether a child should be allowed to be born or not! To be alive or dead! To give life, or to kill – to expose to heartache, a sea of troubles, and the thousand natural strokes and shocks that flesh is heir to, or never to be born - to out of mercy, kill what is alive, to save from suffering, pain, and wretchedness.
SOME, in our age, are exponents of 'mercy killing', and many more believe in the 'institutionalism' of those who 'cannot fit' or who are a 'burden' to society, home, and family! SOME of each group no doubt believe that they are considering the one who is defective or in some other way mentally or physically disabled, incurably ill, et cetera. Others are merely thinking of themselves.
WE BELIEVE IN LIFE, and we believe in the VALUE and SANCTITY of EVERY human being, no matter what their physical or mental condition. We cannot argue with God in this at all. Life is a living, meaningful opportunity to know God, and to reveal God to each other. We are all, regardless of colour, race, religion, politics, or physical/mental handicap, made in HIS LIKENESS. In each one of us is something to be discovered that is LIKE GOD, and that will reveal Him. In each of us is something to reveal and touch off LOVE in another!

"One young man, born with serious physical handicap, without his left leg, and with no arms below the elbow, was asked if he thought

a person born with such defects should be allowed to live – wouldn't he be better off dead?
He replied in part by saying, "I know when I was born, the first thing my Dad said to my Mum was that 'THIS one needs our love more.' An individual with a handicap needs our love and needs us to help him grow into the being that God has made him to be. I'm very GLAD TO BE ALIVE."

A girl aged 14 was watching a programme about pre-natal screening, and abortion for spina bifida – something she herself had been born with, and lived with. She remarked, "I'm GLAD they didn't do that to me, because I've had 14 years of LOVE!"

THERE ARE EXTRAORDINARY GIFTS THAT REWARD THOSE WHO LIVE WITH, AND FOR THE HANDICAPPED.
SUCH CHILDREN TEACH A GREATER DIMENSION OF LOVE WHICH IS IMPOSSIBLE TO LEARN ANY OTHER WAY.
THE VERY EXISTENCE OF THE HANDICAPPED AND IMPERFECT, AND THE LOVE BESTOWED ON THEM BY THOSE WHO CARE, STANDS AS A TESTIMONY TO THE SACREDNESS OF HUMAN LIFE, AND TO OUR CONTENTION THAT THIS SACREDNESS FAR OUTWEIGHS ANY ETHIC CONCERNED WITH THE QUALITY OF HUMAN LIFE."
(Extracted from the Book '*Whatever Happened to the Human Race?*' by Dr. Francis Schaeffer & Dr. C. Everett Koop, M.D.)

IN JULY 1974 A SMALL BOY of four years came to live with us. He had been brought by the Child Welfare Case Worker from Eldoret, who had found him neglected, and suffering from what she had diagnosed as 'Malnutrition'. He was not an attractive sight to look upon. He was wasted and emaciated; stomach swollen and distended, as also were his wrists, knees and ankles. His hands seemed too large for his frail little body. His hair was yellow, sparse and silky in texture, so unlike the usually tight, dark, springing curls of African children, making him seem less able to cling to life. His face seemed screwed up, the skin that of an old person. One eye, unseeing, was swollen to double the usual size, and glazed over, and the other seeing only dimly, making the child cock his head on one side as he grimaced with the effort to look around him. NO, he was certainly not physically attractive.

A rather horrific spectacle. . . YET, as one looked, there was SOMETHING, a heart-pulling something – a force that moved the heart.

"His mother died, you see," the fat and comfortable African social worker was saying. "And when the father went off to bury her at her parents' home in Fort Hall (hundreds of miles away) he did not return. The child was looked after by neighbours, and he contracted measles. I think that's why his eyes are affected. He is unwanted, and there is no one to help. Please take him, and do what you can for him."

Looking at him sitting there, appearing more animal than human being, we felt ourselves a little alarmed and insufficient, and even, quite honestly, a little repulsed! We should have liked to have said "NO, sorry, we have no room!" BUT after all it was ONLY malnutrition; we would feed him up, and then all this strangeness would vanish, and he would put on weight, and be like any other child in a few months. Even his sight might be restorable to some degree! We agreed then to take him in, incontinent, blind, and full of worms. Round worms! He was infested with these as well, internally. A few days after being with us, he deposited most of them in one of the sitting room armchairs as he sat helpless in it. Some of those worms were seven to nine inches long, and as thick as your little finger! His nose ran continually, and as days and weeks went by there seemed little change in his general condition. At last we decided to take him to a retired British surgeon, some 70 miles away. He took one look and said, "GARGOYLISM," and suddenly we found out that little Paul was a victim of Hurlers Syndrome, an incurable, and almost untreatable congenital disease that afflicts about one in ten thousand. Most sufferers die in childhood, or before they are 20 years old. Deformity, blindness, deafness and imbecility are all possible symptoms of the disease in its various stages.

And suddenly we found out that *we cared so much, so very much.* In the weeks and months he had been with us we had come to know the *person* that was inside the body, and we had begun to appreciate the many *beautiful* qualities of life that there were in that person! He no longer looked grotesque to *us*. Yet the doctor was adamant. He would not improve. Look after him? We had no qualified help! How would he grow? How long would he live? Was it fair to let him live together with all the other 'normal' children?

But he was already in our heart. We *loved* him. And so of course we had to *keep* him.

As I have said Paul has remained with us. He is thirty-four this year (2004). His brain is keen and sharp with an immense sense of humour and fun. He is confined now to a wheelchair, and still blind. But he is no vegetable, and he is VERY GLAD TO BE ALIVE. His education suffered due to the fact that although we allowed him to attend Blind School for a while, his physical disabilities made it impossible for him to continue. His disease is still active, but seems to have developed slowly.

He has come to know Jesus as his own Saviour, and he has *lived* amongst us, and been loved and appreciated by the whole family. He has been a special Gift from God. He has never once complained about his multiple disabilities or shown self-pity. Rather he shares in everyone else's life. Why hasn't the Lord healed him? Only the Lord Himself can answer that. We have believed that He *can* heal him, and we have prayed much. Who can tell the future?

We are all handicapped. Perhaps none of us are truly 'normal' – and certainly not whole! Yet we all have something to offer each other, something to *give*, something to *bring*, for He has made us all. And He has sent each one of us into this world to show forth His LIKENESS. We only have to start looking.

But Testimony Faith Homes is not equipped to handle a lot of physically or mentally handicapped children. We are but a few here, and the great majority need, to a great extent, to be able to care for themselves, yet we cannot shut doors any more to a child because he or she is handicapped. From time to time one and another is welcomed in, and we have learnt to be *glad* and not afraid.

"I walked past some kids today, Lord –
Ten year olds making the sidewalks alive
with swirling flag patches,
flashing street-hockey sticks,
yells and pleadings and intrigue.
And right in the middle of them
a boy sat in a wheel chair,
trying to join in,
to yell at the right times,
to be more than a tree stump or a bush.
It's maddening Lord.
That boy is meant to run and shout and chase.
His nerves and glands and muscles are a marvel –
an incredible creation of yours –
but he's like a drenched butterfly.
One damaged gland incapacitates
One pull on a wheel kills.
What a dangerous world we're in
Pascal said it –
'A drop of water or a draft of air
can kill a man!' . . .
. . . LORD, I could look at the wheel chair kid
I could look for the kids who show compassion –
who make him fit in.
I could find the good adversity brings.
I could look for your ultimate purpose –
(didn't you say you counted each hair on
our heads?)

AND LORD, I'll happily admit it –
pain does build maturity in MY life.
But the wheel chair kid,
DOES HE KNOW YOU?"
From the Book '*Is There a Place I can Scream*' by Harold Myra.

Not everyone felt that we were on the right track, nevertheless, and some were quite open, walking honestly like the day, with us about it. One night, it would have been 1973 or 74 I should think, a dear friend and brother was busy warming his rear end at our sitting-room fireplace towards the close of the evening.

"Don't you think this living by faith bit is rather like spiritual blackmail?" he asked. "I mean, when someone *knows* you are out here alone, and without any support or lifeline, well, I mean, they must surely feel morally obliged to put their hand in their pocket, and save you!"

His comment took us back for a moment. But I hope that is *not* how it is in reality. God says (Psalm 50), "If I were hungry I wouldn't tell you." He has no need to tell any of us. The whole world is His, the silver and gold, the birds of the air, the cattle on a thousand hills – the life of man himself – are all HIS.

I did once read a circular letter from a Christian mission which went:

"We are totally without funds, and if you don't put your hand in your pocket NOW, and help us, this work will have to close down."

We have never, by God's Grace, had to say such a thing. We would NEVER say such a thing; for to do so would be to admit that our God is DEAD and NON-EXISTENT. God alone is the confident of our needs. *How* he arranges for our Provision is known only to Him – but the whole world is at His command to do His bidding. I do not think He needs to stoop to a procedure like blackmail – do you? I really hope not, and I hope we don't either, for we would be bringing great dishonour to the name and character of the One we honour most.

Many write or visit and say to us, "It must be wonderful, living by Faith!"

Yes, it IS wonderful!

BUT not always EASY! Faith is, after all, the SUBSTANCE and EVIDENCE of things first of all HOPED and BELIEVED for; things that at first are not near enough to see or touch! The SUBSTANCE and the EVIDENCE is WONDERFUL! The HOPING FOR, BELIEVING FOR, and the WAITING FOR can be very testing indeed. It needs PATIENCE. It needs at times ENDURANCE as well. I have to be truthful about this, and not be too heavenly-minded. The life of faith is often a life of trial. But YES, of course, in the end, it IS very truly WONDERFUL. Praise the Lord.

Others have questioned our wisdom in spending our life in social works rather than in evangelism:

"We do not find anywhere in the Word that we should found schools, hospitals, orphanages etc., to win the lost. It has been said that the lost will not listen to us if we take no thought for temporal things, but this is not true. Ministers are to preach the Word. It is easy to get side-tracked – be careful about this."

This was written to us by a fellow labourer in the Lord's Service. WE feel that all ministers have to be preachers, not forgetting that not all ministers are pastors or evangelists. Some are teachers, some are helps. We are helps! We also do preach as we help. We feel that if more Born Again, Spirit-Filled believers were engaged in social work, then much more would effectively be done for Christ. Social Work without God is like works without faith! It is useless, and from the world's problems around us, we see the truth of that. BUT Social Work WITH God is works WITH faith. It is total involvement of God and Man. But it is not an easy task either.

There are heartaches and sorrows many times. We ourselves are not perfect, and even the homes themselves are not perfect.

We try to be home and family, but not all accept to *belong*, or to make use of what is here. We cry out for the 19% of those who have already passed through the homes, and today seem to be *failures*. Our hearts *ache* for them. But we do not lose hope or faith in the fact that even now God can Redeem them.

We try to be home and family, but there *is* a difference. Most children leaving their own home will always feel their bed is there for them to return to in an emergency. With us this may not be so, for what is left behind when a family member grows up and leaves, is immediately taken up by a newcomer. The homes are open-ended and our families ever growing and expanding. Children are passing through; they *must* leave one day, and although many things are left behind that *can* be found again when re-visited, it can never be the same as it was before. No permanent refuge to return to; only a loving welcome when you visit. Our children are passing through. They go to seek their own life; their own new home and family with God.

Here are a few extracts from letters and testimonies of some of the children who were with us in those years:

" ... *And what you said really burned in my heart as you said that you and Mummy want me to have a good and clean life in which God can Bless me abundantly with Joy, a good wife, and a happy home and family in the future.*
I tell you, Daddy, these words really burned my heart as I just look on the life of men and women, especially in the place next to us here, called Majengo (district of Nairobi). I tell you, young people like me spoil their lives in playing sex, buying prostitutes – as if God created girls to be bought! I just thank God very much because He saved me when I was young and before I came here to Nairobi.
I tell you Daddy, thank you very much for the Word that you been preaching to us. I really know that my body IS a part of Christ's Body; the Temple of His Holy Spirit."

This was written from Nairobi in 1974. Moses had gone there in January of that year to commence a Course in Painting and Sign-Writing. We had feared for him. The locality there *is* very bad and was notoriously immoral and sinful, brimming over with fleshly temptations of all kinds. It was a great joy to us in 1974 to see him standing so firmly on the Rock of his Salvation. Moses Otunga is married now with a large family of his own. He became Departmental Head of a big Polytechnic near Nakuru, and is now pastoring, and running his own children's home in Nairobi.

Another of our boys whose name was also Moses, gave this testimony when he was some twelve years old, early in 1974:

I Praise the Lord very much because He has Saved me.
I like Praising him, and I believe that when He comes,
He will go with me!
I believe He is adding Power to me.
BEFORE I was saved Jesus came to me and said,
'Where are you going Moses?'
And I told him that I wasn't going His way!!
But later on I changed my mind and told Him that I wanted to follow Him.
Jesus saved me then, in 1973.
He saved me because I was a sinner and in darkness.
BEFORE that I used to smoke, and often I was unhappy with myself.
I Praise Him because His Love is not bought.
It is FREE to everybody. I know He will never leave me!

Moses finally went to Bible College, and is now Pastor of a local Christian Fellowship Church right here in Eldoret. In fact he was married in August, 1993, and he and his wife rejoiced to receive a baby boy (Alexander) on 10th July 1994.

NOT ONLY DID WE GROW FAMILY-WISE, but we began to consider providing training for the children.

We had often said that we could not just love and leave.

Love is more than a pat on the back. This attitude led us in 1976 to start a course, within the homes, to train motor mechanics. We called it Testimony Trade Training Centre, and out of it was to grow a much more ambitious educational programme.

The property we purchased in 1972 had included some 800 square feet of workshop space. Many of the children in the homes need outlets at the end of primary school. It was not always easy to find places in secondary school, and so the idea and vision of providing some kind of training in a trade or skill came into our minds.

About this time we received a visit from a total stranger. Indeed two strangers: Dr. Richard Bird, and Mr. Bill Latham of TEAR Fund, England. They were visiting other projects in the area, and also decided to drop in on us. We were delighted to meet them and to exchange our Christian testimonies. We showed them around, and of course we talked of our idea for a Mechanics Training School. And so they left, saying, very little!

A month or so later we received a letter inviting us to submit estimates for the erection of a residential hostel for about 20 students, plus the equipage and extension of the Workshop. We at first hung back from replying to this unexpected letter, but more letters were to follow until, at last, we submitted an estimate. TEAR Fund agreed to the whole cost!

They also supplied a full time instructor/teacher for the course. This was a dear brother in Christ from Scotland, Harry Speedie. Harry was to be with us for two full years, and carried the project on to fame and glory. He was succeeded by John Mattison, a C.M.S. volunteer, who carried on until the course finally closed down in March 1985. More than 140 young men went through the course, and more than 90% of them found employment in the motor trade. But it was not intended to shut down for ever. A wider aim was to be envisaged which it is hoped will eventually enable an even larger Trade Training Facility to come into being. But that was, and still is, in the future.

The year of 1979 dawned. By August, ten years would have passed and from one boy and a mud hut, we were found in possession of two enormous permanent houses, eight acres of land, a Training Centre for teenagers in motor mechanics, and some 60 orphan children. And still we could not be sure where our next meal would come from!

Here are a few extracts from the Diary for 1979:

May 7th
Admitted a new boy today, Joseph.
Went to court to obtain the order for him.
There has been no post for some days, and there is no money available.

May 8th
Having a real problem getting away to pray! A great feeling of necessity always, but no real strength to DO it! This is obviously a counter attack of Satan to all else that is happening.
Still no post!

May 9th
Again no post all day.
All money is now spent, and £656 of NEED facing us.
Electricity may well be cut off soon!

May 10th
Two letters arrived today.
£272 from friends in Denmark!
£82 from friends in England. More than half our need!
Praise the Lord.

May 11th
My 39th birthday. Spent morning writing letters. All shops closed due to the President's visit.
There was no post.
Read in my prayer time Matthew 17v24-47. How Jesus dealt with the need to pay Tax! It seemed to me afterwards that we should just get on and do the work. God will work the Miracle in His time!

May 15th
Took boys to School.
Found £178 in the post from friends in England. Praise the Lord for His continuing care of us.
A further £100 came in later in the day.
Still need a further £700 for School Fees for the secondary scholars, and for building repairs on Jacaranda.
Mr. Newton brought us MILK from his farm. Mrs. Lal brought rice and vegetable curry for everyone's lunch - very hot! Very NICE!
During the evening other Asian friends brought a huge bowl of cooked rice, plus more milk! A bounteous DAY!

May 18th
Had an upset stomach that kept me awake most of the night. ALSO a rat was behind our wardrobe. The cat – with a little help from me – caught it for his breakfast.

July 3rd
Busy with Annual Accounts. Worked throughout the day, and in the evening taught maths to some of the boys. There was no post (in fact there has been little or none through almost the whole of June. Our situation has been CRITICAL, but HE has helped us till now; His right Hand has sustained us).

July 5th
Received £600 from friends in Denmark. Thank you Jesus! Once more, just in time, we are able to pay outstanding monthly accounts, plus giving us a small balance in hand to eat with. Everyone rejoicing. Later received a further £48 from England. GLORY!!

July 15th
SUNDAY
Went to Kapsabet Girls' School in the morning and preached on Psalm 116v1: "I love the Lord BECAUSE". Truly when there is a 'because' then we can truly say we have FOUND HIM!

July 22nd
SUNDAY
Spoke at the Presbyterian Church in the morning. A very large English-speaking congregation. But felt a bit far away from them all – the pulpit is about 20 feet above their heads and about thirty feet from the nearest pew!
£100 from England. Thank you Lord.

Stealing is back in the house. One of the boys lost his bed sheets during the morning! And another lost two of his shirts. Depressing.

July 23rd

Francis Wainaina having a 'problem' with one of his big boys in Jacaranda. He has been truanting from school, and even is involved in theft! I found one of MINE in the same state. I have had to take the 'rod of correction' to him, but I doubt if it will bring any 'light'.

July 24th

£30 from England – EVERY amount is a help beyond expression. And since every gift is a surprise, it is also a Blessing!

Went to see the Headmaster of the Primary School with my problem boy this morning. The Headmaster told me, in front of the boy, that he is very BAD! Goes with bad company, truanting, and very dishonest. I felt suddenly very weary. What does one do with a BAD boy? Father Flanagan of Boys Town fame says 'Love them some more'.

Late evening: found the same boy missing from the house and finally discovered him down the road smoking with others in a mud hut! The hut was ten by ten feet square, blackened with soot and grime. Just a small paraffin wick in a tin can gave the light. A bed was against one wall and was occupied by the husband of the 'family' plus one small child! A woman was trying to cook on a small fire made of twigs, a baby at her breast. Three teenagers, plus my boy, were squatting on the dirt floor. The place was so full of smoke, so dirty, so poor, so squalid. . .

After all these years I found that I could still feel hopeless. . . but only BRIEFLY!

August 27th

10th ANNIVERSARY DAY

This day, ten years ago, our first boy, Wilson, walked into my small home. NOW ten years later HE is a much larger person, almost completing his final year of further training. During the afternoon, dressed very smartly in a suit, Wilson addressed the large crowd that sat under the shady tree of our front lawn. It was a very glad and happy moment for us.

"Ladies and Gentlemen,

We in Testimony Faith Homes are pleased to be with you here today, as we celebrate our tenth anniversary. This all began in a tiny mud house in Maseno, Western Kenya.

In these ten years the Homes have gone through much transition. Time and again we have felt our hopes might not be fulfilled; we're often faced with financial crisis! Yet our sincere thanks go out to those who have so freely, willingly, and unfailingly contributed to our needs of food, clothing, and money. So our hopes were fulfilled.

Ladies and Gentlemen, Testimony Faith Homes was founded on this day, 29th August, 1969. It was founded with one aim: to rescue the orphans, and other young people in need – those who, in our society, might be called outcast, worthless, and 'Takataka' (a Kiswahili word meaning 'rubbish').

Today many sitting amongst us here have grown up in the homes, and comprise some of the healthiest, smartest, and best-educated young people one could wish to see.

Today most of those who have completed their primary education now attend various secondary high, and technical schools, and other institutions in the country, all being equipped with skills and further knowledge, so that they might hope for a stable and prosperous future in our land

of Kenya. Such achievements over the years have only multiplied our joy and happiness together.
Even so it would be unfair of me to dwell only upon the good things without mentioning some of the problems that have faced those growing up in the homes. As we young people have lived here, we have often passed through times of fearfulness also! Some started rushing ahead of themselves in their mind, wondering what life would be like beyond the homes. They became unsettled, and some even ran away and made shipwreck.
Yet the aim has always been to see each young person loved, and helped – and not running away – until they can each one safely leave in a proper and suitable way.
We hope this Anniversary Occasion will mark a new era; an era emphasised by a new determination to save lives; the lives of our young people. It is and always has been the goal."

During the morning hours, we held a Thanksgiving Service in which many of us, including the children, took vocal part in testimony and song. Our long time friend and brother in Christ, one time Chairman of Trinity Fellowship, the Rev. Cuthbert Dawkins, gave the message. During the afternoon, after a buffet lunch under the trees, the sky a cloudless blue, we were entertained with speeches, plays, choirs, and soloists, all organised by the children. There was even a challenge soccer match between Testimony House and Jacaranda Cottage.
It has been a good day - a day to REMEMBER. Thank you LORD!

A DECADE of years had passed like a DAY!! A day full of adventure! There had been plenty of scares, and breath-taking experiences along the way. I had found a purpose in life, a wonderful woman to be my partner and wife, and most of all I had found out more about God, and my own NEED of Him moment by moment. How AMAZING it all has been.

Chapter Six

THE SCHOOL

ONE AFTERNOON in November 1983, the headmaster of one of our local primary schools rang me up.

"Please come to my office right away. There is a serious problem facing us," he said.

I went immediately, and settling myself into one of his office chairs, I asked him what the problem was. He looked most upset, and worried, and started off, "It is a very heavy matter, and I need your help and co-operation."

I began to wonder if he had a personal problem. But he continued, "Daniel and Joseph have been found smoking cigarettes in the school field. I shall have to suspend them from classes."

During the previous month I had had to deal with cases of theft, and even drug-taking amongst some of our older boys. I am sure I almost laughed with relief. Smoking cigarettes! Why that was the least of the present big time temptations overwhelming our local schools.

The next morning the two boys (both 16 years old) took their text books back to the school to be kept during their suspension. No actual time had been fixed for the duration of the suspension at that time. Once they arrived at the school, the headmaster grabbed them, and had them taken to the school parade ground. There, in front of 700 students, they were made to lay face down in the dirt. Then they were given a homily on 'ungrateful orphans' who having no parents, mis-spent public money. They were then given six strokes of the cane each.

Suspended, socially stigmatised, and publicly caned. And this for smoking ordinary cigarettes.

Others in the school known to be taking marijuana remained untouched. This incident, and others like it, caused us to seriously consider opening our own school.

To begin with, in January 1981, we had commenced a small nursery school in the compound of Testimony House. It was started because we could find no nursery or pre-primary school places for our own children in Eldoret town. This posed a problem for children wishing to enter the first grade of primary, since the present law stipulates that they must first have completed a set course in a nursery school.

A young lady from England, Jane Hotham, joined us for a while to take charge of the nursery school in its beginnings. In March 1981 she was to write to friends:

"Writing at the end of the first term of Testimony Nursery School, there is so much to share to thank the Lord for. One particular request was to pray for another teacher, which the Lord has answered very wonderfully in providing Irene, who has been a real blessing to me, and to the children. So now we have TWO teachers, and our school has increased to 20 children, nine of whom come from outside of the homes! As it happens they are girls, which makes a nice balance with all our own little boys! Another change has been in our move to new premises, into two of the Training School Hostel rooms which were no longer being used, and which could almost have been just built for a nursery school!
Looking back over the term, I sometimes wonder who has learnt more, Irene and me, or the children? The Lord has taught us so much, and it is very wonderful to know that each day we can call on Him and His Wonderful Wisdom and Love, to take us through the day. He has blessed us with many joys and encouragements too, as we see the children learning and mastering new skills and taking pride in their achievements. AND SO, whilst I must admit to enjoying the holidays, I DO look forward to next term, and to all the Lord has in store for us."

The die had been cast, and out of the nursery school, urged on by increasing problems within the government schools, affecting our children, we would now go on to open primary. We already had two rooms available in the Trade Training Hostel, where we could initially start grades 1 and 2. We wrote a formal application to the District Education Officer, and took ourselves to prayer. We had no capital available to even think of purchasing necessary desks, tables, chairs, books and so on, and of course there would need to be a certain amount of reconstruction of the rooms to be used, and their re-decoration. BUT, if this was the Lord prompting us then it would all come to pass.

On January 6th 1984, an official arrived to inspect the proposed premises. He liked what he saw, and told us to go ahead and plan to open as requested. Well, then we began to be excited! We rejoiced, and we certainly began to plan!

Before the school was due to open in January 1985, we received a gift of £3000 (kshs. 60,000/-) through the post. It came from an unmarried lady school teacher in England who, as she was praying for us all, felt led in her heart to send us, in her own words, "An encouragement to open your own school, where your children can be ensured a knowledge of God." All the prayers were answered but there were others prayers going up already. We had dreams of a completed school with classrooms, workshops that would provide our children, and others from outside, with better study facilities, and with an opportunity to really get to grips with technical skills that would assist them find their niche in the world outside. We dreamt and prayed for a school where God would be honoured and where teachers could be honourable. Plans were drawn up and donated freely to us by the Eldoret Municipal Architect, Cosmas Busima – plans that could have cost an enormous amount of money. Then AGAIN, detailed engineering plans of the actual structures were drawn up for us by a qualified structural engineer in Nairobi, who charged us only one tenth of usual fees. That was still Kshs. 20,000/- (£1,000).

On the day we were expected to hand over this fee, we received a donation from England in the post for *exactly* that amount! That gift had been sent a week earlier. It is not only the exactness but the *timing* of God's Provision that never fails to amaze us, and to startle us! SO in January 1985, we opened the first two classes, and in the following year we opened the third grade class as building works on the NEW school began! Testimony Faith Homes had a school.

The knowledge of God is being slowly erased from the minds of our young people in our education programmes. It all began a generation following the last Great War, and it has been continuing ever since. All our science text books in school teach evolution now as a fact. Yet fact it is not. As soon as we accept that man is just the last in an evolutionary chain of events that began in the mists of time, then man loses a lot of value. The door is opened wide to questioning every statement that God has ever made through any man anywhere at any time. It is opened to the putting on one side of every moral code that has sprung up from the Mind of God. It is flung wide open to abortion, that murder of the innocent, and child abuse, and to every form of sexual perversion, moral degradation, and human cruelty.

Educationalists have said that if we educate men, then men will become better and better. Well, we have educated man. Is man any better? Is there not more injustice than ever before? More war and violence across the whole wide world?

Is there not terrorism, fear and dread?

Is there not revolution everywhere? Surely the entire world is drunk with blood, satiated with evil, more than ever before. The more man knows, the worse he has become, and lifted up in his vain pride he has consistently eroded the place of the Word of God in his education! Of course charity – love and Godliness – should start at home. If you want your child to be Godly then you have to find out about and learn to know God for yourself, out of a personal experience. Head knowledge is not going to be enough; memories of what your parents may have taught you are not going to be enough. You have to know for yourself.

But then the question arises: what about the teacher at school? I believe the world was created by God, but does the teacher? Will he even permit such an idea to seem credible to my child? Our educationalists are always telling us that they have the greatest responsibility and authority in a child's life; after all a child spends the bulk of his time in school. Well if this is so, if it is true, then schoolteachers should be taking over the parent's task of teaching the child about God. If this was the case then even children from broken homes, or families that lived ungodly lives, would have a chance to gain a knowledge of God.

But is the teacher, averagely, doing this? Will he do it? Do you, as parents take an interest in how your children are being taught? Our children, worldwide, are being taught to mistrust God; to even do without him as a concept in any form! They are being taught to rely upon man's judgement, and that means that they face hopelessness; for all around them in the papers, and on the T.V. we see the result of man's judgement when he is left to himself, without God. We cannot DO without God. We need God at home, and at school. We do not need Him in theory or as a philosophy. We need Him in a real, living, and relevant way. And this is why we prayed for our own school.

CRASH! A slow, tormented creaking and rending filled the air!

W-H-O-O-SH! And the ground GRUNTED at the impact, and a hollow THUD stopped the heart for a moment!

That tree had stood for about 70 years, one of a stand of 20 giant Blue Gums that had stood watching over Testimony House. They had been a windbreak too, but they stood right on the site planned for the primary school buildings. I felt a tremor of sorrow as I watched that first tree fall, and surveyed its broken glory, inert and grounded in front of me. Only minutes before, it had stood gigantically permanent, anchored so proudly in the earth, head in the heavens, confident of the wind. History was in every inch of growth; beauty in every curve of trunk and branch, twig and leaf. I felt for them all, cut down, humbled.

The cost of actually building eight classrooms, offices, toilets, etc., stood at approximately £53,000 (Kshs. 1,500,000/-) in 1986. We had prayed and felt led to ask our bank to give us a loan on the security of the title to Testimony House. Some of our Christian brothers and sisters felt we were and ARE wrong to have commenced this project with a building loan. They have felt, in love, that this is not the way of Faith. We have appreciated their honesty and willingness to walk in the Light with us. The amount of money at stake was considerable, and the risk enormous if the Lord was not in it! We believed that He was in it, and that He had led us thus far. Therefore, we took what, to us, has been the biggest step of faith since we began.

By the middle of October 1986, the new buildings were completed, and all the furnishing and equipment in place, and on January 7th 1987, we began using it. It was a great day for us, but it was not an end in itself. We still dreamt of another primary stream, *and* a secondary technical school. Also the new Syllabus for Primary Schools in Kenya directed that each school should have special classrooms for Home-Science, Arts and Craft, and Science!

During 1987 representatives of TEAR fund again visited us, and the quite unlooked for outcome of that visit was an offer to help us continue with the development of the school. This meant that during 1988 *four* more special purpose classrooms were built for Science, Home-Science, Art, and Technical Studies, plus a school hall to seat 400. These latest classrooms cover the area originally occupied by the old Training School workshops, but we still expect for them to rise again like the phoenix as we continue on in prayer for the advent of a technical secondary school.

Today, in 2004, in the nursery section there are some seven classes in operation. Children between 3 and 6 years attend half day. Some 180 children attend, and those who come from outside the homes are expected to pay school fees each term. These fees ensure that the children attending from within the homes are educated free, and also pay the entire running costs inclusive of teachers' salaries, and all equipment and materials used. However no profit is generated from the fees, since only the actual running cost is sought to be recovered, apart from the provision of free places for the homes' children. More than 70 children leave the school each year to commence their primary education, most of them entering our own primary school's first grade. My wife, Esther, has been the one to build up the nursery school, and was Headmistress until 2003 when she handed over to another, and became Head of primary school instead.

The primary section caters for children from 6 to 14 years in 15 classes of 40 students each. Some 50 children from the homes attend the school, whilst the balance of students comes from the surrounding district. All our teachers are Kenyan, and Christians. They have all received recognised training in Government Colleges but are paid by us out of the fee structure.

In the National Primary Certificate Examinations which were attempted for the first time in 1988, the school came first in the District in competition with more than 20 local schools. In 1993 we were 13th in the Republic. We have continued to do well, and to even progress upwards in the National Examinations. There is a great demand from the general public for opportunities within the school. BUT our greatest joy is to see the children from the homes getting the chance of a good academic education that is God-centred! Thank you LORD.

Early in 1991 TEAR Fund contacted us again to advise us they were willing to assist us continue the school development by providing a second stream of primary classrooms plus new offices for the whole work. These were safely completed and opened in 1992.

Later still, in January 1994, we opened one stream (four classes) for secondary as well. Testimony School, as it is now called, offers educational opportunities from pre-primary through to secondary for all our children free of cost. It offers the same high standard of Christian Education to those outside the homes as well.

IN ADDITION TO ALL THIS, we have seen the Holy Spirit using the school as a 'tool' for evangelism! We have students coming from all levels of the Eldoret populous; many of them Hindu, Moslem, Buddhist as well as Christian in background. Some families have been identified even as Satanists and certainly many atheists! All parents have to agree, before their child is admitted into the school, that their child may not be excused Christian Religious Instruction, and that they must attend all Christian assemblies, meetings et cetera that may be arranged by the school. No parent has ever quarrelled with this. Every week each student is given a printed Bible study based on the short 'message' given each morning in the school assembly. These studies are taken home, and often read by the parent as well, and we have seen many families completely changed and brought to Christ through this facility! Through the school we are reaching into unreached homes and family situations.

The schools are situated on the same compound as Testimony House, separated by an unobtrusive fence. I can look out of the school office window today and see my old front door and just across the lawns, Testimony House, my home for 28 out of the last 35 years we have existed. Still a MUD house! Its 80-year-old walls are just mud bricks baked by the sun. They are some three feet thick those walls, and just covered on the outside with a thin veneer of plaster! As I write there are some 44 in the family, excluding Daryl and Carol and their three children. Esther and I are 'Granma and Granpa' to this crowd of very different children and young people; the youngest is presently about four and the eldest about 20. It's a family house, not very 'posh' but *home* to all who live in it, and there is a sense of belonging. It's an old house too, by Kenyan standards, and needs almost daily attention here and there. The roof still leaks in places! There is continual wear and tear, but we would not like to change it for anything newer.

We once had visitors – in fact we often had visitors – whilst living there, who asked Esther and me where we lived. We were at the time standing in the sitting room, some 900 square feet of family living and fellowship space. "Why here, in this house! This is our home."

Our guests were a bit shocked. How could we live with such a crowd of strangers? How could we be a family lost in such a crowd? Didn't we ever want to 'get away' just 'by ourselves'?

Of course there have been sacrifices; it would be less than true to deny that.

But Testimony House was our home. Our own children were born into it, and into the larger family that share it with us. We had a cook to help us five days a week, and a lady comes in to iron and help with washing, and a man helping in the garden. Now, since 1998, it is Daryl and Carol's home and family. It carries on.

Chapter Seven

OBSERVATIONS ALONG THE WAY

To live in a children's home is not always a bed of roses! There were often trials to go through, and the children were not, as I have said before, automatically born again. Some were to grow up, and leave us, without ever showing any real interest in the Lord, or indeed in any religion. Sometimes without even thanks to anyone at all. Yet we loved them all, and living with them became unavoidably involving. In September 1976 I sent the following letter to friends:

Suddenly one evening the phone rang in my office. One of three 'sons' studying in a Nairobi high school hundreds of kilometres away excitedly yelled down the line that another of their number had been arrested and was even then with the Police.

"He's in terrible trouble," the boy cried. "You've GOT to do something!"
How many times do we 'ring up' our Heavenly Father because one of His Children is in 'terrible trouble'?
My heart missed a beat. One of MY boys in trouble! I rang off, and dialled the Nairobi Police. YES, he WAS in custody. NO, I could not speak to him! NO, they could NOT give me any details, but he had assaulted a man. I put the phone down. I was so far away. He couldn't speak to me direct any more, and he did not even KNOW that I was aware of what had happened to him. I wrung my hands together. Poor boy; all alone. He is not my blood! YET GOD had made him a son. I cared for him – whatever he had done didn't change that.
He had beaten a man. Later he was to tell us that it had been in self-defence; the man had accosted him on the road and struck him first with a heavy stick. He had hit back. He had not turned the other cheek. He had reacted quicker than thought to safeguard himself. He knew the Lord, but he defended himself. He did not think of the other man. He hit back at the enemy and, being caught in the act, was carted away to prison! Yes, he was remanded to prison for two weeks to await the court hearing. He had become separated from home and family and from the whole world.
I was horribly upset.
How often we are unmerciful, hating the one who has wronged us; even willing to have our rights, to defend and safeguard ourselves. How often HE is caused grief because of our merciless actions and attitudes. How often we become separated from His Abiding Presence; the Presence of our Father! So often we wonder if He KNOWS, and if He will come to rescue US from the folly of our own actions.

But He misses nothing. He is on to our trouble quicker than I was on to my son's. He never slumbers or sleeps. He NEVER turns away from loving us, even in our sins. ALL this came so forcibly to my mind as I drove back from Nairobi, having bailed my son out of prison, and put him back in school. I was still troubled though. The case was still to be heard, and the boy was relying more on ME than on the Lord. He had heard my voice on the phone the very night I had called the Police in Nairobi. He had been standing right beside the policeman who had spoken to me. He could not speak to me, but he had known then that I knew what had happened to him, and that I still cared. From that moment he believed that I would not let him rot in jail; that I would come.

Well, I am satisfied that I did what a father would have done.

But how much more our Heavenly Father does for us, and is willing to DO for sinful, rebellious man. His love that will not let us go!! Sometimes it pays off, and oh, then what joy there is in Heaven! And sometimes it pays off here too, in our human family, and oh, what joy there is amongst us. All the grief is worth while then; all the tears, all the wakeful nights, and unutterable groaning! It's worth it all. AND, when I come to Him, when anyone comes to Him, trusting in His Love, honestly confessing the faults and the needs, it's worth it ALL; worth all of Gethsemane, all of the Cross, worth it ALL. God grant us ever to be drawn closer to Him, and to one another!

Some weeks later our boy, Luke, was fully acquitted from all guilt and fault at the court hearing, and set unconditionally free.

Luke finally graduated from secondary school, and trained as a painter and sign writer. For many years he earned his own living from place to place plying this trade. But in 1993 he joined the staff here as Assistant

Maintenance Man; we see him every day, a grown man, married and rejoicing.

IN THE BEGINNING children were often left on my doorstep. David, I remember, arrived like that! I opened door about 6 a.m. just as the sun was rising and found him curled up on the front step, covered only by a tattered blanket. He was just about eight years old then. Others were brought to the door by friends or relatives. Sometimes Government officials would come with requests for help. And in those early days I was very gullible, and easily persuaded of a need, only to discover later that the 'orphan' had a large family including a mother and father; it was just that the family thought their child would have a better chance of free education if it stayed with a European! Well it is not as heartless as it might seem when you understand the material hardship of so many people in this young country of ours. Nevertheless I became more wary as months and years went by, and in the mid-seventies we made it a policy not to take private applications without first channelling them through the Kenya Children's Department. This office has Provincial and District Officers throughout the country now, and they make it their business to officially check all cases of child abuse and destitution reported to them. They then make their recommendation to us. We still reserve the right to accept or reject – there have been cases where even an official 'Children's Officer' has re-arranged a 'story' to assist a relative to get a place in the homes! But on the whole they are most helpful, and do a good job. Children are still sent to us from all over Kenya, and the 'families' in

Testimony House and Jacaranda Cottage are truly a mixed bag, being multi-tribal.

Most of the children we admit into the homes arrive between 0 and 10 years of age. On the whole this age group grow up fairly well, and without a lot of problems. But, on occasion, we do allow an older child to come in, say up to the age of 14. These are usually very special cases of need where we try to assist other welfare agencies who have not been able to settle the child. There is always a risk attached, and not all of such cases can be helped instantly or whilst they are actually with us. Still, even some of the most difficult and currently disappointing cases, do often make a success of life later on, and we BELIEVE that IF the seed IS sown, then ours is to HOPE ALWAYS for a harvest.

Many people ask if we keep in touch with the children once they have left, or if they keep in touch with us. Yes, on the whole there is always an ongoing relationship. I think Esther and I have always found the hardest times are those when we see one and another of the children leave to start their own lives outside, without us. Our hearts really follow them; we worry about them.

One wrote to us a few months after having left Testimony House:

"Up to now I've not found a place to stay. Instead I've been dumped into a tyre store while looking for a 'room' to rent. The only friends I have here are rats, mosquitoes, and malaria!"

He wrote this from 70 miles away. He had taken an appointment as a clerk in a large transport company. Jacob came to the homes way back in 1969 when he was just about eight years old. He was to stay with us for 13 years, not a short time to be in one place and with the same people.

It is not easy to take the plunge into the cold and often cheerless world alone. The average starting wage for an unskilled person in 1982 was about £20 a month. Now in 2004 it is about £25 a month! The minimum monthly rent for a single bare room with no amenities whatever was about £5. That was if you could find one. Such a room even now would probably be constructed of mud and timber. Food would have cost another £10 a month minimally. There was little left with which to save for a better future, and of course there is still clothing to think about. Most of our boys leaving the warmth of family life here, find the new way of surviving a very chilling prospect! But they must leave sometime; must make a start at being on their own. Our part is only to bring them up to be strong enough to survive.

At the beginning of 1982 Esther and I needed to find job opportunities for some six of our secondary school leavers, and that was in the face of increasing mass unemployment. After four months of continual searching we managed to secure four such opportunities, one of which had gone to Jacob.

About a week after receiving the letter quoted above, we felt we just had to find out how Jacob really was. So we motored the 70 miles to see for ourselves. He was *very* surprised to see us, and even more surprised when I slid £5 into his pocket as we left.

"The day before you came, I was on my bed, and I knew I had exactly nothing – not even five cents left. Then I thought seriously

that FAITH is only practised in Testimony, where it works! I could not believe my eyes when I came off duty the next morning and saw you waiting. I couldn't believe me eyes! I was overjoyed; I cannot explain my happiness. AND when you put that money in my pocket I didn't know what to say – but my heart was thanking God!"

He had seemed to have lost a lot of weight to us, as we sized him up that day. He was working, he told us, from 6 a.m. until 7 p.m. six days a week – even on Sundays at times. We thought of him often in those early weeks, alone in a strange place. He became ill with malaria later on, but suddenly showed up at our Sunday morning service, having travelled the distance just to be with us.

"Well, Jesus continues to be my friend, and I'm quite fine now. He leads me in His Truth and teaches me, for He is the God of my Salvation. He picked me up from the deep pit where nobody could tell if that miserable lonely little boy (as I was then) would even live. BUT the Lord of Mercy had His Hand on my life, and that's why I say He leads me in His Truth. I have so many things to thank God for. He FED me, CLOTHED me, and brought me up and LOVED me. I wish the rest of my brothers at Testimony could realise what it really means to belong to God.
I wonder how many remember their lives before coming to Testimony. I used to be very silent at times when with you there. I used to wonder if I would return to the gutter. I have not done so … and I won't."

Sadly none of us know ourselves as we ought! Jacob finally found a place in Bible College, graduating well, and entering into a productive Christian Ministry with Friends of the West. Regretfully, however, he has presently departed from the Lord, and fallen into his old ways. We continue to pray for him, believing that even yet the Lord, who is his Master, will restore and use him.

ON OCTOBER 2ND 1971, a small boy was admitted to the home. He also was just eight years old and small for his age. His elder brothers were already in the home, and they had urged me to look for this youngest one, who had been carried off by his mother when she had run away from her husband years before. The hunt took us many miles into sugar plantations near to Kisumu. But eventually we found both the child and his mother. She was living in considerable poverty with another man. This new husband had no love or care for Teddy, and we found him very neglected and underfed. When we explained that we were caring for the elder brothers, Teddy was almost thrown at us. There was great rejoicing when we arrived home with him.

Teddy seemed very ready to respond to attention and love, and we found it easy to love him. But from the first he seemed to have no natural interest in God.

On Boxing Day 1972, we all moved to Eldoret as I have told before.

Teddy grew into a solid and muscular child. His jaunty and friendly air attracted many friends, and he began to excel in playing football. At the same time he could be stubborn, and as he grew older his attitude became more and more scornful towards God. The more we prayed the worse things became!

In study also he showed a standard lack of interest. He concluded primary school without any distinction, and we found him a secondary boarding school, hoping that he could do better. Up to this time Teddy had never shown us any bad behaviour at all.

In secondary school things began to change. He wrote from school early in 1981, after having been involved in a student riot:

"The PERIL which I was in at school has been settled – by me getting six strokes of the cane, and then digging out three tree stumps from the school field!"

In October of that year he was continuing to make trouble in the school – so much so that he was summarily expelled. We were very deeply distressed by all this, and by Teddy's continued rejection of the Gospel Message in his life. He returned to the home, and we began to consider what his future would be.

After a few days of being home with us we discovered that he had made cigarettes and beer his close companions. On one occasion during this period he was arrested with others for being found in possession of ardent spirits – he was put up before the Magistrate and fined £10 which we then paid!

In January 1982 we managed to obtain a chance for him in the Christian Industrial Training Centre in Nairobi. We watched him go with some apprehension.

On March 16th of that year we received a letter from his new Headmaster:

"I am very glad to write and let you know that Teddy has come right through for Jesus. It was on the evening of the 12th. His conversion has been very public, and very real! Praise God!"

We did.

On the 26th June of the same year one of many such letters from Teddy arrived to thrill us:

Dear Dad and Mum,

I am happy to have this gorgeous opportunity to write a few lines to you both.

The LORD has been Marvellous to me, and I know He Loves me, and I KNOW that when He comes I will have to go with Him!

Yesterday I went to All Nations Pentecostal Church in Nairobi. We had an all night prayer meeting – p we began about ll p.m. and ended at 5 a.m.! I was BLESSED.

We are also having Fellowship Meetings here each Tuesday, and I am remembering you all in prayer.

Sending great Greetings to everyone at home. Your son, Teddy.

So, dear ones, we share these things with you. Many of you may be parents already, with children you pray for and long for. There also may be loved friends and relatives that you covet for Jesus. Perhaps right now you can see only a drift AWAY from God. Do not weary to pray and believe for them. Do not yourselves be so crushed by disappointment about their lack of Christian progress. Our Father loves them, and SEES them. His Spirit is moving and working unseen upon and in them. Trust HIM, in Jesus Name, and give THANKS. He is able to save to the uttermost the WEAKEST ONE!

MANY FRIENDS HAVE ASKED ME if I ever doubt or fear in this life of faith. I must confess and say YES! There have been times like that; like that time I went so faithlessly to Miriam's Wedding! When days go by, as they often do, without post, and the bank balance dwindles more and more, it is never easy to wait. At least I must be honest and say that for me it has often caused a great deal of inner stress! Every day that goes by must find at least £150 to hand or the bills begin to pile up. With no earthly security at all this has its moments of naked fear!

In saying this I am very conscious of NOT having the Gift of Faith. Indeed if I have faith at all, then it cannot be mine, but HIS alone – I must give HIM all the Glory, Honour and Praise. It is perhaps in some measure because of this that every time the need is supplied it becomes the cause of awesome wonder to me; perhaps to all the rest of us here as well! Many have thought it is the faith of John Green that holds all together, but this has to be furthest from the truth – it is altogether the FAITHFULNESS OF GOD ALONE.

I do TRUST the Lord. I DO believe that He IS able do far more than I can ever imagine. BUT I also DO tremble, waiting for Him to DO it; This FLESH is weak, and prone to sin, leaning at times to faithlessness and even despair. But Thank God, through Jesus Christ, I am held up, restored, forgiven, and permitted ALWAYS to see His Salvation! What a privilege!

Finance, of course, may be one of the biggest areas in which we are tested. However, we find ourselves tested also in many other areas of our life and experience.

ON THE 5TH JANUARY 1981, I found myself a hundred miles away from here trying to investigate the background story of a boy we were interested in bringing into the home. As I stood talking to an official, a stab of pain affected my left kidney. I felt sick and giddy. It passed, leaving me weak. An hour later, as I still conversed with officials, it returned more insistently.

I had left home full of vigour, feeling extremely well. Now, just a few hours later, I had to return almost helpless. I was not used to giving in to sickness, and so I fought off the pain, but it gained its own strength, and through the night and the day following it became unbearable. I HAD to go to hospital. I was so uncomfortable that I could barely sit, walk, or stand! My temperature fell to about 94°F, and my blood pressure rose to 210; dangerously high. I was given endless injections, and passed out!

Life – daily routine – was brought to a halt. I had to stop what I was doing until tests confirmed what was wrong; was it kidney disease, or was it my heart?

I was sent to Nairobi to see a cardiologist. I still had rising blood pressure and giddiness, and a certain amount of real apprehension.

After X-rays, cardiograms and a thorough examination, I was bending down doing up my shoelaces having just got dressed. I was then in the specialist's office. He looked up from his notes.

"Mr. Green, we have a problem here. The X-rays suggest you have extensive heart muscle damage; we may have to operate." I just stared at him. "We shall do some more tests just now. But I advise you to take things very easy for a few days until we see the results."

I walked out of his office feeling just like a small child again. The 'legs' of my life had been swept from under me. Esther was waiting for me; there was not a great deal of confidence behind the smile I gave her.

That night I lay in my bed in the dark, sweating it all out, listening to every heartbeat, alive to every new pain or sensation, expecting any moment to leave this present world! Melodramatic? Very! But that was how I felt. Where life had seemed endless and strength ever-abounding, I now seemed plunged into darkness, uncertainty and fear; not a fear of death, but of going!

And then I got up and opened the Bible. I turned to 2 Corinthians 1v9: "But we had the sentence of death in ourselves, that we should not trust in ourselves, but in God, which raiseth the dead."

With that Word came rest and peace of mind. Of course, HE was my Strength, why should I fear? How forgetful we are; how easily we slip into the vanity of self.

I turned then once more to Jesus, my Saviour, consciously giving back the stolen trust and dependence, and at once I *knew* all was indeed well with my soul *and* with my body. I slept soundly.

The results of the later tests were clear! New X-rays showed nothing of the 'damaged heart muscle' suggested in the first set. After a week I was told to go home.

"Your heart is stronger than a horse Mr. Green; you'll not need to return to me!" said the specialist.

But, in January 1988 I did go back!

In the midst of speaking at a Youth Rally in December 1987, the same pain gripped me fleetingly. Throughout Christmas it was to continue to come and go. My local doctor called for more X-rays, and discovered dark areas where none should be. He was concerned. So was I. Within days the pain returned in greater strength, and Esther drove me up to Nairobi in haste. It was a stone in the kidney. My consultant said that it must have remained lodged somewhere since 1981.

"Drink as much beer as you can," he advised, "and you may be lucky and wash it out – otherwise we shall operate!"

Well I certainly was not going back to drinking beer! But I did drink a lot, and the stone was washed out finally. It was painful; I really did think I would die. But the kidney was unaffected and my heart remained a hundred percent, and my blood pressure was stable and at a normal level. Praise the Lord.

But it doesn't take much to jar our 'faith' – or at least MY 'faith'. Like a child I often find myself waking up in the dark and crying out,

"LORD, where are you...?"

"Sssh... I'm right here beside you! Don't be afraid."

I remain British. After more than 25 years, I still remain in Kenya on a British Passport, and by 1982 I still needed a Work Permit in order to remain legally in the country. It had to be renewed every two years. For this reason I had travelled up to Nairobi to the Children's Department Headquarters to ask them to assist me in a renewal, just as I had done on numerous other occasions.

"Mr. Green," began the official. "You have too many people coming from overseas. Even you yourself have been here for many years. Isn't it time to leave everything in African hands?"

He was very serious and in no way helpful. I felt troubled. A week later I had to be back in Nairobi on other business, and I decided to try and see a man high up in the Immigration Department, and to find out just how serious the other man's remarks had been.

"Do you have an appointment? Are you known here?" the severe Secretary to the Commissioner of Immigration asked me.

I had no answer to give, and began to wish that I had not come at all. I felt very small and insignificant.

"I'm afraid he won't see you," she said. Just then a buzzer sounded and she went into an inner office, leaving the door open. A rather portly middle-aged African in a pin stripe suit was standing in the centre of the room, and turning, he caught sight of me.

"Does that man wish to see me?" I heard him ask. "Send him in at once!"

He sat me down in his luxurious office, and asked my business. I told him how God had called me to Kenya, and how the Homes had begun and carried on. He listened very carefully, as I outlined my present fears about being forced to leave Kenya.

He reached behind him, and took a large book from a table nearby.

It was an illustrated story book.

"Read this article out loud to me," he commanded, pointing to a marked page. It was a short article on George

Muller, the founder of Muller's Homes in Bristol, England some hundred years ago. He had also trusted God for everything in the running of the homes, and his own life also, and found Him faithful. The article drew particular attention to this. I finished reading, and put the book upon the desk.

"I was reading that in my quiet time, this very morning!" said the Commissioner wonderingly looking at me. "Isn't it amazing that I should have read about him before you came in!"

Then he took up a Bible from the desk and said, "I was also reading this morning about Hezekiah spreading his letter before the Lord – I think we should spread out this matter of yours also in front of the Lord!" And so we prayed about it together!

"Mr. Green," he said, as he stood up behind his desk. "You see before you a quite important man, but I must tell you that despite what you see, I am only a poor sinner, Saved by the Grace of God through Jesus Christ!" And he gripped my hand in his across the desk.

I was dismissed. He had promised nothing, and suggested nothing. We had just prayed. There was nothing left!

It was a very amazing experience.

But my application was approved, and my Work Permit re-issued, and a year later Testimony Faith Homes was given exemption from the need for its expatriate workers to come under the normal rules.

Let the brother in humble of circumstances glory in his elevation (as a Christian called to the true riches and to be an heir of God): And the rich person ought to glory in being humbled by being shown his human frailty, because like the flower of the grass he will pass away. James 1v9-10

THE LORD OF HOSTS IS WITH US; the God of Jacob is our Refuge – think of that! (Psalm 46v11)

ON THE 1ST AUGUST 1982, some of the children tuned into 'The Voice of Kenya' early in the morning. It was a Sunday.

"THIS IS THE VOICE OF KENYA.

In the early hours of this morning, the Government of President Moi was overturned. A National Council of Liberation has been set up in its place. Further information will be given later. All members of the public are advised to remain indoors and not to travel."

Canned music blared out thereafter. The children exploded into our bedroom, shouting and crying. It was a frightening moment! The whole house converged on the sitting room to listen in for more news. The same message and nothing else was being spasmodically repeated. There was no news of the President. After the initial shock, though, we felt no fear. It was Sunday after all and there were our usual devotions to occupy us.

At mid-day we rejoiced to hear that the Coup had been put down, and that the President was safe. The following Sunday when attending a morning service at the Valley Road Pentecostal Church, Nairobi, that same President was reported as saying that on that fateful morning he had been awake early, and was reading the 46th

Psalm, and that this had strengthened and fortified him for the experience that was in store. Since that time, at the 13th World Pentecostal Conference held in Nairobi, President Moi is further quoted as saying that, "THE ONLY WAY TO HAVE PEACE is to be SAVED" and that it was praying that had sustained him during the long morning hours of August 1st 1982.

Whether we are high or low we see clearly that when trouble comes, and distresses engulf any of us the only Refuge IS Jesus. More than that, God is bigger and stronger than the trouble and the despair, and He will not suffer us to be afflicted more than we can bear.

Economic collapse, physical collapse, political unrest, can all come suddenly across our experience, shaking the very fabric of life, and waking us all up to the real insecurity of our human existence outside of God alone. The Great Enemy of us all is, I am convinced, seeking always to bring us to despair so that we will give up on life. I believe he attacks even the Christian with this in mind.

In December 1983 I went through such an attack. At the time I felt I could very easily have just given up the 'race'!!

I could suddenly no longer sense God's Presence with me in my life. It was as if I had suddenly been shut up in a void. Esther and I had been away most of the year in England and Scandinavia. It was the first time we had been away for almost 11 years, and we had never been away for so long. When we returned it was to discover that almost all we had believed and trusted in was in seeming ruin. Whilst away it seemed many of the children had run headlong into immorality and even Christians had fallen by the wayside and fallen into deceit and lies. We had been shaken to the core. I had looked at my own small family, and my dear wife working herself to the bone, and all of us denying ourselves the 'rights' of family life together and even reasonable living standards, and I found myself asking, "WHAT IS IT ALL FOR?" Supposing God WASN'T there. Then there was no REASON for anything; everything we had set out to do had been for NOTHING! And suddenly I felt as if I was falling down a dark fathomless hole.

"Supposing God wasn't there!" It became a real DOUBT, and then a HORRID fear, and I was in the DARK.

I have never had such an utterly awful, lonely, desolate experience, and it went on for days, and I could tell no one. Yet, when I thought I would never make it back into light, I found rising up within me a tremendous certainty and knowledge, that God *was* there after all. And the darkness faded away before the light of that truth. I knew then that once we are accepted in the Beloved there is no way HE is going to give us up, or let us go, or suffer us to be finally overwhelmed or defeated.

BUT those who are without God – who do not know the Lord – what do they do in face of overwhelming circumstances? In Kenya we are seeing an increasing number of people committing suicide. Indeed whole families are dying. I am sure that this is because of an inability to face the storms of life alone.

In May 1986 I was to tell the story of a little boy called Justin:

We are not sure what really happened.
Perhaps the baby was tied in a shawl, to his mother's back. Mothers here in Kenya, busy about the house or garden with very young babies do often carry them like that, so that they can also be free to work. She was probably preparing food on an open wood fire with the baby by this time asleep. Suddenly she may have bent down to take a pot from the embers of the charcoal fire. Baby slid forward, over her head, and into the glowing cinders.
Screams of pain, and infant terror pierced the air. Smoke, and the smell of burning hair and flesh.
The mother, stunned and shocked, grabbed the child, dragging him from the red hot charcoal, burning particles still embedded in the hair and scalp. He was barely one year old. He ceased to scream. Ceased to even move. Lifeless!
The agonized mother could do nothing to rouse the child. Horror came over her like thick fog, blotting out all sense or reason. Her child was dead, and it was her fault. How would she face her husband. Reaching out, she took hold of a nearby knife, and plunged it deep into her own body, and died! The body of the baby still smoked and smouldered by her side where she fell.
Circumstances overwhelmed her. She committed suicide.

I remember crawling into the kitchen of our little house in Starbeck Yorkshire and finding my mother trying to put her head into the gas oven. I could not have been more than about three years old. She was crying and whimpering to herself, reaching for the gas tap, overwhelmed by her husband's brutality and the load of debt.

And the child stirred, moved, opened pain filled eyes, and began pitiably to cry, and then to scream. Baby Justin was not dead, but alive.

Where was his father all that time? Possibly out drinking, or with his second wife! Later he must have been told, and was one of those who took Justin to the Mission Hospital some miles distant from home. The child must have been an awful sight to behold. His entire scalp within the hair line was raw with burns and blisters, his arms and legs also having burns. He was left, abandoned, at the hospital. He remained there, going through various skin grafts, from late 1983 until May 1986. He did not heal fast, and even by 1986 when he finally came to be part of our family, his head had still not completely healed over. It had to be cleansed and dressed many times in a day. Now it has healed, but he must always wear a hat to protect that delicate head from the direct rays of the sun. He is a bright-eyed, intelligent boy of 14 years. He has found Jesus as Friend and Saviour.

There are so many times when we might wonder about the fiery trials we seem to encounter. Why did He allow this to happen? What possible Blessing can there be in going through this present troublesome experience?

DAVID, in Psalm 124v1 said, "If it had not been the Lord who was on our side, now may Israel say. . ." NOW MAY ISRAEL SAY! After the trial, after the battle, after the overwhelming flood, NOW after it has all happened, and we are still found alive, still standing, NOW ISRAEL MAY SAY, the people of God may say: if the Lord had not been with us we would have gone down!

But He was with us, and He gave us more Grace, strengthened us, succoured us, hid us, brought us through it all.

If the Lord had NOT been with us, then those who turned against us, the situation we found ourselves in, would have utterly swallowed us and we would be totally ruined and destroyed. Life would have been too much for us alone, and we would have been drowned in distress, fear and despair.

BUT we escaped! One there was who, even when all seemed lost and we imprisoned and pinned down, bound and chained up, SPRUNG THE TRAP and set us free; He snapped our fetters, broke our chains, and brought us once more into glorious light and freedom!

Surely, when we look back and see our condition yesterday, last week, last year, then we have to believe that our help is in the Name of the Lord Who made heaven and earth.

And so my heart, my mind
doth sing for JOY.
And sing I must, for Christ I have!
Oh, what a Christ have I!

Yes indeed, if it had not been the Lord who was on our side, what then, I wonder?

"WATER IS DRYING UP ALL AROUND ELDORET. Whole areas are without water. Wells, rivers, lakes are all drying out in the worst overall drought in memory...."

This was 1985. Over the years rainfall has slowly fallen off, water tables have diminished, whilst the population increases and becomes increasingly urbanised, putting more and more pressure on water supplies that were at best small. During that time in 1985 we found ourselves facing severe difficulties. Inside the Municipality one is not allowed to dig wells.Our water supply was piped into the compound, and those pipes ran dry. Our sewerage is water borne; we could not 'pull the chain'. Washing could not be done effectively and neither could we wash ourselves. Even cooking was difficult. Water had to be collected in drums from central taps in town or carted in at great expense. We began to wonder if we would be able to stay in Eldoret. One of our neighbours wanted to evacuate us all to his farm 70 miles away; he had his own spring of water that never ran dry there, but we held on.

We tend always to hold on; it has become a way of life. In 1982 we were hanging on in a different kind of drought.

On August 28th the diary reads:

Open Day.
How we prayed it would not rain, and it has not!
A beautiful day. The homes' 13th Birthday. The children did wonderfully. Some 250 guests attended, and our Guest of Honour, the Deputy Mayor of Eldoret, really enjoyed himself.
No financial gifts now for two weeks!
No post today either! We need £300 (Kshs. 8,000/-) for school fees and the same amount again for other pressing needs.

August 29th

Two donations from UK today totalling £700!! We were flabbergasted! All present needs are met. He is Wonderful.

BUT by 8th September, all available cash for spending had been used up. We had food in the larder for the next two meals, and then we would be cleaned out. There was no money in the Bank!

Two days earlier we had been informed that the Girl Guides were celebrating their 60th birthday, and that they wanted to visit the homes as part of what they termed their 'Good Turn Trail'. They would also have the District Commissioner, and various Municipal Officers with items. We only had a very hazy idea of what they wanted to do, but we knew it would be quite a large gathering. They were going to arrive on the 9th.

The morning dawned fine and warm, and after an early breakfast everyone set out to clean the house and grounds.

We took the chairs from our small chapel and arranged them in the shade of the high tree that stands in the centre of the front lawn. A small table was put in front of the chairs where we thought we might seat the Guests of Honour, with big sun umbrellas to keep them shaded. The National Flag was hauled up the flag-post.

We all waited. We had been warned to expect them at about ll a.m.

All the children from both houses were all dressed in their school uniforms – they had to have special permission to be home from their various schools on that morning. Everyone was excited because the District Commissioner was coming! He had never ever visited before, and he was the District Government Representative of the President; the most important person in our area.

The sun climbed in the sky, and the day grew warmer. The house looked like a palace! Its white and brown painted front facade fresh from the Open Day clean in August.

Well, no one would know, by looking at us, that we were without a cent! We had 'washed our faces, and put oil upon our heads' as in Matthew 6v17.

By mid-day van loads of Guides and Brownies had come accompanied by their Troop Leaders and Officers. Sacks of maize, beans and potatoes came with them, plus many large boxes containing packets of tea, sugar, salt, tins of jam, cooking fat, margarine, together with used items of clothing and even shoes; so many things! The heap grew larger and larger upon the lawn. We looked on amazed at such a shower of blessing upon us! We imagined our empty larder!

At 12.15 p.m. the Commissioner arrived and was duly welcomed with songs and traditional dances. There were speeches, and lastly a presentation to us of 1600 shillings in cash – about £50.

In giving our Vote of Thanks to them all I began by saying, "Do you believe in miracles?"

And thus another drought was ended.

Our driest period is usually December through to the end of February. It is usually the hottest time as well of course; everything is drying out, taking on a parched and weary aspect.

Such was the situation in December 1986 as we prepared to move into the new school buildings. Steven, our eldest son, was enjoying his six month old puppy, a lively, bouncy bundle of fur, with lively eyes and powerful paws. He was an Alsatian pup, and he just loved to run and jump, and generally tear around. One morning I found quite a few children also running about the garden. They were shouting and screaming excitedly. Steven came in saying his puppy had gone mad and was chasing everybody – even biting some. His own hand was bleeding.

I went outside and found the puppy panting on the front step.

His eyes were bright, and he looked normal; just out of breath and a bit over run. I thought the children must have just got him too excited. I put my hand out to him, and he came forward, wagging his tail, and gave me an enthusiastic lick!

"He's alright," I said. "Just let him rest a while."

He seemed quite recovered after that, but that evening he seemed to be running a fever, and soon slipped into a coma and died. I had his body taken to the Veterinary Department so that they could run a check on him. Word came back after a few days that they had found nothing serious – he had probably died of a distemper. We sighed with relief, and went on with our lives unperturbed.

Steven, Michael, and Elizabeth all went off to Nairobi to spend some time with their cousins before school began. The rest of us got busy with Christmas celebrations. The puppy was soon forgotten.

School opened on January 12th. It was an exciting time for us. Suddenly on the 13th the Veterinary Department rang me up.

"About that puppy you sent over to us in December," the voice began. "Just been looking over the file, and I find that although the first set of tests were all OK, there was one, done at the very last moment which showed up as positive Rabies. I'm afraid that pup had Rabies! Hope no one was bitten?"

The blood almost froze in my veins. I went cold all over. Rabies! Steven had been bitten! And how many days had already run by? 28 or 30 at least, and treatment was supposed to begin before any symptoms were seen, and symptoms could take between ten days and two years to appear! We could be too late. Rabies was a killer. I called Steven and we ran a check on how many of us had in fact been bitten or licked by that puppy on that last day of his life. More than 15 including myself – were on the list. We were all possible candidates for Rabies! We could succumb *any moment* to that incurable disease, one of the most unpleasant known to man. None of the medical clinics, not even the government hospital, had any vaccine! We had at last to buy the injections at the local Chemist and take them to our private doctor who then injected us. Altogether we had a total of 43 injections – and each one cost us £13.50, or Kshs. 400/-. Then we had to just wait, wait and see what happened. Nothing did happen, thank God, but it was not easy to wait. But then it is never easy to wait – for anything!!

It is strange too how a trial can continue, and take on a new shape and content. Even before the Rabies scare was ended, other problems were making themselves felt. On the 27th January the water stopped running in the pipes! The town reservoir had virtually run dry!

February 5th
Water off all day.
The mini bus broke down – needs a new block. Now we have no vehicle in working order at all.

February 6th
Still no water.
A primary school child in town died last night of Typhoid. It is reported that seven others have died of the same in the District Hospital!
Later – a dribble of water only in the taps. School and home toilets are blocked! What to do?

Throughout February and March and April we just watched Eldoret come closer and closer to being a 'desert' town. People in hundreds queued for water at public bore holes in the town centre; whole areas cut off totally from all supply. We ourselves were without water for days on end, and for the remainder just receiving a dribble from a single tap. Imagine what it was like trying to keep two homes and a school running with more than 100 residents in the home and another 400 or so coming and going each day in the schools. The flushing of sanitation alone was a nightmare. But then there was the laundry and keeping everyone clean *and* free from Typhoid. It just seemed one thing after another, and then the vehicle broke down! We felt as if we were marooned on a desert island.

March 1st
Situation still very dangerous.

Managed to keep toilets going by flushing with buckets filled from a single tap. Finance also at a low. We now began to count the shillings each day.

This was even more of a 'trial' than all the rest, for the outgoing regular expenses were not small. Much is needed for each and every day that passes. Yet, if we had to begin a day without, we always found enough to pay for that day by the end of it; even though we had nothing left in the hand for 'tomorrow'.

Imagine then our dull amazement when out of the blue, unlooked for gifts of unexpected magnitude began to arrive like cloudbursts upon arid ground. We could not immediately believe it! All at once the vehicle was back on the road, and the whole work entered into a Sabbath.

March 16th
£600 received from UK. How unpredictable are your ways O Lord.

March 23rd
£700 from a school near Nairobi!!!

April 6th
£1000 from friends in Denmark AND a further £1000 from friends in USA. The minibus can be totally repaired now, and we can look a week ahead. The AMAZING thing has been that NONE of these gifts had been promised to us in advance!
Water still dribbles out of the tap!

How humbled we felt, and how secure in His hands. But the water problem remained until May.

ON THE 27TH AUGUST, 1994, TESTIMONY FAITH HOMES celebrated its 25th Anniversary, or Silver Jubilee. Since its commencement in 1969, more than 200 children and young people have passed through our hands. We have managed to acquire and manage two children's homes accommodating some 75 children altogether, and have also built up a top quality school from pre-primary through to high school.

Looking back to 1969 when I was told there were no orphaned children to care for since Kenya still believed in, and practised, an 'extended family system', we have seen more and more children at risk and in need of care and protection. Extended family is less and less practised – especially in the urban areas, and with more and more people leaving for the 'big cities' we see more and more pressure on the need for social action in these areas. Unemployment and poverty have increased over the years, and the incidence of prostitution has also increased, together with a general breakdown of morals unilaterally. This has produced growing numbers of unwanted children, many of them abandoned and left to roam the streets; and also one-parent families providing little or no home life, family affection or discipline. The end result is an up and coming generation of children and young people who have no moral base, and who are out and alone in society without any loyalties except to themselves, and with no ethical scruples to prevent them from acting anti-socially to the general risk and danger of the community at large.

Kenya may not be accused alone in seeing this decline. There has been a marked deterioration worldwide in the quality of life and social ethics. This is due to corrosion of previously held values and standards in favour of a more permissive and licentious attitude by educators and sociologists which has largely gone unchallenged by church and other religious leaders who have themselves become more and more liberal.

The Bible underlines the necessity of a stable home and family, built upon a faithful marriage contract, but in these last 40 years lawmakers have made it more and more easy to destroy and even invalidate this facility. They have done this by progressively relaxing the divorce laws, approving more and more previously illegal sexual offences such as abortion, homosexuality and lesbianism. All of this has devalued and undercut the whole idea of marriage as the proper frame-work for sexual activity, putting sex first, and giving in to human weakness rather than encouraging Man to climb higher. Indeed one wonders if Man is rather devolving instead of evolving; degenerating rather than improving. Surely that 'elite' group of men and women who are able to shape our destiny by law-making and teaching social ethics are responsible for plunging us all into darkness and anarchy. Marriage has also been abused by social economics which (together, in Kenya and other places, with the 'Dowry System') have made it more and more expensive to marry, especially for those in the unemployed or poorer income bracket. It is simpler just to 'live' together, and this opens the door to meaningless, unfaithful, and temporary liaisons which produce nothing of value in society, but rather help to destroy and undermine it, stripping it of the base from which all moral concepts such as honour, integrity, loyalty, faithfulness and trust are grown. Children are being born more and more out of wedlock. Some are just jettisoned into the open field, abandoned to whatever fate might await them. Others are shunted around 'foster parents' or put in 'homes'. And others remain in unnatural one parent families (we now hear of homosexual couples adopting children and 'bringing them up' – or is it down? – in a totally bizarre situation, alien to all well-known and proper concepts of human life and practice). These children are growing up without proper reference points, and promise to bring upon this planet an eventual chaos worse than civilisation has ever experienced.

Some say that Man is evolving, and that this is the age when he will shake himself free from concepts that confined and hampered him, so that he can progress to the heights planned for him, but this is all bunkum of the worst order. We are in fact being deceived and duped! We are being destroyed. We are sliding downwards to the bottomless pit without brakes. We have thrown our forbears' experience out of the window; we have thrown history to the compost heap, and we have relegated the concept of God to the mentally handicapped! What do we have left? Unilateral violence and increasing terror as nations break down to prehistoric tribal entities without natural affection or feeling, willing to kill, rape, and massacre each other for a whim. Sex without love, affection, accountability or honour. Total selfishness without any mitigation. The outlook is grim. Looking back over 25 years is not encouraging.

25 years of civilization has produced uncivilised behaviour. Mankind is not kinder, but more depraved and self-seeking. But this is what the BIBLE says in 2 Timothy 3v1-5:

Men and women will be lovers of themselves,
covetous, boasters, proud, blasphemers,
disobedient to parents, unthankful, unholy,
without natural affection, truce-breakers,
false accusers, incontinent, fierce,
despisers of those that are good,
traitors, heady, high minded,
lovers of pleasures more than lovers of God.

Yet Christians, and other 'godly' men and women of other faiths, will more and more be criticised for standing against this tide of iniquitous life-style.

My wife and I have been married 26 years this August, and we have brought up our own five sons and one daughter together with 40 or more other children in the same house and facility, just an extended family. There has been stability in this home and family. The parents have honoured each other, and loved each other in front of all the family members. We have not seen any immorality in the family. We have not seen violence and hatred in the family. We have representatives of more than ten ethnic groups living together with us in PEACE. No conflict has been seen. Why? Because the parents have always shown the same face and appreciation towards ALL members of the society in the family. We can teach inside the home and family. It is what *every* parent is to do – but to do it he or she *must* be a true parent – married, not free. This is the *only* right environment to teach children a right way. We have not supplied the 'pill' or the 'condom' to our children in tacit acceptance that they will need to engage in sex *before* and outside of *marriage*. We have not seen one of our girls become pregnant before time! We have not heard of any of our boys committing fornication. Yes, yes I know that they may still have done so without us knowing … BUT!

In 1987 I heard a Government Minister of Health encourage all Kenyan mothers to ensure that their daughters had the 'pill' in their handbag/school bag by the time they were twelve. Don't advise them, don't counsel them, just allow them to have sex – they will anyway – and let it be *safe sex*. The world says YES, to safe sex – to fornication, adultery and all immorality.

But what *is* safe sex? The condom is not safe, the pill is not safe. The pill is not prevention to VD or AIDS. The condom is not unable to fail – there is fail risk of 1 in 6. Safe sex is ONE MAN/ONE WOMAN inside the Marriage Bed, for life!

Who will teach this? Not the educationalist, or the sociologist *unless* he or she has put GOD'S STANDARDS FIRST in their life. People are dying – our children are dying – because of the godlessness of our lawmakers. Wake up people, you are being systematically murdered, led to the slaughter. WAKE UP!

Romans 13v8-14
Deuteronomy 4v9
Hebrews 13v4
Proverbs 22v6

This is 1997, and the values are nasty and cheap, unsatisfying and disappointing. Is there another 25 years for Testimony Faith Homes? If there is, it will be 25 years running against the tide, and we shall live more and more in the midst of a depreciated society, geared to humanist, and perhaps even demonic views. Christian concepts, and indeed ANY Godly concept, will be considered anti-progress, and detrimental to the general good. We shall be the enemy! But, for the time being, we shall endeavour to continue to demonstrate that it IS possible for ALL MEN to live in, and at, peace with each other, as we care for children and young people in our two family homes. And we shall continue to use the school as a platform for teaching and communicating the Truth about Man, Sin and the Devil, to the general advancement of moral integrity and spiritual health.

What do we say to all those other organisations concerned in the welfare of the human race? What do we say to parents, to young men and women growing up now in our world?

We say trust yourselves into the Hands of God, and go to Him for Wisdom, and Courage and Strength to put that Wisdom into Action (James 3v13-18).

SOUND THE BATTLE CRY!
SEE THE FOE IS NIGH!
RAISE THE STANDARD HIGH FOR THE LORD.

Chapter Eight

THE END OF A PERIOD

By 1997 the second 28 years of my life was coming to an end. Looking into the future towards the end of that year, it seemed that many things were well established, yet at the same time changes were coming, and looking back, we now see that we did not have a very clear idea of what the Lord was going to do.

I want to state this because I want you to know that John Green is no spiritual giant. No, I have often got things wrong. I have not found myself to have the Gift of Prophecy, or even Knowledge. I have often been rather blind to what the Lord was wanting to do in my life, and often have miscalculated the future. This only emphasises the great compassion and patience of our Father in Heaven, who still is prepared to work His Purposes out in and through people like us without giving up! If this book has any value it must only be in revealing the Wonderful Grace and Mercy of God, and not in promoting John Green, or even Testimony Faith Homes.

To recap a little, towards the end of 1997 we had two children's homes catering for about 75 children in total. Esther and I were still houseparents in Testimony House, and Joshua and Miriam Mbithi were still houseparents in Jacaranda Cottage.

The school, started in 1981 with nursery, was now having two streams of primary, and one stream of secondary high, serving both our own children, and the general public. Esther was Headmistress of nursery school, and I was Principal over the whole school, with two other Headmasters serving under me.

We had a community church.

We had always endeavoured to have an internal Sunday service within the homes, all the children and staff taking part, and even open to any outside neighbours who might have wanted to share with us. Many had asked why we did not join a local denomination outside of the homes, but we live quite far from any church we might have felt one with, and also we had not wanted to identify with a particular denomination (there are more than 200 Christian denominations in Eldoret). We wanted to present Jesus rather than a denomination.

We felt in 1996, that the Lord wanted us to open up this fellowship in a more definite way, however, and we decided to look for a full time 'pastor' to come and take charge. Daryl, one of our three adopted sons, was graduating from his Bible College, and another of our old boys already pastoring nearby, had shown an interest in joining us. We asked them to pray and to seek God for His guidance. Finally it was to Daryl that the Lord spoke. He was also engaged to be married to a very dear young lady called Caroline who had also trained in the same college as himself. She was in fact to be a teacher in our school.

The congregation then numbered about 200 souls, including our children and homes' staff.

We also had two other ministries in place.

The Kingdom Kids run by old boy Charles 'Green'.

In 1995 Charles had asked if he could help us develop a youth ministry using some of the children. Charles had come to stay with us when he was about three. He had been left at a bus stop in Eldoret, alone and stranded. The police picked him up and brought him to us. No one ever came forward to claim him, and we have not managed to trace any family. He could not communicate and we gave him the name Charles. Later when he joined school we still had not found a second name for him, so when his teacher asked his name he just went ahead and said he was Charlie Green. And so he has been ever since though we have never adopted him officially. He was a very quiet and introspective child that we worried about a lot through his teenage years. But then one day, quite suddenly, listening to a street preacher on his way home from school he found Christ, and his whole life changed. After finishing form four in high school he joined 'Youth with a Mission'. After training he had continued on with them, and later he came and approached us. Thus he had come and commenced a Dance and Drama group, which became known as The Kingdom Kids. They presented the Gospel in drama and dance, and were an immediate success, and extra tool for evangelism.

Then there was also SOON Ministries run by old boy Michael Rufroni.

We had been approached by SOON Gospel Literature Worldwide, based in Willington, Derby, UK. They wanted to know if we would be willing to be their representative and agent in Kenya. They already had some 500 Bible Study and Reading Clubs in Kenya, spread all over the country, though the majority, interestingly enough, are all in our immediate area. They wanted help in supervising, and even extending the ministry. We felt this was a definite leading from the Lord, and we agreed. One of our boys was also just then graduating from Nairobi Pentecostal Bible College, and he became the first Assistant Director for SOON, in Kenya. His name is Michael Rufroni. A truly lovely Christian young man, he came to us when he was ten, his mother having been struck dead by lightening as they sat together in Church one Sunday morning. The Church was made of mud and wattle, and the lightening struck through an open window. It was a terrible experience for Michael, and it was some many months before he could even speak, so shocked he was. He has no other family. He feels that the Lord was even in this! So, SOON Gospel Literature became part of the overall ministry of Testimony Faith Homes.

Finally, we also owned and ran another property known as 'La Chacra' some 15 kilometres away, managed by Peter Mwema, and his wife, old girl Jane.

It had belonged to a retired C.M.S. missionary, Miss. Caroline Martha Drakely, M.B.E. She had originally been sent to Uganda in 1925, and there she had commenced a girls' school (The Gayaza Normal School), which went on to become the Lady Irene College (a teacher training college for women) in 1936. Miss. Drakely (Patty to all who knew and loved her) became Principal of the college until her retirement in 1960, when she moved to Kenya. She had been awarded the M.B.E. in 1952. Once in Kenya, she took various 'retirement' teaching jobs in Mosoriot Teachers' College, Nasakol Girls' School, and finally at Kaptagat Preparatory School. We first met in 1973 when she was some 72 years of age. We visited her at La Chacra, her home in the forest, though in fact the property was by then on the receding edge of it! It comprised a small brick-built bungalow with two bedrooms, where Patty herself resided, plus two timber chalets that she had had built as holiday accommodation for friends and tired missionaries! Surrounding these dwellings were nine and half acres of river-side gardens and lawns. It was a little paradise, and we often spent a few days there in one of her chalets, and came to know and love Patty very much. She also loved children, and became very interested in all that we were doing in Eldoret, and often came down to visit us whilst she could drive, and played a portable organ for us in our Sunday Services. But with the passing years, of course, she aged, and by 1991, she had lost most of her sight, and was getting rather deaf. Christmas 1991 she had a nasty fall, and fractured her hip. She never walked again, and after a short bout of bronchitis she passed quietly away in her sleep. It was the 3rd July, 1992. She left Testimony Faith

Homes the entire property of La Chacra, un-entailed, in her will. It is just about 15 kilometres away from Eldoret, and we continued to use it as a holiday/retreat centre both for the friends and missionaries that enjoyed it before, and also for us and the children. Later, Peter Mwema tried his luck at starting a flower business, but it came to nothing. By 1997 Peter and Jane were still managers there, mainly looking after the property and trying to raise vegetables for the homes on some four acres laid down for agriculture, but it was not paying for itself, and was in fact running at a heavy loss annually. It was cheaper for us to buy the vegetables we needed from the local city market than pay the cost of transport and labour to grow them in La Chacra.

BY 1997 I HAD HIT 57 and Esther celebrated her 53rd birthday. We were both fully occupied most of every day, and by the time we returned home to Testimony House and our family of some 40 children, we were feeling a bit unequal to supervising home-works and other chores, as well as providing love and fellowship. Additionally we felt that with almost two-thirds of the family almost through with College, they would soon be ready to fly. We would then be taking in a whole new bunch of very young children, even infants, into our house again. It would be good to have a change of houseparents – a younger couple who would be able to see the children through to their adulthood. Perhaps this would be a good time for us to retire? Esther and I talked about it. But it was easier said than actually done. We did not want to leave the homes, but just withdraw from being Mum and Dad in Testimony House. But Testimony House had been OUR home for

28 years, half of my lifetime. Our children had all grown up there. It would be hard to leave. Then again where would we leave to? There was no spare housing, and we had no personal means to rent a house elsewhere.

Some weeks after we first talked together a letter arrived from very dear friends in the south-west of England. They felt it might a good time for us to think about retiring from being houseparents. "Why not build a 'Retirement Cottage', and hand over to a young couple?" They would contribute the bulk of the cost towards this venture provided our Board agreed to let us live in such a cottage rent free for the duration of our lifetime – whereupon it would be free to be used as part and parcel of the homes.

It was an astonishing offer. Our Board agreed. I drew up a plan and presented it to the local Town Planning Department for approval. They approved, and our friends send a cheque for five-thousand pounds sterling to start us off. It was September 1997. Before October ended, the foundation had been laid and the walls put up. It was a miracle! But the nearer it came to completion the more we had cold feet, and wondered if we could in fact actually make the break and leave Testimony House.

The question of who would take over from us was another matter that occupied our thoughts and prayers. We had three possible couples. One of them was our adopted son Daryl who was still pastoring our church fellowship, and his wife Caroline who was teaching in the primary school. We had shared our thoughts with each couple, and they had gone to pray – once again it was Daryl and Carol the Lord spoke to finally. We were very relieved. We knew we could not try to persuade or influence them ourselves, but we had felt in our hearts that they would be the ones. But we were still not too sure emotionally if we were actually doing the right thing.

Christmas came and went. The New Year dawned.

On the second January, about noon, I had gone to my office door. It was a beautiful day, cloudless and hot. I was in my office, and Esther was in the school home-science room. Suddenly I heard loud frenzied screams, and running outside, I saw a great column of black acrid smoke ascending into the sky above Testimony House. Running across I found one of the bedrooms at the rear of the house thoroughly afire, with flames already up to the rafters. Crowds of people were already gathering to 'sight-see', as well as to help. We had fire extinguishers to hand fortunately, and the contents of these together with hurriedly gathered buckets of water were being directed at the fire. But it had such a grip in the roof that we feared we would not prevent it spreading to the main living area. Such an old house, so dry and vulnerable. The Fire Brigade arrived, the Police and more and more curious people from the neighbourhood all milled around in the mess and the smoke, and general chaos.

It seemed that the fire had started in a dormitory right next to our own bedroom. No one ever discovered how it started. The dormitory was completely consumed to the rafters, and the fire had travelled across to our bedroom bringing the ceiling down and generally making it quite impossible for us to enter. Hardly anything was salvaged from these two rooms, and Esther and I had to move out of the house into makeshift quarters. The NEW house was ready, but we had not wanted to move, and furniture had still to be bought and arranged. We had in fact been on the verge of back-pedalling and staying put – the fire insisted we move out. A nod was as good as a wink after all – if we HAD tried to stay after that perhaps the entire house would have burned down!!

On the 24th January, all being finally ready, we moved ourselves into Green Cottage – our 'retirement' home. It was not just me and Esther that went to live there of course. We still had two of our adopted children, with us, James 'Manu' aged 14, and Helen, aged 9. Additionally we also took Sarah Magio with us. You can read of her story in the next chapter of this book. She was by this time 15 years old, and going through a very difficult teenage stage. After the fire, Daryl and Carol had gradually taken over from us but Sarah would not accept them as parents, and had been virtually impossible to live with. She and her brother Abraham had been with us almost since they were born, and we had suspected she would not take kindly to our apparent desertion. We had hoped that since she was almost ready to think of a future without any of us she would manage. We were wrong. So in the end she also moved in with us. We were a family of five still. Fortunately I had planned four bedrooms: one for us, one for Manu, and one for the girls. The fourth was for visitors – and just as well since we have had a steady and continuous stream of them since moving in. In fact we have seen Green Cottage to be a special blessing in bringing people to stay with us, and to get to see and understand Testimony Faith Homes from inside.

Green Cottage is only 50 metres from Testimony House – just across the lawn.

The night we moved we had a wonderful prayer and fellowship in Testimony House with all the children. It was a blessed time. We officially then became grandparents to all the children in all the homes, and left Daryl and Carol as Mum and Dad in Testimony. Daryl was 28, the same age as I had been when I first entered Kenya in 1968. He and Carol had much to learn. He had grown up in the home of course, and knew the routine and the atmosphere, but now HE was Dad. It was quite a daunting challenge. The first years were not so easy for either of them, but the LORD helped them – perhaps one day they will write their own book.

Many did not quite understand about our move and 'Retirement'. People got the idea we had actually left Testimony Faith Homes altogether, and were either occupied elsewhere in a new field, or that we had just gone out to pasture so to speak? We had done neither. I was still fully occupied as Principal of the School, and as Director overall. Esther was still Head of the Nursery School. We were busy. And of course Esther was still a wife and mother. The Fellowship had also begun making radio programmes for the local Christian Radio Station, and I was heavily involved in that work and ministry. Both of us were still heavily committed to the work, in fact more than ever we had been before. And we continue to be so. We expect to go on going on till He comes or calls.

Chapter Nine

INTO THE FUTURE

Since first writing the end of chapter 8 almost ten years have gone by. It is now 2008, and as I wrote at the beginning of this Edition, there have continued to be changes. There have been comings and goings. The Millennial Year has come and gone. The world has changed, and is changing. WE are changing – and expanding. The homes and the children have continued, and each day the Lord our God kept us, and provided for us, and does continue to provide for us!

We have four homes now, and residentially care for 125 with expectation to raise that to 145 by Christmas 2008. In 2006 we rented two houses nearby, and turned them into children's homes: Drakely Cottage and Trinity

Cottage. And in 2006 we built two new homes in the compound of Jacaranda Cottage into which we have transferred the children from the rented houses.

We sold La Chacra and purchased two acres of new land adjoining to the school for recreational purposes. The school had long been without any playing field, and we had our eye on the adjoining land for some years. The owner finally being found willing to exchange some of her land for La Chacra, we felt it was good to agree. Although La Chacra had been a beloved haven for us it had cost the homes almost ten-thousand pounds a year to keep up and secure with almost no profitable returns. Peter Mwema left us to become a Town Pastor.

National interest in SOON Ministries slowed down and eventually died. Michael Rufroni has now taken on a lecturing position with The Pentecostal and Holiness Church Bible School nearby.

Esther has been prompted to become the Headmistress of the primary school, and I handed my post as School Principal over all school departments to Anthony Ndungu who had helped me start the primary school way back in 1985.

I remain Director overall, and have become quite involved in District matters related to children as well. I am currently Chairman of the District Board of Medical Management, Chairman of the District Children's Officer's Committee and a Gazetted Member of the District Probation Case Committee, the District Public Service Case Committee, and The Eldoret Juvenile Remand Home Panel of Visitors. More recently I was appointed General Secretary of the Uasin Gishu Children's Services Forum, a conglomerate of more than 50 Children's Organisations within our immediate district. All of these commitments have taken me into a much wider area of service, and opened countless doors of opportunity to witness for Christ in all areas of public service.

Joshua and Miriam, as I mentioned have left us to start a new ministry just three kilometres away. Everything looks and feels the same – but the outside world is changing.

THE WORK OF TESTIMONY FAITH HOMES is ongoing. More and more children are at risk and needy. This year the Government of Kenya put a new Children's Act through Parliament – the last one was passed in 1963. This will greatly change the way children's institutions are set up and run. This has come out of the U.N. Children's Charter and The Rights of the Child. Some of it is very good indeed. Out of it has come a need to consider how to accommodate children. The Government is not enthusiastic about using rented property, and this prompted us in May to go ahead in faith that God would supply, and we set about building our own new homes. As we began we had no funds to hand, yet in less than nine months all the money came in without appeal, and the two new houses are now up and accommodating 60 children. Now we are thinking of going on to believe for a way to renovate and expand Jacaranda Cottage itself so that it can increase its capacity from 30 to 50 children. To prepare for this we began to build a 'Guest House' to accommodate those children now living in Jacaranda while we rebuild their home. We completed this in June this year, and it is already being used to provide extra space for some of our older teenagers who are in college completing their professional education for some nine months of the year (when one leaves for college, we usually take in a child to fill the space. When the college boys and girls return for holidays it is good for them to find a bed still available for them).

The situation in Kenya and in Eldoret today is one of increasing poverty and distress following the New Year political strife and racial tension during elections.

But we are a very tiny work, a very small contribution to the business of alleviating the material and human need around us. And we are also not a wealthy work from the point of view that we do not have financial backing or support enough to do GREAT things materially. We have remained HIDDEN, and UNKNOWN to a large extent, and our existence has depended entirely on God, and the fact that He sees our need, and hears and answers our cry.

Many friends have asked me if I ever doubt or fear in this life of Faith in God. I must confess and say YES I do! There have been many times in fact.

Not long ago I was asked if I would not consider ways and means of making the work more financially secure and steady, perhaps by presenting our needs more definitely, or by putting the children up for sponsorship. A lot of very good arguments were put forward up with these suggestions, and I found myself willing to consider them. It was a temptation. Just at that time finances became quite strained as well. I picked up a book by Francis Schaefer, and found myself reading:

"Whatever is NOT an exhibition that God exists misses the whole purpose of the Christian's life now on this earth. In matters of Christian service HOW we are doing it is at least as important as what we are doing!"

It was SO relevant to me. When we had started the homes, we did so as a testimony of WHAT God can do when we believe. We took in the first children without any material security, and without any material assets in hand. But as soon as the children came in, we began to SEE the Provision of God. We have always believed BEFORE we have actually seen. We have not obtained our need FIRST and THEN believed, but first we believed and THEN SAW what we believed for. It is a point of difference between us and many other charities. I felt rebuked for thinking it should be otherwise.

At the same time we were immediately pressed to pay some £600 of bills due. There was not even £1 to hand. That day I had been invited to attend the official opening of a new bank in Eldoret. The function was to be attended by the President of Kenya, Daniel Arap Moi. I went. After the ceremony was concluded the Chairman of the bank got up and made a speech of thanks to the President, at the end of which he said that to mark the occasion his bank had decided to make a special donation to a local charity of £1,000. He then took up a cheque and handed it to the President to be presented.

It was then that I was asked to step up to the dais to receive this cheque on behalf of Testimony Faith Homes. I was so unprepared I almost fell off my chair. My spirit soared. We were saved and delivered.

But then I heard that the cheque could not be cashed for ten days!

What mean trick was this? We needed the money IMMEDIATELY, not in ten days! It was so cruel to actually have the cheque but be unable to cash it. I felt disconsolate with God, with the bank, and with life in general. I am being very honest here. I don't want you to imagine me to be more than I am. I am also flesh and blood.

I returned home depressed.

The following morning a letter arrived from England from a small Church in Brixham Devon. Inside was a cheque for £600 immediately negotiable! I was chastened indeed. It taught me a lesson I still find hard to remember. Our Father in Heaven wants us to TRUST in Him, and not in man. He wants us to do this ALWAYS, no matter what is happening around us.

And it is in many ways forced upon us almost unavoidably because we are being challenged to take in children daily – whether we have money or not. Sometimes, even if we have the accommodation or not. If we can squeeze one in we never say 'No'.

But not everyone finds a place. Christmas 1989 found two ragged boys knocking on our door and asking for a place to stay. They certainly looked in need of care and a good meal, but the truth was they were just 'trying it on'. In reality they both had a home and a family not far away from us, and before the day was through we found them out and returned them home again. It was a poor home and life was certainly nowhere near a prosperous one, but it *was* home, and they had concerned parents.

It is often hard to turn away those who come seeking escape, purely and simply, from poverty. But 'blood is thicker than water' and we feel that children need to stick to their roots, and be close to their families no matter how poor the circumstances might be.

We often help such a family to stay together with a little financial relief instead of taking a child into the homes and causing distressful separations.

But some DO find a welcome, and a refuge – mainly those who have lost every vestige of home and family; lost and lonely children; children at risk; children adrift.

Such were the twin offspring of a poor beggar girl.

She had shuffled and dragged herself up and down the dusty streets of Kabarnet Township almost the whole day. It had been so hot, and she was tired. Born crippled in her hands and feet, she was very unable to help herself a great deal. Her mother was given the drug Thalidomide during her pregnancy, and the result had been a seriously deformed child. She had only one arm. A stunted hand joined the other shoulder. No legs, only feet joining the trunk. She was nevertheless loved and cared for until one night there was a raid by a gang of cattle rustlers, and in the early morning light both her parents were found to have been slain. She was alone then. There were no brothers or sisters to care for her and no relatives either. She was destitute and unwanted. From that day she became a beggar. By 1983 she was 26 years old, ragged, hungry and tired. She crawled into a shady copse and slept.

Suddenly she was roughly seized, shaken, dragged. She opened her eyes in terror as the man ripped apart her ragged dress, forcing himself upon her. His big hand covered her mouth, she could not scream.

All was still. People came running as she began now to call out in distress and fear. They gathered around her, looking at her from a distance. She lay exhausted upon the ground a shapeless and abused, piece of human refuse. They all turned away from her. She was after all only a deformed beggar – an orphan. Why should anyone care about her?

A few months later she realised she was pregnant. She crawled to the Government Hospital where she was let in, and there on the 9th October she gave birth to twins, a boy and a girl. She was a simple person and had never been to school. Her mind was still that of a child herself. She reached out to her children, but to her they were as dolls to play with. She soon lost interest. The nurses named the children Sara and Abraham. They were perfectly formed in every way, beautiful children. Initially it actually got into the newspapers – deformed beggar gives birth to perfect twins! It was news in a crude, sensational way. The poor woman died soon afterwards. The children were alone.

"Will you take them in, Mr. Green?" asked the middle-aged social worker pleadingly. "Please do let them in, as if you don't we just do not know what will become of them."

We took them in. By this time they were about 9 months old. Sarah is 21 now and just completing a course as a Beautician, in Nairobi. She had a hard time growing up, seeming to feel rejection of herself deep within. She was vicious in temperament, rude, rebellious and antagonistic to all idea of God. Only now is she beginning to blossom, and to reveal her real self. The hurt within her is healing, and it is something especially beautiful to see. She is not academically bright, but she has a bright and humorous personality. Her twin brother, Abraham has done well in school and is now in university studying medicine.

THE SUN WAS FAST GOING DOWN IN ELDORET. A thin mist was swirling over the fields near the Water Cleansing Works just a few kilometres from the town centre. It was Easter Saturday 1981, and it was getting cold. No one was in sight as the Water Engineer cycled along the main road on his way home. Suddenly he heard a baby cry! It startled him. There it was again…shrill, fearful, alone. He stopped by the curb and strained his eyes into the gathering gloom to look across the fields from where he thought the sounds had come. He caught sight of something small and dark near the middle of the field amongst the tufts of long grass. Nothing else. Did he see movement? He was not sure. He left the bike at the roadside and climbed over the barbed-wire fence and made his way across the field. As he came close to the bundle he had seen, he saw that it was a little girl of about two, wrapped up in a blanket. He looked around again, and called out to see if anyone else was nearby. Only silence and the unfolding sea of grassland all around him. He shivered in the damp evening air, and stooping down, lifted the child and carried her to the roadside and to his bike. He took her to the local Police Station and left her there – an abandoned child. The Police went straight back to where the child had been found and sought around and about for any knowledge of her from scattered farms and homesteads. No one could shed any light on the matter. No one could say how she came to be stranded in that field, but someone had thrown her away; had purposely lost her.

A few days later she was brought to us and we let her in to be part of our growing family. Now she is a young woman of 23 who works as an accountant. She loves Jesus, and although she knows how very lost she was, she understands how very glad she has been to be found. The Water Engineer found her first, and brought her to the Police who brought her to us, who brought her to Jesus. She may never know her true name or origin, but she has been FOUND by her Heavenly Father and adopted into His Family.

SO MANY CHILDREN, so many lives. So many lost and astray children, lonely and abused children. How to care for them? What to give them?
Do you remember the old Nursery Rhyme?

There was an old woman who lived in a shoe:
She had so many children she didn't know what to do.
She gave them some broth without any bread,
She whipped them all soundly and put them to bed.

The prescribed poverty and attending stress in a cramped overcrowded home can and often does produce hardship and suffering without a lot of comfort or affection. On the other hand too much ease may produce an opposite affect. How to provide the right balance is a big problem when it comes to assisting needy humanity – especially children.

In Testimony Faith Homes we have found it hard to find this balance. Often the children we help outside of our homes, who still live with their families yet in often severe poverty, actually progress better and further than some of those who reside within the homes themselves. Is this because the discomfort and poverty provide a spur for hard and industrious effort in school in a desire for a better life? Is it because three good meals a day and comfortable security without anxiety produce a state of satisfaction that leads to a certain laziness or lack of effort to get on? I am sure that a more basic standard of living is healthier than one that is too well-heeled. Nevertheless it is still not easy to find a happy balance between the two extremes. Finding houseparents who are willing to share that optimum standard of living totally integrated with the children in the homes and with themselves and their own children is not easy either. For us there has had to be a lot of self-questioning and willingness to sacrifice before we could set up the individual homes as they are. Each one is not just an orphanage, or extended African family home, it is also the family home of the houseparents and their own individual family. It is all one and the same – one family living together at the same level. So far so good, but we are still learning from our mistakes, and from seeing the results in the lives of those who have been through their time with us.

And in the early days when children were coming to us almost daily, and our needs increased apace moment by moment, I often felt myself to be like the old woman who lived in a shoe. With the first two boys, the Provision came so instantaneously that I had not had time to be apprehensive as to how I would care for them, but as the numbers increased the Provision needed became increasingly greater, and there were times when we had to WAIT. At such times I found, and still find even today, that my faith can be wanting! But so He teaches us to grow, and to learn patience and trust through hope.

In January 1990 I wrote:

We were suffering from rather straightened circumstances through October last year, until just before Christmas, and at one point we received no material gift of any kind for more than two weeks, so that we were in some difficulty, though still very much alive. Tell me the old, old story! Yeah! Well it's true – this IS our often experience, and in it we Glory! Praise the Lord! On 16th December friends arrived from Australia, and brought with them a gift they had collected early in September. It was VERY welcome. It was almost £1,000! We did indeed Praise the Lord! It was like the Relief of Mafeking!

In September of the same year I wrote again:

August was a very thin month financially, and by the time school opened for the third term we had fees for the eight who were returning to boarding school (some £700) still to find, but it was all on the way to us, and arrived the very DAY that it was needed. All from very unexpected, and in one particular case very unknown sources. But if we waited for school fees, we also have waited on our Daily Bread. We endeavoured not to let it show, and we did our

best to 'anoint our head, and to wash our face' as per Matthew 6v16-18. This life of faith! It is a constant testing.
Once, Abraham was tempted by the King of Sodom (representing the desires of the flesh and world) who suddenly offered quick, ready wealth, very reasonably. He did this at a time when Abram was tired and weary, and perhaps a bit low both physically and spiritually. But Melchizedek stood not too far away, and not long before had re-affirmed to Abram God's Blessing upon his life. And so Abram resisted the King of Sodom, and turned down the offer of ease in Zion. He said, "I will not take a thread or a shoelace, or anything that is yours, lest you should say, I have made Abram rich" (Genesis 14v22-23).
It might be said that Abram was 'looking a gift-horse in the mouth', but the truth was that he was against giving glory or praise to the world, or to man; he wanted it ALL for God. And after this the Lord gave Abram a vision in which he spoke to him and said "FEAR NOT, Abram. I am your Shield, your abundant compensation, and your reward shall be exceeding great" (Genesis 15v1). Isn't it even more encouraging to know that our Father in Heaven understands our human fears without condemnation, willing to make known His Protecting and Shielding Power; willing to underwrite all our liabilities. How can we go wrong, if He is with us?

But some things continue on, and continue to be difficult lessons to learn to perfection. In September 1992 I wrote:

It is a fact that over the last 23 years Testimony Faith Homes has proved without doubt that God answers prayer made in the Name of His Son Jesus Christ. But it is also a fact that He is not always in a hurry to do so. Daniel of course waited for his prayers to be answered, and David seemed to often suffer distress of spirit due to delayed answers to his prayers. In Psalm 22v1 he cries out, "My God, my God, why have you forsaken me? Why are you so far from helping me, and from the words of my roaring? O my God, I cry in the daytime, but you do not hear."

And in Psalm 28v1 he says, "...be not silent to me lest if you be silent I become like those who go down into the pit." David was often requiring SPEEDY ANSWERS to his prayers; he was often in a hurry to get help...and at times God was NOT in a hurry to give it – although there is no doubt at all that the answer did come, and that it was always 'in time'! In Psalm 40 he says, "I waited patiently for the Lord [to answer], and he did bend His ear toward me, and heard my cry." Hallelujah!

In late May this year (1992) the homes had almost nothing in hand for the week ahead. For twelve days into the month of June there was no income at all. Then on the 12th June provision arrived. Then nothing more until the 21st...and so on. We found ourselves on the 1st July with £350, less than a third of what we needed in that first week. Each day we prayed our provision in, but by the end of July we had nothing in hand. Not until the 14th August were we delivered. Then we were suddenly faced with demands from the various boarding high schools and colleges to which 18 of our teenagers were returning for their third term; they were all increasing their costs for the term ahead. We immediately needed £600 to cover it all. We had a day's provision in hand. Days passed and the Prayers of Faith went apparently unheeded. We experienced knots of apprehension in our stomachs. We seemed to be running a series of 'Ten Day' trials. Suddenly, on the very last day of August, a Kenyan brother home from studies in Denmark called upon us and presented us with 37,000 Kenyan shillings in cash – the equivalent at that time of £569! It was a miracle!

I finished up by adding:

We cannot say that we always find ourselves full of faith. It is not automatically with us. We are not always calm, patiently waiting for the Lord to deliver us. There are often times of dearth, but every day, money has to be spent, bills accrue. Do we weary of this lifestyle? Yes, at times, like Peter, we might feel tempted to return to 'fishing'. But our confidence is in God, and not in ourselves, or in others. It is too late to turn back and try another way. God alone has to be our refuge, a very present help in times of trouble. We do not regret accepting to be led this way.

George Mueller, that man of faith, never suffered unpaid bills! Many have intimated that John Green is yet another Mueller, but this is not so. Our Visions, I think, may have been different in some ways, and certainly George Mueller is far ahead of me both in the scope of the ministry given to him, and in the dimension of faith that he wielded. Yet it is true that we serve the same Jesus and Lord, and that we have both believed and trusted in His Word, and found it unchangeably true. However we often have unpaid bills on the table, and see many days go by before we are able to pay them. Funds have not always been there, as I have previously demonstrated. We have prayed and believed, but we could not always wait since life went on around us moment by moment. Before a week ends we have had to commit ourselves for more than £1,500 in outgoings. And finally, the bills ARE always paid.

We did not scream to man for help whilst we waited, but we often felt and feel like doing so. But we left our plea with the Father alone in Jesus' name. Our faith and knowledge of His Faithfulness is growing.

One associate of ours wrote a short while back and said, "Although your ethos for the last 30 years has been one of absolute reliance on the Lord, it may be time to consider reviewing that ethos...It may be time to start considering alternative ways forward for funding..." The writer went on to hint that if we did change the ethos of 30 years it might well open the door to more definite funding of a more abundant and regular nature. It was a real challenge to us since at the very time the letter was received we were also needing funds, and feeling the need. Yet God had NEVER failed to supply the need; in all the years, bread has always been on the table for us all, and our clothes have never turned to rags. BUT it has been and remains true that it is not always a 'delight' to walk through the desert on survival rations; it can be distressing, humanly painful, even depressing at times, but to see His Presence walking with you, to see His Hand providing for you...THIS IS SOMETHING WONDERFUL. It cannot be compared to the hardness of the way – the hardness of the way is nothing! Yes it is possible we might be richer if we turned more openly to help from Man. But would we be closer to God? Would we know Him in a way that would increase our Faith and Confidence in Him Alone to fulfil ALL our need, and be ALL our satisfaction? I do not think so. Better be poor and KNOW His Salvation at every turn, than to be rich and without any assurance of safety or final well-being in His Hands.

And what does George Mueller have to say? He writes thus:

"The increase of faith is the work of God in the human heart. God delights to increase the faith of His children. By this Means God is glorified before an ungodly world and the Powers of darkness. Furthermore, the confidence that His children show in Him in times of trial, discouragement, pain and sorrow gives great encouragement to other Christians. God delights to do good to others through them that they themselves, through the exercise of faith, may obtain an increase of it. Difficulties, limitations, hindrances, bereavements, and losses, though we shrink exceedingly from them, are the very agencies that God uses to cause us to grow. As an infant has its limbs developed by means of exercise and nourishment until ultimately they possess the power of a man's, so, in a spiritual sense, is the Christian made strong by adversity. I am not one who believes that we can attain to strong faith instantly, any more than I would affirm that a weak infant can spring into manhood at once. Our faith which is feeble at first is strengthened more and more by use.

Again the increase of faith is dependent upon the individual's attitude toward the methods God uses for this purpose. Instead of wanting no trials before victory and no exercise of patience, the child of God must be willing to take these things from His hands as means of expanding his Christian life. Trials, difficulties, obstacles, griefs, necessities – all are the very food of faith.

I get letters from so many of God's dear children who say, "Dear Brother Mueller, I'm writing this because I am so weak and feeble in faith." Just so surely as we ask to have our faith strengthened, we must feel a willingness to take from God's hand the means for strengthening it. We must allow Him to educate us through trials and bereavements and troubles. It is through trials that faith is exercised and developed more and more. God affectionately permits difficulties that He may develop unceasingly that which He is willing to do for us, and to this end we should not shrink."

We remain conscious that Testimony Faith Homes is something God has set up, and that whilst we reach out to children in need our very real purpose is to reveal the reality of God in our midst, and in the midst of society in general. In a failing world and a more and more corrupt and selfish society we are to remain unmoved by the trends around us, and to STAND. To do this is already, and will yet become more difficult, and it is conceivable that we shall have to endure even opposition from an unbelieving world that no longer puts either God or the Bible first.

We shall not shrink from such a challenge. And in the meantime we will do as much as we can with whatever God puts into our hands, to rescue children from adversity as we also introduce them to God's unfailing and everlasting Love.

What are our needs? Too many, and some too pressing to mention. He will undertake. One of our biggest challenges is related to the future of the School. We employ Government Trained Teachers, and must pay them Government Rates. These increase from time to time, and are considerable. Although outside parents pay for their children to come to school with us the fee is high, and 80% of it goes entirely to pay the teachers. Fees cannot for ever be increased since there is a limit to what parents are able to pay. So far the Lord has not given any indication that He will provide against this – we are not in immediate danger, but within a few years we must see an answer.

Our daily needs to feed, care for and provide medical care, education and security to 120 children in four cottage homes are considerable, and the cost increasing annually due to rising prices of all basic commodities. There is not a day when we have no need, and thus we continue daily to PRAY for our DAILY bread, and remain DAILY appreciative in seeing it supplied. He remains Faithful, our only Hope and Expectation.

We remain a LIGHTHOUSE and indeed we have been set even geographically upon a high hill. We will endeavour to keep the LIGHT shining – till He comes!

Epilogue

UPDATE TO THE PREVIOUS EDITION

The first printing of this book was completed in 1998 – ISBN 0 9534593 0 6, printed by REDWOOD BOOKS. It was published by the AENON trust and ran to a thousand copies only. All were sold.

At the time of going to print many things were projected for the future and set out in the last chapter of the book. Some of the things mentioned did in fact happen, but in some ways did not always continue.

For example we were, at the time, hoping to expand the usefulness of a property left to us by Miss. C.M. Drakeley, M.B.E. In the end this did not become viable, and Peter and Jane Mwema left us for other activities. We sold the property and put the proceeds to the purchase of extra land for the use of our School. Peter Mwema went on to pastor a Church in town.

We had also opened an office for SOON run by one of our old boys, Michael Rufroni. This reached a great many people but did not actually take on, and eventually in 2003 it was closed. Michael is now a lecturer at the Pentecostal & Holiness Bible College in Kisumu District.

The Kingdom Kids, a ministry directed by another of our old boys, Charlie, also came to an end, and now Charlie is working as an evangelist for another Christian organisation, both in Kenya and also Tanzania.

The projection of more development on the side of the school did not happen. Instead the orphanage work has increased and expanded.

Finally, Esther and I retired as house parents in the main home, but did not leave the work. Instead, Esther is headmistress of the primary school department and I am still director overall. Daryl and his wife Carol took over as house parents in Testimony House for some eight years but then left and now live in their own rented house nearby. Carol is still teaching in the school, and Daryl has become more involved in general administration as my personal assistant.

Joshua and Miriam also felt the Lord leading them into something new, and two years ago left Jacaranda Cottage to commence a new ministry caring for HIV positive babies and infants. They are not too far from us and we have been glad to see the Hand of the Lord still upon them. Now we have new house parents in Testimony House and Jacaranda Cottage.

This briefly sets out the changes that have been taking place as the years have passed. A little more will be said towards the end of the book as it now stands.

Seven years have passed since the original manuscript was finished. Many have asked for a revision of the book, and after some thought I have felt led to just update it, and see whether or not we can once again find a publisher. If you are reading this then, of course, we will have been successful. Not a lot has been changed or added to the bulk of the original text. I have just tried to bring things up to date.

J. A. Green
October 2008

A final Reflection and Comment on the Work and Ministry of Testimony Faith Homes.

Why did I have to leave England to travel to Africa? What was so different about the need of children in Kenya to those I left behind in England? Well to start with there were so few looking out for them – and they were a growing percentage of the population.

Even today this is the picture with more than 50% of Kenya's thirty-one million people being under the age of 15! More than 3,000,000 between the ages of 6 and 14 have been given up to child labour, and 10% are below the age of 10. More than 800,000 have lost mothers or both parents to AIDS – one in 15 boys will die of AIDS.

The figures are still growing. More than 250,000 are needing care and protection, many out on the streets as early as four years old – mainly boys, but increasingly also girls. Many are exposed for years of their life to self-survival through theft, traffic in drugs, prostitution, extortion and blackmail. Many are delinquent before they are ever 'found'. Others 'learn' to be delinquent from an ever-increasing exposure to a breakdown in respect of home, parents, religion and morals, all promoted and demonstrated in modern world literature, films, T.V. and video. Not a happy scene. And there is little or no moral restraint either from Church or State. Indeed, there is often more than merely tacit encouragement to please oneself, no matter the risk there may be in doing so.

It is even worse in other places quite apart from Kenya, and the trend is not yet showing signs of improvement. Indeed it is much worse than 20 years ago. For this reason we continue to reach out to these lost young people.

In 1984 I was asked to address a Christian Perspective Forum here in Kenya on the topic of 'Juvenile Delinquency'. It very clearly set out the problems, the need, and the Christian need to ACT. I include it here as part of the background to all that may have gone before in this book. As a backdrop, perhaps, to many lives lost and later found!

DELINQUENCY is failure or omission in the doing of your duty. The dictionaries variously define a delinquent as one who has failed to do what was expected of him; an offender against society; a drop out. Chambers

20th Century Dictionary depicts a delinquent as 'a person lacking in moral and social sense, yet without showing impairment of intellect.'

Dr. Erastus Mugo, in his book '*Crime & Delinquency in Kenya*' published in 1975, defines a juvenile delinquent on page 96 of his book. He writes:

"A juvenile delinquent is a child between the age of seven and sixteen who commits an act which, when committed by persons beyond this statutory juvenile court age, would be punishable as a crime, or as an act injurious to other individuals or the public, that is the state or the government; an anti social act.

Thus we are discussing anti-social behavior, and in particular such behavior that applies to juveniles between the ages of 7 and 17, though I would personally raise the upper limit of the age grouping considerably. The phrase 'anti-social' is a very good one. It means behavior that is against society, and in rebellion to the general rules of acceptable social patterns, both at home with the family, and outside the home in the world at large. Another word often applied to delinquents is 'maladjusted'. This simply means to be badly adjusted or 'tuned in', to normal and acceptable society. Such youngsters become unco-operative with others, and unable to apparently cope with the life-style of the rest of the family, or other people around them. They may become destructive, seeking to destroy, break up, and deface public or even private property. They might go even further and commit violent offences against others, such as theft, assault. Or they may just take off and live their own free, uninhibited, lives in their own way; abandoning old values and cultural traditions in favour of free sex, drugs, and a generally nonconformist pattern of behavior."

There is [circa 1984] a worldwide increase in juvenile crime and delinquency. Dr. Mugo, dedicating his book, writes, "This book is Dedicated to my son, Daniel D. Aroka, so that he may live to see a less criminal society in Kenya." Dr. Mugo seemed to feel that the publication of his research into Crime and Delinquency would somehow stem the tide, perhaps even turn it back upon itself. He notes in his book that during the years 1965-1971 (the years that he conducted his survey) there had been an overall increase in juvenile delinquency in Kenya of up to 63%. It would be good if I could tell you differently. I cannot. In fact in the years 1971-1983 from figures extracted by me personally form the individual Annual Reports of the Kenya Children's Department and the Kenya Probation Department, an increase of more than 350% can be found. Instead of the hoped-for decrease and reversal of this 'tide of iniquity' amongst the youth of Kenya, we see a surging high tide that threatens to overwhelm us. This only reflects the state of things worldwide. It is not just in Kenya; the entire world is suffering.

Long ago in British history we are told of a Christian King who was greatly admired by his courtiers. His name was Canute. One day his courtiers came to him, seeking to flatter him, and said, "O King! There is none greater or more powerful than you. Why even the very waves of the sea must return from the shore if you so command them." Canute thereupon commanded that he be carried on his throne to the nearby seashore. The tide was coming in upon the sandy shore. He told them to set down his throne facing the incoming waves. There he sat, and loudly commanded the waves to go back, and cease to come further up the beach towards him. But the waves continued to beat upon the shore, and slowly, little by little, continued to come towards him until the sea began to lap around his feet. Then The King turned to his courtiers and said, "There, do you see my friends? It needs One greater than I am to command the tide to recede." In all of this he had hoped to humble his courtiers and to teach them a true lesson. We are little better than those courtiers. We put our faith in research, statistics, surveys, and our own inventiveness and wisdom to stem the tide of immorality and crime and rebellion all around us. None of these things will do. Not all the intellectual knowledge of mankind, his institutions, Academies of Learning, nor his political science, technologies and ideologies can change things for us. We cannot change this ourselves. We have to look beyond ourselves. We need to look to God Himself, if we want to see a reversal of this flood tide of anarchy and civil disobedience in the younger generation.

In Kenya today more children than ever before have opportunity of education, good health, peace and prosperity. Yet still children run away from home to the town and the city. Indeed it has been like a stampede in some places. We still see children arrested for theft and vagrancy – indeed they roam about in gangs, preferring the risky life of 'cops and robbers' to that of being with their families or going to school. What is wrong? What is causing this instability, this world-wide instability? Some say it is poverty – and certainly there is a deep poverty in many areas of Kenyan life. But is it only poverty? No, I believe there are other factors. Jesus, speaking in Matthew 24v6-7, points to some of them. He says "...ye shall hear of wars and rumours of war…for nation shall rise up against nation, and kingdom against kingdom; and there shall be famines, and pestilence, and earthquakes in different places….” In the 1940s we saw the end of the Second World War. The atom bomb was dropped on Hiroshima. Twenty-million lives were lost in the last Great War. Yet WAR is still very much with us. Not only violence fills the earth, but man is also busy killing his environment, busy putting his very existence in danger. He is upsetting the world ecology so that – over-population apart – famines, earthquakes and other irregular natural disturbances are on the increase year by year. The whole planet seems to be staggering uncertainly in its daily and seasonable course. As forests dwindle to make way for roads and domestic or industrial development, the deserts multiply and expand. As industry abounds so our seas and rivers, even the very air we breathe, become steadily more polluted. There is less and less land for the multiplication of Man to stand upon, and less and less for him to eat. Newspapers and news reports throughout the media are full of this, plus the spectre of unemployment and civil unrest. Where is there to go? What is there to do? Mankind seems to face a new brand of hopelessness – and many are running from it.

Hard to see a secure and predictable future. I had felt the same in the 50s in my own teenage years, but then I had met up with the reality of Jesus Christ, and found a Personal Saviour, Who immediately delivered me from all my carnal fears and apprehensions. And He has seen me through. He alone has been my Stay, my Refuge, and my Strength in times of dark despair, doubt, and fear. I have often thought this through, and I know definitely that if I did not know Jesus, and have a personal faith in Him, then I would not be the man I am today. I would either have killed myself, or I would have lived the life of a delinquent until now! Yes I can understand how the world around one can suck hope out of life's expectations and hopelessness results in many anti-social acts.

Many have said that it is 'ignorance' and 'illiteracy' that is the root cause of social breakdown in human experience. They use this opinion as a valid reason for pointing out how crime and revolution are on the increase in the Third World where poverty is still a deep and widespread problem – poverty that of itself prohibits education and social advancement.

Dr Billy Graham in his book, '*World Aflame*', published in 1966, said:

"It is the assumption of some educators that the cause of world tension lies in the lack of knowledge, and that if we can only educate man, peace will come to the world. They say that if man knows better, then he will do better."

Well man has continued to learn, and he progressively knows more and more. Especially in the more developed nations. But is he any better? I think not. The lure of knowledge has been the pitfall from the beginning, since Adam's Day. Yet Man still cannot raise himself up. He cannot save himself.

Dr. Martin Lloyd Jones, writing in his book '*The Christian Warfare*', published in 1976, ten years later, writes of the British scene at that time. He says:

"…Medical Officers of Health are reporting that there is an appalling increase in venereal diseases and especially amongst adolescents and juveniles. Such is the problem confronting us. This moral problem has become the most acute and the most urgent – there is a serious breakdown in morality. They tell us that we are confronted by an amoral generation; by people who do not seem to have a moral sense at all. But let us not forget that this situation must be considered in the light of the exceptional educational facilities and opportunities and advantages that have been increasingly prevalent over the last hundred years. MANY HAVE BEEN THE lectures and the lecturers that have said that Religion is not the only solution. Yet here is the problem still – immorality and vice and evil. The world has multiplied its institutions for dealing with the moral and social problems in this present time more than ever before. Yet there are men saying one after another that moral standards are deteriorating almost hourly, week by week, and that the problem is becoming appallingly difficult to solve. They are asking what can be done!"

In Deuteronomy 6v4 we read these words:

Hear O Israel; the Lord our God is one Lord.
Thou shalt love the Lord thy God with all thine heart, and with all thine soul, and with all thine might. And these words which I command thee this day, shall be in thine heart. And thou shalt teach them diligently unto thy children, when thou walkest by the way, and when thou liest down, and when thou risest up.

THIS is a Family situation. Here the parents are being told to teach their children, and to talk to them about the Word of God at every opportunity in order to instil right standards and precepts for daily living.

Educationalists in Kenya are always saying that they have the greatest responsibility and authority in a child's life, since the child spends the bulk of his time in school. Well if this is in fact the case they must also take over the responsibility of instilling the Bible into the minds and hearts of their students. They must each teach that the Bible, The Word of God, is true, standing Alone and Incomparable to any other word or teaching. Can they do this? Are they doing this? Do they desire to do this?

(In Kenya today, and at the time this lecture was given, the Educational System is called 'The 8-4-4 System'. Children mostly commence the first grade of primary education at the age of six, spending eight years in primary school. Then four more years at secondary level, and hopefully four more years in university. It is now also compulsory to attend a pre-primary school from age 4.)

The current school syllabus in Kenya questions more and more the Authority of the Bible. The bulk of teachers are unmindful of teaching Bible Concepts. Thus children hear little more than the opinion or view of their teacher, a view that is often liberal and without faith. If parents do not bring up their children from the cradle to hear and learn God's Word, they will perhaps never learn it. Without it there is no alternative but a continuing moral decline into chaos.

If we would obey Deuteronomy 6 from the word 'go' with our children, then delinquency would soon be restrained, perhaps even eliminated.

"Train up a child in the way he should go, and when he is old he will not depart from it." So says Proverbs 22v6. The brethren of the Roman Catholic Communion say that if they are given a child to train in their doctrine from infancy until five years old, then that child will never depart from the Catholic Faith. They prove the truth of this continually. God's Word does not tell us to send our children to the Sunday school, or to a teacher at school to learn about God. Instead the Bible says to the parent, YOU teach! You Train! You talk! Do it at home, within the family circle and routine. When parents cease to do this, things will and must go astray. When children have no direction at home they lose their way and become LOST. The homeless, destitute and orphaned child is immediately at risk because of this, and may not be able to avoid becoming delinquent.

In Testimony Faith Homes we have found this the case time and time again.

Children are brought to us at all ages, and from varied backgrounds. Some are runaways, having hidden their past under a tissue of lies and falsehood. They have home and family somewhere, but because of poverty, abuse, or just plain rebellion have deserted them. Others are truly alone, orphaned, without tangible family or material home. Some are abandoned in open fields, at bus stands, public toilets and even city streets. They are often babies and infants up to three or four years old. Some lose everything to AIDS, their parents both dying, their relatives backing away from the offspring in fear they too might become tainted by touch or association. So very few come to us knowing anything about God. We have to do what we can to teach them!

Do they hear well? Which age group hears the best and responds well? Why the youngest! They easily believe and accept, and take hold of Jesus in their little lives and hearts.

The older ones often come in with the wisdom of their own conceits – the self-assurance of their own tried ways, and long experience outside, alone. Apart from those who had a previous upbringing with Christ and the Bible as a foundation, we find these older ones do not accept new concepts so easily. They are more shut up and shut in upon themselves; already well started on their own way far away from the Truth. Thus many arrive to stay and live with us already delinquent!

We are not always able to change this trend in their life. But some that are lost are eventually FOUND, and there is a moment in their lives of RECOGNITION, and they suddenly see where they have been heading, and realise that there is another way. Then there can be real change. Faith in Christ, and in the Bible, does make a difference – a difference that nothing and no one else can achieve.

Children and young people also need security. We all do – throughout our life. But a child in particular needs security and stability in its life. When there is LOVE in the home – love between the parents for each other, love for the children, for God – this gives a firm foundation for a child to feel safe with. If he knows his parents love each other, for example, therein there can be no fear of a family split, a divided home, perhaps no home at all. He knows by what he sees and hears that his parents are together and can be depended upon to be there for him. Marital splits, separations, divorce, are all prime causes of a great deal of juvenile delinquency. These days in the developing world around us, divorce and marital breakdown is climbing. Three in every five marriages are ending in divorce or separation. More and more relationships do not even begin with marriage, and children are born into a one-parent situation, to be brought up in various ways, all of them unbalanced and without the security and discipline that stems from a well-grounded and acceptable parental authority that makes for a stable home.

In Kenya too this is a trend that is on the increase.

We have discovered that a lack of God-consciousness, and Bible-based teaching, and a lack of a stable and loving home and parents contribute greatly to a young person becoming delinquent.

There is also a third factor: the lack, or even the improper use of correction. In our present sociological world outlook physical correction has been out of fashion for some time. Little Johnny must not be smacked, caned, even touched! Away with the cane, and away also with the hand. Corporal punishment is taboo, banned in the home, in the school, and in the prison. No smacking, no beating, no death penalty. This will make Johnny a better boy, and the world a better world. Yet everywhere people are crying out that there is no control, no safety, no security. Crime, murder and public disorders are on the increase. Is this so surprising? After all, our hands are tied. Mum and Dad may not smack, teacher may not cane, and the Judge cannot take away life. Kenyan society is finding this hard to agree with in the main, since its heritage has demonstrated the good sense of all that modernists say is unhealthy. Parents still discipline their children. Teachers, even though there is officially a ban on the use of the cane, still cane, and the death penalty is still, for the moment, on the Statute Book of Kenya's Laws. But erosion in all these areas is taking place in Kenya, and problems amongst young people – and adults – are expanding.

In the Bible, Proverbs 22v15 tells us that "foolishness is bound up in the heart of a child; but the rod of correction shall drive it far from him." This 'Christian' view is diametrically opposed to the current worldview. And even Christian parents tend to forget scriptures of this nature as they learn to compromise with the Word of God, and become more liberal and worldly in their attitudes.

In Eldoret, a town of some 300,000 young people under the age of 20, and the town I have lived in here in Kenya since 1972, we have many children and teenagers walking, and living on, the streets. Some of them may have drifted in from outlying areas to scavenge and get away from poverty at home. Others, however, have home and family right here within the town boundaries. Many of their parents are both working all day, or else they just cannot cope with their children and let them roam. Perhaps they are even glad to see them out of the house, or communal family room, for a while. Some just send them out to beg! And some use them in their own market stall businesses. Few are asking questions. Others are looking for whatever is available to promote their own independent life style. They form gangs on the streets and beg, rob, solicit, prostitute, and indulge in drug abuse and traffic. Seldom are any picked up or corrected in any way.

Man has said that punishment is BAD, and for this reason many back away from any form of capital or corporal punishment in our modern society. But crime and delinquency have not decreased because of this humane moderation. In many parts of the U.S.A. the death penalty has been re-introduced in States where it had previously been removed. Immediately the numbers of murders and other violent crimes have reduced! We may not LIKE the rod of correction, but we cannot do without and live. Discipline is part of the laid down pattern of creation. There is no freedom without discipline. Freedom without discipline, in our world, is unlimited terror; it is chaos. Its fulfilment is to be found in HELL.

Then again there can be no full expression of the knowledge of God's Love without discipline, and to my mind this means ultimately that one can have no real stability or security without it. The Bible says again in Proverbs 13v24, "He that spareth his rod hateth his son; but he that loveth him chasteneth him early." No use closing the stable door after the horse has bolted. If you do not act early you will definitely be too late. Can you want to see your child make a shipwreck of his life just because your sentimental desire not to hurt him makes you ignore his waywardness? Even God – in Whose likeness we are made – has no pleasure in the death of one human being. Indeed "...for whom the Lord loveth he chasteneth, and scourgeth every son whom he receiveth." Solomon the Wise says a little more when he writes in Proverbs 29v15, "A child left to himself will cause shame." We may NOT hold back our hand for giving discipline – we MUST take the Word of God seriously.

Now let me share a story with you. A tale of one particular boy. A true story. A narrative to start us off on this journey homeward, filled as it is with twists and turns, sorrows and joys.

THIS IS THE STORY OF STEPHEN – the story of a lost waif. Stephen's mother was unmarried. She had had many lovers. After being found drunk and disorderly she was put on a Probation Order. Within a few days she vanished, leaving two small children, boys of three and five years old abandoned on the street. She was never heard of again. The boys remained on the street and were eventually picked up by police some months later. They had survived by eating whatever they could find in dustbins. They were ill, dirty, and alone. A woman in another town, our own town of Eldoret in fact, came to hear of them, and applied to the Children's Department to foster them both. And so Stephen aged 3 and Joseph, his brother aged 5, were taken from the Police Station where they were being held and transported to their new home. The woman that fostered them was an elderly married businesswoman with grown up children living away from home. She seemed to have good intentions initially for she was paid nothing by the Government to foster the children, and arranged for them both to attend school. Life seemed assured. But she was not a Christian. After three years her husband died, and she travelled with the two boys to her husband's ancestral tribal home 150 miles away to have him buried. She was losing her sight by this time, and shortly afterwards became completely blind. She did not return to Eldoret, and the boys did not continue with schooling. They became her eyes and eventually her slaves, running the small infertile farm and tending the lean cattle. Steven ran away. He was by then 12, and returned to Eldoret, to the streets. There he began to fend for himself. He was lean, sharp-eyed, and mentally very alert. He became a consummate pickpocket and thief. One afternoon he was about his usual business when a car ran him down, and he suffered severe head injuries. He had no identification papers, and having been admitted to the government hospital lay there unconscious for many days. Eventually he recovered, and returned to his old occupations, only to be arrested and sent to the local Juvenile Remand Home where after some weeks of uncomfortable residence he was to meet me.

I am a gazetted and official visitor to the Remand Home and was making one of my periodic visits to check on the health and state of the young people pent up there. It was November, 1978. I noticed Stephen immediately.

He was a very attractive personality, full of humour, and intelligence. But he did not confide his past to me that day. He said he had lost his memory after the motor accident and could remember nothing prior to that. He was lying, but it was a good story!

Esther and I had a vacancy in our home, and so we arranged for him to be given over into care until he was 18. We felt sure that once in school he would do well, BUT we reckoned without those ten or so years of thinking for himself and planning for himself. Ten years without any real direction or discipline. It soon began to show.

We ran our house just like a family home. Esther and I were ever-present as Mum and Dad, and our three children lived totally integrated with some 35 other children aged from 0 to 20. We ate together, sat together, and interacted in every way as a family. We read the Word of God together, prayed together (even those who did not believe in what we did). Stephen joined this household. He also heard the Word of God. But it was a very new and strange experience for him, since he had never known a truly Christian family life, or observed set routines or a need to obey simple rules. He was rebellious from the start, and did not settle at school. He discovered discipline, but it made little impression upon him at 13. He had endured a lot of hardness, and was not impressed by physical correction at school where he was regularly beaten for misdemeanours. At home it was the same. He began to truant from school, and then absent himself from home all night. Things began to be missed. He was stealing.

After many attempts to steer him into a different attitude and behaviour we gave up and had him committed to an approved school. We had failed to help him. He was still as lost and alone as when he first hit the street at three-years-old. We wept to see him go.

He ran away from the approved school four times. He always returned to us!

AND left us again after a few months. He turned up in 1981 and 1983 and then in 1986. He was 20 years old by then, often the worse for taking marijuana or drinking raw spirits. Still stealing. Still the same attractive personality, humorous and carefree. He never took life seriously. Our hearts broke many times because of him. Of course he left again, and this time did not come back into the family home. He was just too old! He ran back to the streets within a few months of his return. He joined in with a team of open-air car washers. Then one day in

August 1992 we heard he had been arrested again. This time he was accused of stealing a briefcase left in one of the cars he had been washing. It had contained twelve-thousand Kenyan shillings (approx £100 at that time). By this time Stephen was 24.

We had known nothing of the matter until one day in October a prison officer from Eldoret Prison phoned me up. He knew me, and although he was officially not supposed to communicate what he saw inside the prison, he felt I should know that Stephen was there and that he was very ill. He said he was not being treated, and that I should try to intervene. I went immediately to the prison, and found that indeed our wayward son was seriously unwell. He could not walk! Could not so much as stand on his own. His body was swollen in many places, especially so in the region of his left breast and his buttocks. He had been in prison for two and a half months. When I asked the Governor what had happened I was told that the Police had beaten Stephen up before bringing him to the prison – ostensibly to find out what he had done with the stolen money.

I arranged for him to be taken to a local hospital for X-ray and paid for it. They refused to let me take him myself. A week later I returned to see how he was getting along. They had still not taken him for X-ray and he was now weaker than before. I had armed myself with a Production Order from the Court this time, and took him out of the Prison. This time I took him to our home's doctor. He confirmed that Stephen had been seriously assaulted at some time and that two ribs had been broken and healed again of themselves in the interim period.

During this assault blood vessels had been broken in the area of his left breast. This formed blood clots which subsequently became septic and caused ulcers which had now swollen with infection to a very dangerous state. Similar results had ensued from further beatings received in the area of his right hip. More than two cups of pus had to be drained immediately. The Doctor said if we had not got him to the surgery that very day he might not have made it. He survived. We found a safe job for him.

After six months he had saved enough to set himself up in a second-hand clothes business in town. For a while things seemed good.

A year later we heard he had left, sold up his business, and gone to Mombasa.

Soon after that we heard he was in hospital there having been beaten up for theft.

Is there any light in this saga? Is there any suggestion that the Word of God was working for this lost soul, this throw-away piece of humanity, this orphan? The Bible says clearly to the orphan, "When your Mother and your Father forsakes you I will make you mine – I will adopt you." That sounds so positive so safe. It was true in my own life and experience. But was it true for Stephen? It is true for every orphan? Could I see it in long years of Stephen's life as I had witnessed it? Well I could NOT see it in some ways. YET on the other hand I could see that somehow, as he had continued to encourage his own ruin and destruction, he had always been preserved and kept alive. WHY – if not because God in Heaven had his eye on him?

Returning eventually from Mombasa, Stephen continued a life of booze, and sex.

Doctors warned him that he was destroying himself. He was seriously ill again with venereal disease and was advised clearly that if he did not reform himself AIDS was the next step for him. He came to us and prayed for our forgiveness, and asked us to pray for him to be saved. Once more we found employment for him. But in 1999 he proved to be HIV positive. He was soon unable to work, and we stepped in once more to make sure he was fed and medicated. Most weeks he would call in to see us. Then suddenly we missed him. He had fallen ill and shut himself up in his hut. For eight days no one saw him, and no one enquired of him. Then he was discovered and taken immediately to hospital. We were notified and Esther and I went to see him in the terminal ward. He was very obviously dying, but when he saw us he smiled, and cracked a joke or two. He had always been able to make me laugh on the dullest occasions, and I had always loved him. I could barely keep back my tears as I sat down on his bed and took his hand in mine. He could not even sit up or raise his head. Later, as we were leaving, he called softly for me to go back again. As I bent my head to listen to what he had to say, he whispered,

"Dad, I know that all this, all my life, has been my own fault. I have told God so. But I have not done so well. Dad, don't worry for me. Jesus found me, and I know He is taking me home."

He died peacefully a few hours later. He died of AIDS. I cried out for his apparently wasted life down here on earth, but then I suddenly knew that it was not at all wasted. He had been blind, and weak, and easily led astray. He was more and more lost. Yet somehow through the haze of his life, Stephen had glimpsed the Truth. God's Love found him, and he began to see. He had been FOUND, and is no longer lost and away. He had suffered. Suffered insisting on the wrong way and the wrong style of living. But every hard blow had somehow hammered home a TRUTH he could not avoid seeing.

He was 37 when he passed away. A long time to be lost. But great JOY to be FOUND.

Jesus came to SAVE the LOST – He came to FIND them, and to show them the way HOME. He found me. And He found, after a long search, Stephen.

Waweru.

THIS SOCIETY BEGAN CARING for orphaned and destitute children in 1969, in Maseno, Western Kenya, moving to Eldoret, in Uasin Gishu District, North-West Rift Valley, some hundred miles away from Maseno, slightly south-east, in 1972.

In 1969 the old cultural traditions of the extended family, where care and shelter were extended to all members of the family in need at any time, were still visibly practised. But they were also beginning to break down in the wake of increased urbanization. Additionally the gradual emancipation of women in society to stand equally alongside men, so that many have increasingly been able to pursue education leading to professional and other full-time occupations instead of the old confines of 'home and family' has been another contributing factor.

In 1972 we found in Eldoret Town a community of some 40,000 people, and not a street child or beggar in sight. The Department of Social Services in Eldoret at that time could not advise us of one destitute child needing residential care.

Today in 2004 Eldoret's population exceeds 600,000. More and more continue to come in from the rural areas seeking their fortune. Satellite towns and slum neighbourhoods are increasing all the time. Unemployment has also escalated to match a general rise in crime and prostitution as a means of income. Street children as a factor in the society were still barely noticed in 1985, but by the middle of 2002 it was estimated that more than 2000 were wandering our streets. The majority of them have 'home and family' and are basically the victim of poverty. In 2003 a new government implemented free education nationwide, and this has immediately reduced the numbers seen on the streets to only a few hundreds.

BUT there are still children being abandoned, and their incidence is on the increase.

Many of these children come again from severe poverty, prostitution, and AIDS.

There is an increasing need to re-educate our society on the old concept of the extended family, and the responsibilities of the family in general, as well as parenthood. More children's homes and institutions are now being built, but these alone cannot achieve a conclusive answer to the problems at large.

It is the lack of a sound home and family base that puts a child at risk in the first instance. And this is true of any place on earth at this time. The reasons for lack of such a base are many and varied. Any building that is to rise up to endure the wear and tear of time and elements must be built on a strong and sure foundation. Likewise, if a child is to grow into a mature, responsible and productive adult, it will also need a strong and sure foundation; a strong and sure home – a home where both the Mother and the Father together play out their respective roles in front of the children. Not a lop-sided family; not a single parent situation. This is not a properly balanced home.

It is at home, and in the home, that children are to learn and be taught certain definite things. It is a child's parents that are basically and primarily responsible to do this for their offspring. It is my belief that this is clearly set out for us in the Bible. Let me draw your attention to some of the Scriptures dealing with this important fundamental matter concerning the upbringing of children in the home and family.

In the Old Testament in Deuteronomy 6v4-7, we see that the responsibility to teach a child about God and His Law, family, and even local social history is the parents:

Hear O Israel (people of God) the Lord is one!
You shall love the Lord your God with all your heart, with all your soul, and with all your might. And these words which I command you today shall be in your heart. You shall teach them diligently to your CHILDREN, and shall talk of them when you sit in your house, when you walk by the way, when you lie down, and when you rise up.

And Proverbs 22v6:

Train up a child in the way that he should go,
And when he is old he will not depart from it.

It is at home with the parents that child will be taught about right and wrong, good and bad. It is at home with parents that a child will receive advice and council in the choice of friends – yes and even what he should read or view.

My son, if sinners entice you, do not consent.
If they say, "Come with us, let us lie in wait to shed blood;
Let us lurk secretly for the innocent without cause…
… My son, do not walk in the way with them,
Keep your foot from their path; for their feet run to evil
And they make haste to shed blood.
Proverbs 1v10-19

There is much in the Bible, God's Word, that teaches what is good, healthy and RIGHT.

It is for the parent to teach his children from the word go as much as he can find, no doubt commencing with the Ten Commandments. It is the parent's responsibility.

But it is not the only one that he has. He has other things to ensure on behalf of his children. They are also part of providing a safe, secure, and dependable home.

The parent is responsible to discipline.

Yes, both parents are expected to take up this responsibility seriously as part of good training and upbringing. And where painful discipline becomes needful the parent is not encouraged to run away from administering it.

He who spares his rod hates his son,
But he who loves him disciplines him promptly.
Proverbs 13v24

The rod and reproof give wisdom,
But a child left to himself brings shame to his mother…
…correct your son, and he will give you rest;
Yes, he will give delight to your soul.
Proverbs 29v15&17

There was always a cane somewhere to be found in my parents' house. I can only remember it being used on me once, and that once was enough. It was not used without reason, and the justice of it was explained to me carefully before I received it.

I respected its justice for the rest of my life, and regarded it carefully. It was not wasted on me, and I was not abused by it. I learned from it.

Many parents today (I am talking about good and caring parents) fight shy of going that far even when it is obviously necessary. They are afraid of being accused of being abusive, and indeed society itself is now poised to condemn any such discipline, labelling it 'child abuse.' In Testimony Faith Homes, and with my very own children, we have made it clear that the cane is there, and may be used and felt if the occasion calls for it.

My wife and I have not had to use it often. It has proved its worth even so, and provided substance to prove our sincere and determined care of our children's growth into serious and law abiding adults. Especially the godly parent is exhorted to "have his children in subjection with all gravity" (1.Timothy 3v4).

The parent is also supposed to be the provider for his children. In this is security for the present and even for the future.

Children ought not to lay up [provide] for their parents, but the parents for the children.
2 Corinthians 12v14

It should be obvious even from these few citations from Scripture that the home and parent is the prime source of knowledge and a sense of good discipline and security

When it fails to be there it needs to be replaced as soon as possible. However this does not mean that every child that has become somehow destitute of home and family can be assured of a successful future when it is taken into an institution or children's home. Neither can it be said that every child living at home with its parents will live an exemplary life, or turn out well. Things do go wrong, and generalities are not without exceptions to the rule. Some family homes are godless and dangerous. Some institutions are far from providing surrogate family life. My wife and I have tried to do our best, but we know that in many ways we have been unable to replace what has been lost to a child we have taken into our own home.

In June 1984 the Chairlady of the Kenya Child Welfare Society stated that:

"Nothing can replace a child's natural home and family, and children's homes should only be used as places of temporary shelter whilst parental or home situations remained in difficulty."

I was to reply in an open letter published in the national Press as here below:

It is true that nothing can perfectly replace a child's natural home and family, and this is true even when that home and family may be experiencing poverty, hardship, and even marital disturbance. Roots are important to all of us and especially to a developing child.
Thus we would go even further than the Child Welfare Society on this point, and say that it would be better to see NO child admitted to a children's home when that child has any ability at all to remain in his or her own family home.
We believe this to be so even when there might be some deprivation materially or otherwise. The important factor here is the on-going security and mental stability of the child. To be deprived and separated from one's known home and family, knowing that it is your true home, and that your very own family is being left behind in difficulty can be a very serious emotional upheaval.
A child so separated and placed in a children's home or even into a foster home, will always be looking back and waiting for the day it can return; it will not easily settle anywhere else.

Of course we know from experience that we cannot expect the world to do what we would like it to do. As much as we like to see more children able to remain at home with their families, we know full well that there IS parental abuse of responsibility and that this often results in children having to be removed from their authority in order to protect them from further abuse or hurt. Also divorce and marital separations dismantle normal family life and sometimes also necessitate children losing their home. We know this. We regret it.

Many of the children that come to us have suffered because of such things.

The older they come to us the worse it is for them, since they find it difficult to accept our home as their own, or us as their parents. They may understand why they are in an institution, but they will wish they were not, and this affects their attitude in many ways. This can be very difficult for those of us that live with them, and demands a great deal of prayer and understanding.

The world society of our age is, on the whole, one that disregards personal responsibility. And this is especially true in respect of our children. More and more are at risk. More and more are unwanted, abandoned, and abused.

The lack of a sound home and family base is increasing. Children are being born and thrown into the world untaught, unclothed, and unattended because more and more parents fail to provide what is needed.

And it is not only instruction, discipline, and security that parents should be providing, but also an example in human relationships as they grow in love and mutual respect and faithfulness toward each other in their marriage. This most of all outlaws the wilful practice of single parenting.

It is in marriage that a home is built, and offspring succoured.

The springboard of life is MARRIAGE. It is in the coming together of a man and a woman that TRUE LOVE becomes visible and tangible. A home and family are created and an environment built up that can demonstrate every facet of God's character and personality. This is why God initiated marriage in the first place, and there was an order to it. God did not turn to the dust from which He had made Adam in order to create Eve. No, He took instead one of Adam's ribs and Eve became ever so mysteriously bone of Adam's bone, and flesh of his flesh. She was individual but not separate from Adam; she belonged to him in a very real, basic, and physical way. And it had the ring and organic necessity of permanency about it, as a living relationship.

YET in 1990 it was stated that:

Up to a third of all marriages in Western Countries break up. In Britain the divorce rate – the highest in the EEC – is still rising, and legal costs alone add up to two billion pounds a year. In West Germany half of all marriages in the big cities fail. There is hardly a family anywhere, from teeming housing estates to royalty or bishops that has not been affected by family breakdown.
One in seven British children live with only one parent – double the 1971 figure.
Last year (1989) a quarter of all births in Britain were illegitimate.
A host of social evils can be traced back to breakdown in the family: Aids, child and drug abuse, teenage suicide, runaway children, a rocketing crime rate, and violence in the home.
Projections for the USA show that by 1991 the total number of AIDS cases will have risen to between 300,000 and 485.000. In

New York City an estimated 50,000 to 100,000 children in this generation will lose at least one parent to AIDS. Health authorities there say that by 1995 20,000 orphans will need either adoption or foster care.

Present statistics for the commencement of 2002 show that the total number of AIDS cases was put at 816,000.

In Kenya we have upwards of 15% of the population living with HIV/AIDS with more than 800,000 AIDS orphans. In this figure alone it can be seen how hopeless it has become to safeguard children from loss of home and family, and how necessary children's homes and foster homes have become in Kenya alone. Not a happy picture.

When I asked Esther to marry me in 1971 I was also inviting her to be a mother to the 28 youngsters I was then caring for in rather primitive circumstances. She only had a vague idea of what this would mean, for I really had it in mind to build a real home for homeless children. By the time our first child was born we already lived in with 36 kids of all ages and backgrounds. Steve, our first child, was literally born IN to an existing family – a very extended family – of which he now became part. So also with our other two children, Michael and Elizabeth, and later our four adopted children, Daryl, Edward, Manu, and Helen. Our particular home was always a fairly packed family of no less than 40 children. We have three homes now, and that is the pattern for each.

We do not help many compared to the need – just scratching the surface really. But we have tried to demonstrate a concept and to reintroduce in a very practical way the old cultural habit of an extended family. Many have come in and gone out. More than 200 in fact up to date since we began. Many are presently with us. Some still remember their own homes and parents that have been lost to them. Some find it hard to settle in. Some come to accept the Love that God has put in our hearts for them, and become truly 'family'. So we experience heartbreak and sorrow at times. And at times joy and happiness.

ON THE 29TH AUGUST 2004 we celebrated 35 years of family with hundreds of men and women that grew up here. When all is said and done, we look back and we say, "This is the LORD'S doing, and it is MARVELLOUS in our eyes!" NEXT year we shall celebrate 40 years. Dark clouds of despondency seem to be rolling over the world with dire predictions of economic collapse, famine and disaster on every front. Humanly this is already affecting charities. Charity will suffer more and more the pressure of having to begin at home. How will God undertake for the financing and securing of His Works of Love and Grace worldwide? Will He be unable? Will all His work fail, and those that trust in and upon him be brought to shame?

Look at Luke 21v25-26 as written in the Amplified Bible Translation:

...upon the earth there will be distress (trouble and anguish) of nations in bewilderment and perplexity (without resources, left wanting, embarrassed, in doubt, not knowing which way to turn ... Men swooning away or expiring with fear and dread and apprehension and expectation of the things that are coming on the world...

This could be an apt description of the current world crisis now beginning to be experienced and forecast in our media at this time.

A hopeless future? Let me leave you with this quote from Habakkuk 3v17-20. It says it all for me.

Though the fig tree does not blossom, and there is no fruit on the vines,
Though the product of the olive fails and the fields yield no food,
Though the flock is cut off from the fold and there are no cattle in the stalls,
YET I will rejoice in the Lord:
I will exult in the victorious God of my salvation!
The Lord God is my Strength, my personal bravery, and my invincible army;
He makes my feet like hind's feet, and will make me to walk (not stand in terror, but to walk)
And make spiritual progress upon my high places of trouble, suffering or responsibility.

12th October, 2008